W9-BBK-154

DISCARD

Quantitative Measurement and Dynamic Library Service

Quantitative Measurement and Dynamic Library Service

Edited with a Preface
and Introduction by
Ching-chih Chen.

A Neal-Schuman Professional Book

Prof,
025.1
Q1

ORYX PRESS
1978

Operation Oryx, started more than 15 years ago at the Phoenix Zoo to save the rare white antelope—believed to have inspired the unicorn—has apparently succeeded. The operation was launched in 1962 when it became evident that the animals were facing extinction in their native habitat of the Arabian peninsula.

An original herd of 9, put together through *Operation Oryx* by five world organizations, now numbers 47 in Phoenix, with another 38 at the San Diego Wild Game Farm, and 4 others which have recently been sent to live in their natural habitat in Jordan.

Also, in what has come to be known as "The Second Law of Return," rare biblical animals are being collected from many countries to roam freely at the Hai Bar Biblical Wildlife Nature Reserve in Israel, the most recent addition being a breeding herd of eight Arabian Oryx. With the addition of these Oryx, their collection of rare biblical animals is complete.

Copyright © 1978 by The Oryx Press

Published by The Oryx Press
2214 North Central at Encanto
Phoenix, AZ 85004

Published simultaneously in Canada

All rights reserved
No part of this publication may be reproduced or transmitted in any form or by any means, electronic or mechanical, including photocopying, recording, or by any information storage and retrieval system, without permission in writing from The Oryx Press

Printed and Bound in the United States of America

Distributed outside North America by
Mansell Information/Publishing Limited
3 Bloomsbury Place
London WC1A 2QA, England
ISBN 0-7201-0826-8

Library of Congress Cataloging in Publication Data
Main entry under title:
Quantitative measurement and dynamic library service.

  (A Neal-Schuman professional book)
  An outgrowth of the proceedings of a two-part institute held at the School of Library Science, Simmons College, Nov. 1976 and Mar. 1977.
  Includes bibliographies.
  1. Libraries administration—Addresses, essays, lectures. I. Chen, Ching-chih, 1937-
Z678.035   025.1   78-13066
ISBN 0-912700-17-3

Reprinted January, 1980.

Contents

109009

Charts, Figures and Tables

Preface

In November 1976 and March 1977, a two-unit, i.e., two-part, Institute on Quantitative Measurement and Dynamic Library Service was held at the School of Library Science, Simmons College. During the first unit of the Institute the participants were introduced to some of the basic statistical methods and some of the concepts of system approaches used in evaluating library services. Presentations on the subject were made by several authorities in the field. There was much group discussion and examination of selected examples of these useful quantitative techniques. There was a great deal of enthusiasm about applying quantitative methods to library managerial problems among participants. During the interim period many applied these techniques to their own libraries to evaluate some aspect of library service. During the second unit these participants reconvened to share their experiences and critically evaluate their efforts to date. This two-part approach was used rather than the traditional one-shot conference because it gave the participants the opportunity to not only learn something new, but also to attempt to apply this knowledge and then to discuss and share their experiences with others. The follow-up experience provided the participants with critical direction and confidence.

This publication is an outgrowth of the proceedings of the Institute. It documents the positive experiences that result from such a conference. More importantly, it demonstrates that library managers can practice and benefit from scientific management, provided they are motivated and enthusiastic about this type of approach. Most of the participants do not have sophisticated statistical knowledge, yet this publication shows that even within a very rushed time period, many library managers can learn quickly to apply whatever methods are needed to help them to evaluate their library service.

Because of the extremely brief period of time given to the participants to do their studies, the methodologies they used can undoubtedly be improved. Even so, the potential benefits of a quantitative approach to library management were easily realized by all of us.

Several studies have been modified since the Institute ended. Several others have led to more exciting new investigatory projects. Four papers (by Turner, Ungarelli, Varnet, and Parker) have been included because they are relevant to the Institute; they were prepared under similar rushed circumstances.

Ching-chih Chen

Introduction

No one in the library profession has to be convinced that the current economic crunch in which we all find ourselves warrants new approaches to evaluating and justifying our services. With the limited resources available, library managers are forced to seek new modes of operations in cost-beneficial terms and to investigate new ways to maximize the available resources—money, staff, space, etc.

With the ever increasing amount of information sources or knowledge records, library users' information demands and needs are increasingly difficult to satisfy, particularly in light of the shrinking budgets for library collection development and other activities. Thus new evaluative methods must be developed and utilized in order for library managers to make wise decisions in providing necessary library services and programs. In other words, the old way of administering a library by past experience and intuition has to give way to scientific management, which requires accountability. It is clear that the current library financial situation propagates interest in quantitative methods in library management.

The scientific approach is problem-oriented. Various problem-solving tools, such as statistics, probability-theory, and systems analysis, are frequently employed. These techniques and tools can assist library managers in many ways including user needs assessment, performance measurement, forecasting and prediction, priority-setting, selection of viable alternatives, cost-benefit study, improvement of library effectiveness and efficiency, resource maximization, and many others. It should be pointed out that some librarians seem to have the notion that the techniques will tell them what they should do and will make decisions for them. Actually, on the contrary, the librarian must never allow any method to replace him or her as the ultimate decision-maker. This implies that the responsibility for decisions must rest with the person, not the tool. The techniques have no magic. They are just guides and aids to the decision-maker. Knowing what will result in the future, if certain decisions are made now, will enable an administrator to make wiser decisions for the future.

In addition to the above-mentioned advantages, one of the most obvious by-products of a quantitative approach to library management is that if one is going to justify one's library budget, program and services, or some aspect of these to financial managers, it helps to be able to present one's arguments in quantifiable terms. When the benefits of supporting certain library services or the consequences of certain library cutbacks can be clearly stated in figures, library managers find themselves in a more favorable position when competing with other nonlibrary organizations for limited available funds.

This book is intended for those library professionals who have *no* background in statistics but who are interested in applying quantitative methods to various library managerial problems. Thus, most studies included involve the use of simple statistical methods. This publication demonstrates that one does not have to have an extensive background in statistics to take advantage of these methods. The various studies included in this book show that one is free to choose whatever method one decides is best suited for his/her purposes in his/her particular library situation. The point, after all, is not for us to be mathematically fancy, but to improve our ability to evaluate library services and thus to make more intelligent management decisions.

This book is divided into two parts. Part I consists of four papers dealing with different aspects of the quantitative evaluation of library services. All four authors are very familiar with library statistical studies.

Chen's article is a general background analysis of the nature and purpose of scientific inquiry and evaluation. She acquaints the reader with some of the basic concepts of quantitative evaluation and indicates some of the broad areas of library service where they may be usefully applied.

Lancaster provides a more detailed discussion of the nature of the evaluation of library services. His examination of many of the quantitative procedures that have been used to evaluate library services does not hesitate to point out the serious limitations of such efforts at the present time. He also attempts to define the proper goal of information services.

Hamburg is concerned with exploring statistical methods that will aid library managers in their basic planning and decision making. The usefulness of such tools as sampling techniques and prediction models is examined.

Leimkuhler deals with the application of systems analysis and analytical techniques, such as operations research, to the evaluation of library services. He discusses the history of this application and isolates some of the areas where it has been most fruitful. These include document usage, storage, availability, core literature, shelving, etc. Leimkuhler is very much aware of the philosophical and human problems raised by the application of operations research.

Part II presents various types of practical library statistical studies—from the simple to the more sophisticated and analytical; from small public library to large academic—on a great variety of topics. The statistical and systems approaches discussed in Part I of the book were applied by numerous library managers to different library environments. Naturally the use to which these new tools were put and the skill with which they were handled reflects the previous backgrounds and the particular interests of the people involved at each level. The results of the studies demonstrate that statistical and analytical tools can be picked up by any librarian and used in the manner and to the extent s/he desires.

Five relatively simple and straightforward applications of statistical methods to generate quantitative measures of library services are represented by the study of reference services at a public library by Melissa Chait, the measurement for space utilization in a medium-sized public library by Leila-Jane Roberts, the investigation of the use of journal back files in a special library by Julie Long, the survey of user demands at an industrial corporate library by Karen Feingold and Jane Ward, and a statistical study on the nonresident borrowers of a public library by Anne Turner. Although some quantitative studies involve complicated statistical analyses, this need not be the case. For example, Chait's study utilizes a simple tally sheet survey method to produce a single-faceted evaluation of reference services in a small to medium-sized public library. This study shows that as long as one's methodology is viable and resulting inferences can be supported by the collected data, an unsophisticated researcher can implement a basic quantitative study to justify library activities. Roberts also applies a simple tally method of collecting data on the use of a given library space, in order to generate information for a long-range plan for alternative spacial-design of the library.

One of the simplest methods of reducing a mass of data into a manageable form is to construct comparison tables. "A Journal Use-Study in a VA Hospital" employs this technique to analyze circulation statistics of journal use in a VA medical library. On the basis of these easily assembled statistics, Long is able to justify a policy decision as to which journals are to be put onto microfilm in order to maximize valuable shelf-space. The comparison tables also allow the author to relate circulation figures to another parameter, the size of the bound journals in terms of linear shelf-space. The author also suggests a further use of her methods: a study of current circulation data could be made to determine if heavily used backfiles can be predicted on the basis of current use of journals.

Feingold and Ward conduct a simple survey of information requests at their corporate library. They analyze the results in terms of a scheme for categorizing library services. Their purpose is to get some hard data that could be used as an aid in planning for future staff expansion projects. Their study is in the nature of an internal report, since it defines a specific problem indigenous to an individual library environment, with results useful only to the original organization. It does illustrate, however, how techniques of quantitative measurement may be profitably utilized to solve problems in decision-making areas, such as forecasting user demands.

Anne M. Turner conducted a simple study of the nonresident use of a medium-sized public library in order to make various significant administrative decisions regarding library service programs to non-residents and the appropriate allocation of LSCA funds. The methodologies used are simple and straightforward and can be applied by every librarian with little statistical background.

Two more studies that involve an easy-to-understand and direct methodology are Sheila Testa's study of journal use in a community hospital library and the work of Joan Stockard, Mary Ann Griffin, and Clementine Coblyn in academic library settings. Both studies attempt to measure in-library use of their respective libraries using the pick-up method. In her study, Testa is able to determine which policy areas may be affected by the results of use measurement figures. While the technique is simple, and has been adapted to a policy already operating in the library (i.e., the non-reshelving of materials), conclusions drawn from the gathered statistics may influence major decisions concerning future management of the hospital library in question. Stockard, Griffin, and Coblyn use the same simple pick-up technique to produce tabulated data about their particular libraries. The authors manipulate this data in order to propose a correlation between in-library use to circulation figures to substantiate the more easily obtainable circulation statistics as a valid measure of in-library use (via the resulting ratio). Their paper shows how an uncomplicated methodology can yield useful results. They also indicate other areas to be examined in the future. This multi-institutional study provides valuable results for cross comparisons, thus overcoming one of the limitations of user studies by gathering data from three locations.

The companion studies of Ungarelli and Varnet of the cost benefits of book detection systems in their respective libraries also represent basic statistical approaches to the evaluation of a new library service. These studies will certainly be of interest to any library manager who is considering the installation of a similar system in his or her library. They are also of interest because they utilize different methodologies. To get a handle on the extent of losses in a large academic library, Ungarelli took a random sample of the shelf list of the library and checked it against the stacks, materials in circulation, and materials on reserve. Varnet, however, working with a much smaller library, was able to use the figures of the actual annual inventories of materials. Both authors attempted to correlate age and use of materials. The fact that their results are very similar is an interesting indication that one methodology can be tailored to different needs and that it can still be viable.

Sometimes the collection of data to be used for the quantitative measure of library services is even easier and faster than in the previous eight studies. This is illustrated by Myra Carbonell in a study that demonstrated the kind of analysis that is possible when library operations are controlled by computer. In compiling an acquisition profile for an academic library, Carbonell found that relevant data could be readily accessed by computer programs. Once the files were read, the analysis consisted only of correlating information. She also presents topics and a comparison which could be part of a later in-house or inter-library project. Further useful studies could also be generated.

A more sophisticated use of the tools of statistics than has been mentioned up to this point is represented by Ethel Apple's four-part quantitative study of library use at a community college, utilizing the Statistical Package for the Social Sciences (SPSS), a statistical analysis software package. Using various data gathering procedures, the following areas were examined: title availability, equipment and facilities use, in-library circulation, and user characteristics. This Learning Resource Center survey is the result of four separate studies, each with its own implications, which when combined give a total picture of library use.

More sophisticated analytical statistical methods, such as operations research, are employed in the final two studies. These studies employ probabilistic techniques in measuring library services and are a "test" of the applicability of these methods to specific library contexts. The first study by Sandra Spurlock and Ellen Yen examines library life sciences book use in terms of a predictive operations research model developed by Morse and Chen. Their paper stresses the adaptability of this model to a subject collection in a large academic library system and the ease, rapidity, and accuracy of the data gathering procedures associated with the model. The authors discuss the implications of their study, demonstrating how future measurements would be able to show the success or failure of policy changes made on the basis of the results of this initial study.

The second study by Andrea Hoffman is also an effort to build on the work of Morse and Chen. Their models and procedures are used to sample the circulation of a special library collection at a teaching resources center in a small college in order to measure it. These results are used to help arrive at a better monograph duplication policy. This study concludes in specific recommendations for book duplication and is an excellent example of how some of the latest techniques in statistical methods in library management can be applied to a particular problem in library services.

The last paper by Parker included in Part II is not really a statistical study. Nevertheless, it is included because it raises some of the larger questions of deciding which analytical tool to use in a specific context. It provides background information, since the author discusses basic types of methodologies suitable for quantitative studies. In addition, five specific performance indicators are explained in detail. Parker undertakes such a project to show how operational performance measurement systems could be adapted to reflect an altered library organization and activity structure (in this case, a Canadian government health sciences library network).

Part II is followed by an appendix which describes briefly the Capitol Region Library Council Study (Connecticut) to develop a data management system for use in the measurement of library services. The study is the product of a successful grant proposal (LSCA) developed by Dency Sargent, Richard Akeroyd and Barbara Gibson when they participated at the Institute on Quantitative Measurement and Dynamic Library Service at Simmons College in November 1976 and March 1977. This should serve to point out yet another benefit and advantage of quantitative approaches.

A glossary of frequently used terms on quantitative methods is also provided for the readers' convenience. Finally, at the end of the book, an extensive bibliography on statistical applications to library management is provided. The bibliography describes all useful and up-to-date references in seven major categories, which include basic statistical texts, bibliographies, "state-of-the-art" update, "state-of-the-practice" update, recent articles on the use of library statistics, selected statistical sources on libraries in the USA and Canada, and specific statistical applications. The last category is further sub-divided into nine topics.

Ching-chih Chen

Contributors

Ethel Apple is Librarian of Learning Resources Center, Elgin Community College, Elgin, Illinois.

Myra Carbonell is the System Librarian at Yale University, New Haven, Connecticut.

Melissa Chait is Assistant Director of the Wayland Public Library, Wayland, Massachusetts.

Ching-chih Chen is the Assistant Dean for Academic Affairs and Associate Professor, School of Library Science, Simmons College, Boston, Massachusetts.

Clementine Coblyn is the Circulation Librarian at Hayden Library, Massachusetts Institute of Technology, Cambridge, Massachusetts.

Karen Feingold is the Head Librarian, Digital Equipment Company, Maynard, Massachusetts.

Mary Ann Griffin is a Doctor of Arts student at the School of Library Science, Simmons College, Boston, Massachusetts.

Morris Hamburg is Professor of Statistics and Operations Research, Wharton School of Business, University of Pennsylvania, Philadelphia, Pennsylvania.

Andrea C. Hoffman is the former Director of the Teaching Resource Center, Leslie College Cambridge, Massachusetts.

F. W. Lancaster is a Professor at the Graduate School of Library Science, University of Illinois.

F. F. Leimkuhler is Professor of Industrial Engineering, Purdue University, West Lafayette, Indiana.

Julia L. Long is the Head Librarian at the Boston VA Hospital, Boston, Massachusetts.

Deanne McCutcheon is at the Graduate School of Library Science, University of Illinois.

Joy McPherson is a Librarian, School of Library Science, Simmons College, Boston, Massachusetts.

Sandra Parker is the former Librarian, Health Protection Branch Library, Health and Welfare, Canada.

Leila-Jane Roberts is Director of the Winchester Public Library, Winchester, Massachusetts.

Sandra Spurlock is Assistant Science Librarian, Massachusetts Institute of Technology, Cambridge, Massachusetts.

Joan Stockard is at the Library, Wellesley College, Wellesley, Massachusetts.

Sheila Newlands Testa is Director of the Health Sciences Library, Lynn, Massachusetts.

Anne M. Turner is Director of The Jones Library, Amherst, Massachusetts.

Donald Ungarelli is Director of Libraries, C. W. Post Center, Long Island University.

Harvey Varnet is Assistant Director of Public Services, Learning Resources Center, Bristol Community College, Bristol, Massachusetts.

Ellen Yen is Assistant Science Librarian, Massachusetts Institute of Technology, Cambridge, Massachusetts.

PART

I

ASPECTS OF QUANTITATIVE EVALUATION OF LIBRARY SERVICES

Statistical and Systems Applications in Library Management

by Ching-chih Chen

The concept of quantitative evaluation and measurement of library performance, effectiveness and efficiency has been introduced to librarians and library managers for quite some time. For instance, as far back as 1947, Ralph R. Shaw advocated scientific management in the library. Yet, prior to the 1970s the library economic climax was relaxed and comfortable and librarians were seldom required to justify their existence, to defend their budget requests, to account for their support, and to find ways to maximize their resources. As a result, few library administrators were either willing or capable of applying statistical and systems methods in their library decision-making process.

On the other hand, since the late 1960s, the inflationary spiral and tight economy have become more and more serious; the costs of managing libraries, developing library collections, delivering needed information, and providing helpful library services have reached unprecedented levels. As a result, few budget officials are willing to accept the value of library services without convincing justifications from the library administrators and detailed accountability for the money spent. Thus, it seems fair to say that the present economic climax has promoted librarians' willing and unwilling interests in quantitative measurements.

Furthermore, there are other factors for increasing concern with quantitative measurement of libraries and their services. Some of these factors, as Orr suggested are:

- Success of these tools in other fields;
- Adoption of these techniques by the organizations supporting libraries;
- Increasingly explicit character of competition for funds at all levels;
- Complexity and critical nature of decisions on alternatives created by technology and by formalization of library networks.

This paper represents an edited version of a talk presented at the Institute.

INQUIRY

Prior to any discussion on how statistical methods can be utilized in library management, it seems necessary to briefly discuss "inquiry" in general. Northrop stated that "inquiry starts only when something is unsatisfactory."[1] He further stated that inquiry begins with a *problem.*

However, an inquiry does not have to begin only when a problem exists at the present time. It can and should begin when a potential problem begins to surface. For example, library space has always been a big problem, and librarians should start looking for viable solutions for the next year even though there are still sufficient numbers of shelves to accommodate this year's new acquisitions.

A Problem Oriented Inquiry

To conduct a problem oriented inquiry, one generally follows the following steps:

1. Identify the problem;
2. Define the problem;
3. Discover the basic theoretical root of the problem;
4. State the long-term goals and short-term objectives of the inquiry;
5. Identify relevant and controllable factors involved in a problem situation;
6. Project relevant hypotheses;
7. Plan the investigation of the problem;
8. Collect relevant data;
9. Analyze the collected data, logical deduction and verification of the hypotheses;
10. Present proposed solutions on recommendations to the problem.

The first three steps seem to be self-evident, and librarians need not be reminded often about them. In other words, any inquiry must start with a problem, whether existing or potential, and one simply does not go around collecting data for collecting's sake. Yet, in reality, few librarians do look seriously at the kinds of statistics they keep.

Most library statistics have been collected for a long time without anyone knowing the usefulness of these data. They are being collected because traditionally they have been collected for years (kept in the head librarians' filing cabinets). We frequently hear the sad remark, "It isn't that we do not have statistics. Our problem is that we have too many unusable figures."

The setting of goals and objectives is essential to the success of any inquiry. In literature and actual practice, we have found that the two

---

[1]F.S.C. Northrop. *The Logic of the Sciences and the Humanities.* New York: World Publ. Co., 1971. p. 1, 17.

terms—"goal" and "objective"—have been frequently interchangeable. Here, goal is generally considered to be long-term and general, while objectives are short-term and quantifiable in a functional way.

Projecting hypotheses is also a necessary initial step, so that one can possibly predict the potential outcomes of a study. However, librarians should know the difference between setting hypotheses and pre-determining the study results. It is not uncommon to locate some library studies which have been conducted in such a manner merely to prove that the pre-determined results are correct ones.

One of the most difficult parts of any study is probably the planning stage of an investigation; and during this stage, the appropriate methodology to be used for the particular study needs to be established. It seems appropriate to stress that *methodology* is not method. Kaplan (1964, p. 23) stated that "methods" include the following procedures:

1. Forming concepts and hypotheses;
2. Making observations and measurements;
3. Performing experiments;
4. Building models and theories;
5. Providing explanations; and
6. Making predictions

and he succinctly defines "methodology" as "the description, the explanation and the justification of methods." Thus, in the process of describing, explaining and justifying the methods used in an investigation, one needs to carefully explore and describe the various methods used by previous related studies; to present the reasons for selecting specific methods; and to point out the limitations of the selected method. Furthermore, one needs to define the data elements involved in the study; to determine the study sample(s); and to discuss the existing difficulties, bases and problems of the study. Each of the planning stages deserves a careful and detailed consideration. For example, the planning of a study sample involves at least the following areas of consideration:

● Scope of the sampling;
● Sampling unit;
● Sampling period;
● Sampling size;
● Sampling methods (random, etc. . .)

Once a healthy methodology of a study is set, the data collection process is generally relatively easy but frequently tedious. Once the data collection is completed, it is necessary to organize, categorize and deduct these gathered data by using various statistical and analytical techniques, whether descriptive or inferential. This is a difficult but essential step because without it, the big mass of data would yield no meaningful results or findings.

Thus, it seems quite apparent that librarians would benefit a great deal by working on these types of projects with a team approach. A systems analyst with statistical and systems knowledge can be most helpful to library managers in almost all stages of an inquiry.

It also seems appropriate to stress the importance of making viable recommendations and presenting alternatives to a problem. Library administrators should be open-minded enough to be willing to accept and to test the new alternatives, and thus generalize a continuous reviewing process.

From the above discussion, it should be clear that all quantitative evaluative studies should follow the basic research methodology. The Recommended Texts following this article are advised for further information on the subject.

EVALUATION

Evaluation and measurement have been frequently used in an interchangeable way, yet they are not really synonymous. Lancaster (1977) considers that there are three possible levels of evaluation of library services: effectiveness, cost-effectiveness, and cost-benefit. "Effectiveness must be measured in terms of how well a service satisfies the demand placed upon it by its users. . . . Cost-effectiveness is concerned with its internal operating efficiency. . . . A cost-benefit evaluation is . . . concerned with whether the value (worth) of the service is more or less than the cost of providing it."[2]

King and Bryant (1971) consider that there are at least two types of evaluation. They are macro-evaluation and micro-evaluation. The macro ones are mainly descriptive in nature and generally relate to the state of the arts, while the micro ones are diagnostic in nature and go further to seek viable solutions to the existing problems. For example, a great deal of library evaluative studies attempt to measure library effectiveness. Figure 1 shows that those studies dealing with the first two categories of problems are generally considered to be macro-evaluative ones while those dealing with the diagnostic aspects of the problems are micro-evaluative ones. Naturally, the latter studies are more useful to library managers. For a more detailed discussion on this topic, readers are referred to Lancaster's recent book (1977). To follow up on the above discussion of an inquiry, the evaluation process is summarized in the somewhat over-simplified diagram shown in Figure 2.

PURPOSE OF EVALUATION RESEARCH

Weiss considered the purpose of evaluation research is "to measure the effects of a program against the goals it set out to accomplish

[2]F.W. Lancaster. *The Measurement and Evaluation of Library Services.* Washington D.C.: Information Resources Press, 1977. Chapter 1.

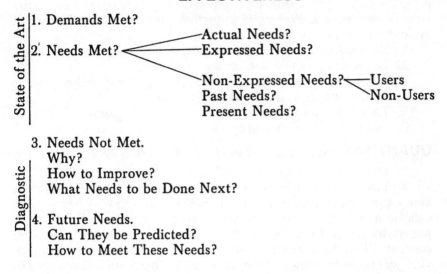

EFFECTIVENESS

State of the Art

1. Demands Met?

2. Needs Met?
   - Actual Needs?
   - Expressed Needs?
   - Non-Expressed Needs? — Users / Non-Users
   - Past Needs?
   - Present Needs?

Diagnostic

3. Needs Not Met.
   Why?
   How to Improve?
   What Needs to be Done Next?

4. Future Needs.
   Can They be Predicted?
   How to Meet These Needs?

FIGURE 1

EVALUATION PROCESS

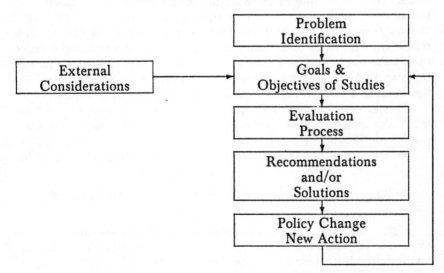

FIGURE 2

as a means of contributing to subsequent decision making about the program and improve future programming."[3] This seems to be quite clear from Figure 2. Weiss (1972) further points out that the uses of evaluation can be summarized as follows:

1. To continue or discontinue a program;
2. To improve its practices and procedures;
3. To add or drop specific program strategies and techniques;
4. To institute similar programs elsewhere;
5. To allocate resources among competing programs;
6. To accept or reject a program approach or theory.

QUANTITATIVE EVALUATION IN THE LIBRARY

"Statistics," "systems analysis," and "quantitative methods" are all familiar terms to librarians, yet librarians are generally unclear about the applications of statistical methods in libraries beyond the collection of common statistics for reporting purposes. While several papers by the institute faculty have specifically dealt with the basic concepts of statistics and systems approach, this paper hopes to provide general discussions on how statistical methods can be employed in every aspect of library work for various managerial considerations. Prior to this discussion, it seems necessary to restate the role of the library in terms of *information*. Figure 3 provides a simple model which illustrates that the library serves as an intermediary or a transmitter between the world's big mass of information (or knowledge records) and the information consumers. To fulfill this transmitter's role, the library's basic functions are the selection, acquisition, organization and dissemination of the available information. Thus, in order to improve the effectiveness and efficiency of the library's role as an information transmitter, evaluative studies employing both basic and analytical statistical methods can and should be conducted on all entries illustrated on Figure 3. Since time and space do not permit a detailed discussion on every possible type of study, the potential sample investigations are briefly categorized in Table I in order to heighten the librarians' awareness of statistical applications in libraries.

It is essential to identify input variables for any type of measurement. For example, some of the useful input variables for library users can be identified as the following:

- Age;
- Sex;
- Race;
- Socioeconomic status;
- Academic status if applicable;
- Affiliation;
- Educational background;
- Experience

Once the input variables are defined, the possible outputs can be expected. For example, in studying the use behavior of library users in an academic library, if one of the input variables is academic status of

---

[3]Carol H. Weiss. *Evaluation Research: Methods for Assessing Program Effectiveness.* Englewood, N.J.: Prentice-Hall, 1972.

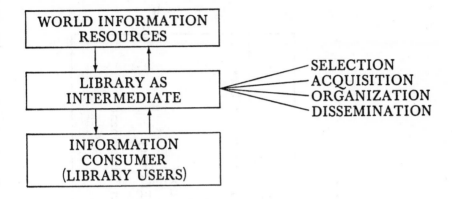

FIGURE 3

a library user, then one can expect that the study results will show the various use patterns of faculty, staff, researchers, graduate students and undergraduates.

Looking at the "library" itself, every aspect of a library function — selection, acquisition, collection development, organization, and dissemination — can be an attractive target for quantitative measurement and evaluation in order to enable librarians to find better ways to provide more dynamic library services to their library's users. The following are a few sample listings of possible studies related to library functions:

CATALOGING
- Use of catalog
- Access point of information to users
- Need of subject headings
- Time and motion study
- Catalog output and by-products
- Benefit of OCLC cataloging

CIRCULATION
- Reserve collection use
- Loan period
- Need for automated circulation system
- Fine policy
- Missing items and inventory problems
- Inventory

COLLECTION DEVELOPMENT
- Budget required to satisfy:
  1. Minimal collection need
  2. Appropriate collection need
  3. Optimal collection need

TABLE I

POTENTIAL LIBRARY QUANTITATIVE EVALUATIVE INVESTIGATIONS

Areas of Study	Factors Related to Each Area of Study	Evaluation Criteria
Information Sources	Quantity	Exposure of Information to Users
Libraries	Quality	Accessibility
Librarians	Effectiveness	User Satisfaction
Funders	Cost	Operational Efficiency
Library and Nonusers	Cost Effectiveness	Money, Effort, Time Spent
Information Users	Cost Benefit	

- Collection policy
- Citation studies
- Use studies—journal, book, other materials
  —Past circulation
  —In-house materials left on desk
  —Random sample of total collection
  —OR studies for prediction purposes
- Core collection development
- Duplicates
- Weeding
- Networking

REFERENCE

- Use of the library resources
- Alternatives to increase use
- Assessment of answering effectiveness
- I.L.L. needs and collection assessment
- Delivery time of I.L.L. material
- User groups and their respective needs
- Time study of answering reference questions
- User satisfaction to information services
- Failure analysis of searches: manual, machine
- Training and success
- User orientation and training
- Enumeration and classification of reference questions
  —Type, subject, source, time spent, etc.
- Study of reference collection
- Reference personnel and organization
- Cost analysis

ADMINISTRATION

- Budget—PPBS vs. Line vs. ZBB
- Budgetary allocations
- Use of physical facilities
- Storage problems
- Staffing allocations
- Mechanization vs. manual
- Queueing of library services
- Economics of library operations

SAMPLE EXISTING LIBRARY EVALUATIVE STUDIES

Quantitative library studies are not really new phenomena. Library literature shows that this type of investigation can be traced back to 1911 when inventories of books were studied at the Grand Rapids Public Library (1911). Since then, hundreds of library studies have been conducted by utilizing statistical methods. In 1970, Atkin listed over 700 studies in her bibliography (1971) of library usage alone. Although the quantity of these studies is great, most of them are descriptive in nature at the macro-evaluative level and few are substantial, diagnostic and predictive by utilizing modern analytical techniques.

Furthermore, several other common problems have been found in library evaluation. They are:

- Vague objectives (not in functional terms);
- Uncertain methodology;
- Uncertain measures;
- Half-formulated standards;

In Professor Lancaster's paper, he has succinctly provided a quick overview of existing library evaluative studies by types of library functions and operations. A detailed review of the state of arts of library quantitative measurements and evaluation can be found in his recent book, entitled *The Measurement and Evaluation of Library Services* (Lancaster, 1977). It categorized library evaluative studies as follows:

- Catalog use;
- Reference service;
- Literature searching and information retrieval;
- Collection;
- Document delivery capabilities;
- Range and scope of library services;
- Technical services;
- Automated services;
- Library surveys;
- Physical accessibility to ease of use;
- Cost-performance benefits.

Thus, the book should serve as a background reference tool to those who are contemplating any library evaluative studies.

CONCLUSION

In spite of the increasing acceptance of and reliance on applying quantitative methods in libraries, there are still conflicting attitudes among librarians and library administrators toward this type of management approach. These attitudes can be summarized in two categories:

1. One school feels that some of the major benefits derived from libraries are intangible and not measurable. Each library is unique and should be assessed in the context of its own particular history, constraints, users, and environment; and the subjective judgment of professionals should be respected. Members of this school view quantitative measures as a "necessary evil."

2. The other school believes that it is possible to measure objectively the goodness of most library services. Imperfect measures can be useful if their limitations are appreciated. The libraries are no more varied than other organizations where the tools of management science have been applied profitably.

With this conflict in mind, it is our hope that an institute such as this one can promote more dialogue and better communication between these two groups of librarians, stimulate careful reappraisal of traditional approaches in library management, and convince the library managers that quantitative methods can be not only valuable tools for research, but also practical aids in the management of libraries.

REFERENCES

Atkin, Pauline. *A Bibliography of Use Surveys 1950-70.* London: The Library Association, 1971.

Grand Rapids (Michigan) Public Library. *Report.* (Samuel H. Ranck, Librarian.) 1911. (Listed in *Library Journal* 37 (May, 1912):291).

Kaplan, Abraham. *The Conduct of Inquiry: Methodology for Behavioral Science.* San Francisco, CA: Chandler Publishing Co., 1964.

King, D. W. and Bryant, E. C. *The Evaluation of Information Sciences and Products.* Washington, DC: Information Resources Press, 1971.

Lancaster, F. Wilfrid. *The Measurement and Evaluation of Library Services.* Washington, DC: Information Resources Press, 1977.

Northrop, F. S. C. *The Logic of the Sciences and the Humanities.* New York: World Publishing Co., 1971.

Orr, Richard H. "Measuring the Goodness of Library Services: A General Framework for Considering Quantitative Measures." *Journal of Documentation* 29 (September, 1973):315-332.

Shaw, Ralph R. "Scientific Management in the Library." *Wilson Library Bulletin* 21 (January, 1947):349-352.

Weiss, Carol H. *Evaluation Research: Methods for Assessing Program Effectiveness.* Englewood, NJ: Prentice-Hall, 1972.

RECOMMENDED TEXTS

Ary, Donald, and others. *Introduction to Research in Education.* New York: Holt, Rinehart and Winston, 1972. Pts. 1 and 2.

Goldhor, Herbert. *An Introduction to Scientific Research in Librarianship.* Monograph No. 12. Urbana, IL: University of Illinois, Graduate School of Library Science, 1972.

Northrop, F. S. C. *The Logic of the Sciences and the Humanities.* New York: Macmillan, 1947. Reprinted by World Publishing Co., Meridian Books, 1959.

Some Achievements and Limitations of Quantitative Procedures Applied to the Evaluation of Library Services

by F. W. Lancaster and Deanne McCutcheon

Most of the achievements in the application of quantitative and semi-quantitative methods to the evaluation of library services have occurred in the last decade. The purpose of these quantitative methods is to evaluate the services that libraries provide and the degree to which these services meet various demands of users. This paper will explore these methods, first by defining the various levels of evaluation, and then presenting a survey of the application of these methods to various facets of library service, including evaluation of the collection, document delivery capabilities, reference services and catalog use. The focus of this discussion will be on the achievements as well as the limitations of the methods used in the measurement and evaluation of library services.

In discussing the application of quantitative and semi-quantitative methods, we need to recognize the existence of several possible levels of evaluation and the differences among these levels. An evaluation of the effectiveness of a service is an evaluation of how well the services meet the needs or demands of the community to be served. The results of an effectiveness evaluation can be expressed quantitatively. For example, the document delivery capability of a university library may be measured and determined to be 72 percent, which would mean that, when a user comes into that library, there is a 72 percent probability that the user will find the needed item in the collection, and available on the shelf. So, effectiveness evaluation relates to the extent to which user demands are satisfied and can be expressed quantitatively in many instances.

This paper is a more or less verbatim transcript of a talk presented at the Institute.

Cost-effectiveness evaluation, on the other hand, is concerned with the relationship between levels of effectiveness and costs. This 72 percent level of achievement in document delivery might be achieved in several ways, each having different costs associated with it. A cost-effectiveness analysis of the situation would be one that, assuming, for example, a document delivery goal of 72 percent, investigates which of several possible strategies can achieve this level of performance and what costs will be associated with it. We can improve the cost-effectiveness of an operation by keeping the effectiveness level constant and reducing the cost, or we can improve its cost-effectiveness by holding the cost constant, but raising the effectiveness level. Cost-effectiveness expresses a relationship between levels of performance, which may be expressed quantitatively, and their associated costs.

A third level of evaluation is cost-benefit evaluation. Cost-benefit studies are concerned with the perceived or measurable value that accrues to the community to which a service is provided. This is a higher level of evaluation than either of the other two. In fact, the three have been mentioned in a sequence of increasing complexity, cost-benefit being the most difficult simply because the benefits of library service lack tangibility and are extremely difficult to express in cost-benefit terms. In the literature of information and library science, the terms *cost-effectiveness evaluation* and *cost-benefit evaluation* are used rather loosely, and frequently interchangeably, as though they were the same, when actually they are not.

Another distinction that needs to be clarified is between macroevaluation and microevaluation. Macroevaluation is simply concerned with the level of performance of a particular service or system. If we did a study of the document delivery capability of a particular library, and by taking an appropriate sampling of user demands, found that this library was operating at a level of 72 percent success (72 percent probability of an item being on the shelf when it was needed), this would be a macroevaluation. It tells us how we are performing now and it gives us a benchmark against which changes in the system can be measured. But macroevaluation, while valuable in itself, only goes part of the way towards evaluation. Knowing that a library is achieving 72 percent success is an interesting figure, but it tells us nothing about how to improve the service. We need to ask ourselves why it is operating at 72 percent and what would we have to do in the future to raise this level of performance to some other goal, say 80 percent or 85 percent.

Many of the studies conducted in the last ten years, that can be grouped under the general heading of quantitative methods, are pure macroevaluation because they rarely go beyond producing data. In order to improve the service, we need microevaluation. Microevaluation deals with the most important level of evaluation, the diagnostic level. Why are we operating at 72 percent? What is the difference between the 72 percent that represents our successes and the 28 percent that represents our failures? This kind of analysis, although we use figures in our analysis, is more or less non-quantitative. It is interpretative. The investigator is very much involved with using the figures, acquired through quantitative procedures, to make reasonable decisions on what needs to be done to raise the level of performance.

Before we evaluate any service, we must have in mind the objectives of the service, and this immediately raises some problems in the library world because libraries in general tend to lack clearly defined statements of objectives. In considering the objectives of libraries and information services, a careful distinction must be made between long-range objectives and short-range objectives. The long-range objectives of libraries, and, in fact, of other kinds of service institutions, are largely unmeasurable. It is difficult, if not impossible, to evaluate the performance of a library in terms of what we might consider to be long-range objectives; therefore, we must concentrate upon the short-range objectives.

The importance of this distinction was stated very well by Peter Drucker (1973), the management expert, who noted that any public service institution has both long-range and short-range objectives. The first group, the long-range, are largely unmeasurable. For example, he pointed out that the long-range objectives of the church can be said to be saving souls, while the long-range objectives of education might be viewed as developing the whole personality. These objectives are unmeasurable. Similarly, the long-range objective of certain aspects of library service can be said to be helping citizens become better informed, which is also largely unmeasurable. Therefore, we must focus instead upon the short-range objectives. If, instead of focusing on saving souls, we recognize that a reasonable short-range goal of the church is getting young people to attend church, that is an objective which is precisely measurable and quantitatively qualifiable. Teaching a child to read by the time he finishes third grade is an objective which is quantifiable and susceptible to precise measurement. In the same way, answering successfully 95 percent of all requests for factual information made to the library is precisely measurable. Although it is not easy to measure, it is susceptible to quantitative analysis, whereas the long-range objectives of libraries are not.

In thinking about the short-range objectives of libraries, it is perhaps an oversimplification, but a convenient oversimplification, to regard the library as an interface. That is, the function of the library or information center is to act as an interface between some community of users, which is defined as the population to be served, and the universe of bibliographic resources. At the interface, then, we obviously have inputs and outputs in both directions. The role of the library is to bring the bibliographic universe, or at least that portion that is of most relevance, to the community of users. The library attempts to organize this universe and to make it available at various levels of accessibility. Certain items in this universe are more accessible than others because they are collected by the library and put into prime locations on open access shelves. Others, which can be assumed to be less in demand, are acquired by the library but put into stacks. Still others may be in a warehouse, while some items are not in the library at all but accessible through interlibrary loan or photocopy.

If we concentrate upon regarding the library in its role as an interface between these communities, library evaluation is simplified because we then evaluate library service in terms of how this interface role may in all cases be improved. This has been expressed very clearly by Morris Hamburg (1974), when he speaks of the role of the library as one of improving exposure.

When we speak of the role of the library as one of exposing users to materials, we are saying that the library serves as an interface between the community of users and the community of materials. Rather than simply considering exposure as a single entity, as Hamburg does, it is helpful to split the objective into two aspects, exposure and accessibility. The exposure of users to materials involves a dynamic kind of information service whereas accessibility of materials to users is a more passive service. The role or the goal of improving the accessibility of materials to users implies organizing the materials in terms of their accessibility so that when a user needs a particular item, the probability of its being available is maximized. It also implies that the user has to initiate the process, that is, the user has to come to the library and be seeking material, whereas exposure implies continually informing users of new documents, new information, which match their interest profiles. Maximizing exposure of users to materials involves a dynamic service such as a selective dissemination of information service, while maximizing accessibility of materials connotes a more passive situation. Both are important and need to be regarded as two sides of the same coin. The difference between exposure and accessibility may be related to Ranganathan's Five Laws of Library Science which distinguish between exposure and accessibility in different terms. The second of Ranganathan's Laws of Library Science was "every reader his or her book," implying the need for accessibility of materials to users, while the third law, "every book its reader," promotes the idea of exposure, of a dynamic information service.

The criteria that can be applied to the evaluation of the public services of the library eventually have to be related in some way to user satisfaction: that is, we have to have some measure of the extent to which the user demands or needs are satisfied. When we are concerned, on the other hand, with evaluating technical services, it is not usually possible to assess technical services directly in terms of user satisfaction. In evaluating technical services, we are more concerned with evaluating their internal efficiency: productivity, speed of processing, the general efficiency with which materials are acquired, processed, and made available to the public services. In addition to this evaluation of internal efficiency of technical services, we must also look at the effect of the technical services on public services. Most evaluations of technical services concentrate entirely upon output in terms of the efficiency of the operation, the unit cost of cataloging a book and getting an item processed and on the shelves, the length of time needed for these tasks, and the delays. These are all measures of internal efficiency. An issue that is equally important, but generally neglected, is the effect of internal efficiency of the technical services on the public services. What is the long term impact? For example, what kind of evidence can we collect to show that delays in through-put of materials are significantly affecting the success rate in document delivery?

In evaluating any kind of service, whether a library service or an airline service, the people who are being supplied by this service generally will evaluate it in terms of cost, time, and quality considerations. These general groupings of evaluation criteria apply equally to library service as to other types of public service. Cost criteria can be cost in terms of money, or cost in terms of user effort. There is an obvious cost if money changes hands: how much it costs per literature search, how much it costs the user when the library is providing, for example, an on-line search for material, how much it costs for an SDI profile. But there is another cost factor which is important, namely how much effort the user must spend to use the service; what is the cost to the user in time? The time factor that will be most important to the user is the waiting time (how long it takes to obtain the results of a literature search, the results of a reference inquiry, or an interlibrary loan).

In evaluation, the qualitative considerations are the most difficult ones with which to deal. In applying qualitative criteria to library services, there are two basic situations. One can be expressed in terms of "It is the service's success or failure." This is the easier one, as represented by the known item search. The user comes into the library looking for a particular bibliographic item, for which he or she has the author or title. Evaluation of this service involves a binary situation because the library either is successful or not; that is, the library either has the item the user wants at the time it is needed or it does not. The second situation, involving other kinds of services that libraries provide—such as subject searching—is not susceptible to this binary type of evaluation. In evaluating a subject search, we are faced with degrees of success which is a more difficult evaluation situation. For the user coming to a library or an information center for materials dealing with a particular subject, it's not a yes or no decision of whether some are found or not but rather the question is: how much information is found? Subject search evaluation gets into questions of relevance, of which is the most relevant or valuable material, making this evaluation situation much more complex than the known item search.

One of the biggest limitations of all evaluation efforts applied to libraries so far is that they tend to focus on a very small tip of an iceberg. Most studies are of a very limited scope because they apply evaluation procedures which focus upon the present users of the service and they largely ignore present non-users. In terms of assessing the value of the library as a service to the entire community, concentration upon the present users gives, in many ways, a distorted picture of the success of the library. Not only do we tend to concentrate on present users and exclude present non-users in our evaluation, but even in focusing on present users, we tend to identify the *demands* made by this group of users on the present library service. In this way, we ignore two important issues. First, what are the needs of the present users that are never converted into demands on the library, and why are some needs (information needs, document needs) of the library never converted into demands? Secondly, almost all studies that have been done so far assume that the demands made upon a library actually represent the needs of the users. If somebody comes into the library looking for information on a subject, we can evaluate how well the library performs in satisfying the stated need but, because it is extremely difficult to measure, we do not know how far this stated need actually represents the real information need of the user. Studies of the performance of information retrieval systems have shown clearly that, in many cases, there is a substantial gap between what the user states as a need and what is actually needed, that is, the latent need behind the expressed need. We face the danger of a distorted situation because one part of the picture is looked at intensively, while other parts are largely neglected. The most that is usually achieved is a relatively good picture of how well the library or information center satisfies the demands of the present users. Most of the studies that have been done of library services cannot be said to have measured the degree to which the library serves or is able to serve. Rather, they are actually studies of the degree to which this service meets the expressed needs of those individuals who are present users, which in many cases is a very small part of the iceberg. A danger exists in this type of evaluation because it creates a kind of self-reinforcing situation. If we always evaluate library service in terms of the expressed needs of the present users, then as a result of our evaluation, when we attempt to improve the service, we tend to move the library service toward the demands of the present users, and away, perhaps, from the unexpressed needs of the users and the needs of those who are not presently using the library.

This evaluation of services in terms of the expressed needs of the present users is the most serious defect of all the work that has been done in the evaluation of libraries in the last ten years. The concentration on present users and their demands is understandable because we know who the users are and what their demands are, while it is much more difficult to recognize needs that are never converted into demands either by present users or present non-users. It is easy to see demands and to quantify demands, thus measuring the performance of the library against the demands of the present users. There is a serious danger of getting a false impression about how useful the library is and of reinforcing an existing situation and continuing to move the service away from the people who apparently are not using it.

Another problem is that certain facets of library service are difficult to measure objectively. Ideally, we would like to be able to measure user behavior in the library by unobtrusive means to counteract the danger that behavior may be altered if the individual knows s/he is being observed. In most aspects of library usage, there is no way of measuring the performance unobtrusively. We certainly cannot evaluate how well a patron uses the catalog unobtrusively. Generally speaking, we have no unobtrusive way of finding out how successful the user who is looking for a particular item is. User success can only be determined by asking the individual patron. Because most aspects of library service are not susceptible to unobtrusive measurement there can also be the danger that the procedures that must be applied will affect the results and will influence the performance of the people observed.

If we believe in the future, this situation will change because the more that libraries become mechanized, the easier it becomes to evaluate library performance objectively. If, rather than consulting a card catalog, a user comes to a terminal, to search an on-line catalog of a library or group of libraries, performance can be monitored completely unobtrusively.

On-line circulation systems provide, if they are properly monitored, vast sources of data on what is being borrowed. All kinds of statistics can be produced unobtrusively through monitoring mechanized circulation systems, on-line catalogs, and library union catalogs in network operation, so we are just beginning to reach the possibility of a level of objective evaluation of library service that never existed before. When we reach a point where a very large number of libraries are using mechanical procedures, specifically on-line procedures, and we have a large impact of on-line catalogs on libraries, most of the measurement of a library's service that we must now do obtrusively, can be achieved unobtrusively.

In examining some of the techniques that have been applied to various aspects of library service, we need to consider their achievements and their limitations. The services that libraries provide can be divided into three major groups: (1) the document delivery services (the situation in which a user is coming into the library looking for a particular known item); (2) reference service; and (3) literature searching service, both retrospective and current-awareness. The following discussion shall focus on the document delivery capability, as a most important example, in an attempt to point out the complexity of the factors which influence whether the user coming to the library is successful or not. There is a danger in viewing any library service which looks on the surface to be a very simple situation of failing to recognize all the underlying factors which determine the success of the user. Determining the probability of an item being available when a user comes into the library looking for it is not a simple situation. There are many factors influencing this probability, and consequently, many factors that have to be considered in a comprehensive evaluation of the degree to which successful completion of this event is likely to occur.

First of all, when a user comes to a library looking for a particular item, there is the question of whether an entry for that item will be located in the catalog, and secondly, if an entry for that item is found, whether the user is then able to find a copy of the item on the shelves. Whether or not an entry is found depends, first of all, on whether or not the library owns a copy, and this obviously depends on the relevance of the collection to the needs of the community served. The second factor is whether or not the item has been cataloged. If it has been cataloged, and there is an entry for it in the catalog, can the user find that entry? Finding an entry depends upon a large number of factors, including how familiar the user is with the use of the catalog, how good the cataloging is, and, very importantly, how many access points are provided in the catalog. Is it a catalog, for example, including title entries, author entries, subject entries, etc.? Other factors which affect the ability of the user to find the entry in the catalog, assuming that the entry exists, are the information the user brings to the catalog search, such as a full bibliographic description for the item or just partial information; the accuracy of the filing; and the intelligence and perseverance of the individual.

Assuming that the entry is found, what is the probability that the patron will find a copy on the shelf? Finding a copy can be divided up into two aspects. First, is it on the shelf at the time that it is needed and, secondly, if it is on the shelf, can the user find it on the shelf? Whether it is on the shelf is dependent upon such factors as the duplication policy of the library and whether or not the policies of the library on duplication match the needs of the users. Duplication policy and the length of the loan period both affect the probability that the item will be on the shelf when it is needed. Security factors affect the probability of the item being on the shelf when it is needed, that is, the extent of theft. Assuming that it is on the shelf depends on the person's ability to transcribe and/or remember call numbers, the number of shelf sequences in the library, the guidance of the shelves, whether materials have been filed or shelved accurately, and how much staff assistance is available.

Consequently, we have a whole series of factors which affect this probability that a user will be successful when coming into the library looking for a known item. Some of these factors are collection factors, relating to the quality of the collection; some are catalog factors, relating to the quality of the cataloging and the patron's ability to use the catalog; while others are related to document delivery capability, based upon duplication policy, loan period, and security.

Catalog use studies focus on one aspect of this total evaluation problem. There have been many studies of the use of catalogs in libraries, but some of the most important are: a very extensive study done by the American Library Association (Mostecky, 1958) in 1949, which involved a rather large number of libraries; a very extensive study by Lipetz (1974) at Yale University, involving about two thousand interviews with catalog users; a series of studies done at the University of Michigan libraries, Tagliacozzo (1970); and a study done by Maltby (1973) in a number of libraries in the United Kingdom. Maltby's study is a rather different one because his investigation had to do with the extent to which library patrons use the catalog. The other three all concentrated on library users who were known to use the catalog. Much commonality exists in the methods used in these three studies. All of them were based upon interviews with actual catalog users, using an established questionnaire or interview schedule. As was pointed out, if you want to find out how successful people are in using the catalog at the present time, you must ask them. Without an obtrusive study, there is no way of finding out what people are looking for when they use the catalog, no way of discovering how successful they are, or of identifying the factors that influence their success and failure.

Until we have on-line catalogs, we will need to continue interviewing catalog users. The interviews can vary in their level of obtrusiveness depending upon when they are conducted. The least obtrusive interview would occur entirely after the search, although this might not tell us as much as we would like to know. Interviews can also be from before and after the search; or before, during, and after the search. Two of these studies did a before and after approach; that is, when a patron was seen to approach the catalog, s/he was interviewed first to determine what material was needed, then interviewed again later to determine the degree of success experienced. In one case, there was a kind of running interview, in which the interviewer actually accompanied the catalog user throughout the search. Obviously, this becomes the most obtrusive type of interview.

The purpose of this is essentially to identify what it is the user is looking for, how much information s/he brings to the catalog, how good the information is, how complete and correct it is, where the user looked, in what sequence, and how successful the search was. The successes are then divided up first into those that represent collection failures, that is, items which the person needed that were not in the collection and were confirmed not to be in the collection by later searchers, and secondly, into the catalog use failures, items in the collection for which the individual had been unable to find an entry, but were found by subsequent users. The questions that these studies attempt to answer are: what is the success of catalog users in known item searches and in subject searches; what are the principal factors that affect success and failure; and what can be done to increase the success rate in the future.

Collection evaluation is another aspect of the total evaluation problem. The emphasis on methods used to evaluate library service collections has changed rather considerably in the last few years. The literature on evaluation of library service, up to about ten years ago, reveals that collection evaluation used to be, almost exclusively, an evaluation of a collection against some external standards. When people in the 1950's spoke about an evaluation of collections, they meant an evaluation of the collection of the library against some external standard. This external standard could be one or more outside specialists. A common technique to evaluate the collection of the library was to call in one or more subject specialists who examined the collection and attempted, subjectively, to assess its adequacy. A somewhat less subjective method was using a standard list as the external standard instead of a subject specialist: a standard list of best books, a basic core collection for hospital libraries, a basic core collection for undergraduate libraries, etc.

An improvement on this technique was the creation of specially prepared lists of titles for evaluation purposes. One of the best studies of this kind was one by Coale (1965) that was done of the collection of the Newberry Library in Chicago in Latin American history of the colonial times. Coale came up with a very interesting and valuable technique. It still involved evaluation against a list, but, by the way he derived the list, he developed a technique which is potentially applicable to many other situations. Essentially what Coale did was to identify a few recently published monographs discussing various aspects of the subject of Latin American colonial history which had been well reviewed. He took the bibliography at the end of these monographs, merged them and created a rather large bibliography on Latin American colonial history from these sources. He used this bibliography as a check on the holdings of the Newberry Library.

His justification for this method was simply this: if these scholars had been writing their books in the Newberry Library, what proportion of these resources that they would have needed could the library provide? He was able to evaluate the collection of the Newberry Library in this light by asking not only how much could have been provided, but also what kinds of things did these scholars need that were not in the Newberry Library's collection, as well as identifying the kinds of documents, historical periods, materials by language groupings, in which the Newberry Library was weak.

It was an extremely interesting approach and a technique that is potentially relevant in many other situations. For example, if one wanted to evaluate the adequacy of the coverage of *Index Medicus* or the MEDLARS data base in some specialized aspect of medicine, such as tropical medicine, one could go to the *Bibliography of Medical Reviews,* pick at random ten or twelve review articles covering various aspects of tropical medicine, take the bibliographies at the ends of the papers to form a bibliography of tropical medicine, representing the items that current authors are citing, and simply use this as a checklist against the adequacy of the coverage of *Index Medicus* in this field. It is a very simple technique to use. Preparing evaluation lists for special purposes has much greater applicability than trying to prescribe a standard list of materials that should exist on tropical medicine or on Latin American colonial history. These have very limited applicability, while the specially prepared lists have a much wider range of application.

Whereas the idea of the external standard for collection evaluation was universally accepted for many years, we are now beginning to get much more emphasis on evaluation of the collection in terms of the amount and type of use it receives, either by drawing a sample of the materials from the collection itself (a collection sample), and examining the data labels to find out which categories of materials are most used, or by taking a sampling in a particular time period and observing what kinds of materials are being borrowed over a particular period of time (a circulation sample or a check-out sample). Both techniques have value and applicability under certain circumstances.

The classic example of the collection sample, of course, is the Fussler and Simon (1969) study at the University of Chicago. Examples of studies from circulation samples include the work of Trueswell (1966), Morse (1968) and Chen (1976). Jain (1967, 1969), at Purdue, had a rather interesting technique in which he drew both a collection sample and a circulation sample, and compared the two.

The purpose, presumably, of analysis of this kind is 1) to improve selection of materials and 2) to optimize space utilization. Most of these studies have been concerned with optimum space utilization in the sense that the studies have been done to determine which materials are likely to be most in demand and therefore should be in prime storage locations and which materials are less likely to be in demand and therefore can be retired to less accessible storage areas. More specifically, techniques of this kind can be used to identify portions of the collection that can be considered to be most active, as well as portions of the collection which can be retired to less accessible storage areas. If properly used, they can identify parts of the collection that may be regarded as weak, when, for example, the ratio of use of particular categories of materials is low in relation to the volumes available in these categories or the ratio of use is low in relation to profiles of interest of the user community. They can also be used to identify the need for duplicate copies, where the ratio between the number of copies available and the number of days in which these copies are circulating indicates inadequacy in terms of the probability of the item being on the shelf when needed.

Document Delivery Studies: One of the limitations of any study of a collection, by any procedure, is that collection evaluations generally tell us a lot about our successes, but not much about our failures. Document delivery tests are designed to tell us about our failures rather than our successes. Since we're likely to learn more from our failures than from our successes, document delivery tests, in one form or another, are particularly important. There are two basic methods that have been used to assess the quality of the document delivery service of the library. One method was developed by the Institute for the Advancement of Medical Communication by Dick Orr (1968) and is referred to as the document delivery test. It involves creating a citation pool which is used to evaluate the probability of an item being available at the time needed. The result of this is a test set of citations whose most useful application is in comparing the performances of a number of libraries. The second method is one that attempts to measure the actual performance in document delivery of a particular library or group of libraries. Most of this work has been done in England by Urquhart and Schofield (1971), by Buckland (1972) and by Maurice Line (1973).

The idea of the citation pool method is to arrive at a representative set of bibliographic references that can be used as a standard test set to evaluate the capability of a library or to compare the performance of a number of libraries. The citation pool that was used by Orr was derived in order to evaluate the performance in document delivery of medical libraries. What he did essentially was to take a large sample of recently published articles in the medical field, take the bibliographies at the end of these articles to create a bibliography of several thousand sources that were being cited by current writers in medicine, and drew a set of three hundred completely at random. This test set of three hundred bibliographic references, drawn from a much larger universe of sources being cited by current writers in the field, was used to test the document delivery ability of medical libraries.

The questions asked by this study were: does the library own a copy of each item, and if it does own a copy, where is it located at the time when it is needed? The person administering the test acts the part of a library user coming to the library with a list of citations, in this case the test pool of three hundred citations, to be checked against the catalog. If the library does hold it, the person finds out where it is at the time s/he is administering the test, which is assumed to be the time that the item is needed. Is the item on the open shelves, in the stacks, out on loan, in binding, etc? Depending upon whether or not the library owns the item, and if owned, where it is located, the library gets a score which reflects the degree of accessibility, the more accessible the item, the higher the score.

The most accessible item would obviously be one that the library owns and has on the open shelves, and therefore is most accessible at the time it is needed. Other situations would represent lower levels of accessibility. If the library scored 100 percent on the document delivery test, it would imply that all three hundred bibliographic references were found to be in the collection, and on the open shelves at the time that they were needed.

The document delivery test, originally devised for the National Library of Medicine for evaluation purposes, has turned out to be a useful tool in discriminating among the performance capabilities of various libraries. When the test was applied to university medical libraries in the United States, as one basis for evaluating the probability that these libraries would be useful as regional medical libraries, some libraries scored in the 90's, meaning that there is a 90 percent probability that the item wanted would be in the collection and on the shelf at the time needed, and some libraries scored as low as the 30's. Thus the test can be used to compare library performance because it is a standard which can be maintained from one library to another.

Another technique which studies the performance of the particular library has been used by Urquhart and Schofield and by Buckland at the University of Lancaster. This technique involves asking users during a specified period of time to complete failure slips. Users coming into the library are given a piece of paper or a card. If they are looking for a particular known item and fail to find it, they fill out this slip, and drop it into a box (an alternative is to have them put it on the shelf where a book should appear) as they are leaving the library. The box is emptied every half hour and the staff involved in the study determine the reason for the failure at the time that it occurs. From these failure slips, the staff may identify items that are not in the collection or, more importantly, items that are in the collection, and the location of these items when they were needed. Were these items out on loan, in the bindery, in use in the library, etc?

This test is more difficult to administer than the document delivery test because it involves a high level of user cooperation. There are some problems associated with the test. First, in order to arrive at some overall figure for the rate of failure, one must estimate the rate of return. What proportion of all the users entering the library are cooperating? If we want to be able to say there have been a certain number of failures in this two week period, we need to know what proportion of the users failed to cooperate. The users (or a sample of them) have to be interviewed to determine whether or not they filled out a failure slip.

At the same time, we would like to know how many successes occur to counter-balance the failures. This is a difficult task. If we measure the failures, what do we use as a comparable estimate of the successes occurring in the same period? One method that Urquhart and Schofield used was simply to count the number of circulations. Within a two-week test period they extrapolated from the number of circulations the number of failures by interviewing a sample of users and estimating what proportion of all the users coming into the library during this two-week period who encountered failures actually filled out a failure slip. They were then able to compare the number of failures with the number of successes by the number of circulations. But this gave a distorted figure, biased against the library, because they had no comparable figure for the number of times materials were consulted in the library and not borrowed. Thus, the failure rate was inflated and the success rate deflated.

The figures themselves are less important than the analysis, the micro-evaluation of why the failures occur. These studies generally have yielded extremely useful results in terms of identifying what can be done to improve the probability of success in the future. For example, if we can find, from a study of this kind, that the document delivery rate is 72 percent, and we want to raise it to 85 percent as a reasonable goal, what is the best strategy to use to raise the present level of performance from 72 percent to 85 percent? Do we purchase duplicate copies, and if so, duplicate copies of what titles? That is, what are the titles most in demand and what are the titles or categories of titles for which most failures occur? Or, do we improve our rate of performance by variable loan periods? If we can identify the categories of items that are most in demand, can we change our loan policy so that we can establish a short loan period for those that are known to be most in demand and a long loan period for those that are less in demand. There have been some very valuable studies, notably at the University of Lancaster, done by Buckland and others, which have shown that the librarian's ability to vary loan policy is a very valuable tool for improving the document delivery capability at very low cost. Variable loan periods at the University of Lancaster could raise the average document delivery capability by 10 or 15 percent at almost no cost to the library. If those items in greatest demand can be identified and put on a shorter loan period, then the library has a possibility of raising the performance level very substantially at essentially no cost, whereas the duplication policy would involve rather substantial costs to the library to achieve the same results.

Since these two methods—the document delivery test using a citation pool and the actual analysis of performance within a library—are intended to accomplish the same things, it is useful to consider the advantages and the disadvantages of each. First, the latter is more difficult to administer because it requires more effort and a high level of user participation. On the other hand, one can reasonably argue that the document delivery test is an abstract situation because the underlying assumption in citation studies is that items cited in recent literature are items that are going to be most in demand by library users. Some studies have shown that this cannot always be taken to be true, that items most cited in the literature are not always most in demand in libraries.

Studies of the performance of libraries in terms of what is actually demanded have had another limitation: the study based on the citation pool is very definitely related to potential needs whereas the other study is restricted to actual demands. This is focusing on the tip of the iceberg because we are assuming that people coming into the library looking for particular items are typical of all the users that the library is designed to serve and we assume that the items for which they are looking are typical of all their needs. We are ignoring the people that do not come into the library and the people who do come but do not convert all their needs into demands. The citation pool method is much more a reflection of what can be assumed to be latent needs of users because it is not influenced by the people that come in and place demands, and it can be reasonably assumed that it represents things that people can be expected to need because they are items that are cited by current writers in the field.

While both of these methods have their advantages, each also has limitations. Maurice Line, in his study at Bath University Library, attempted, although not completely successfully, to assess the capability of the library to meet the latent needs of users. That is, he attempted to get beyond an evaluation of demands to an evaluation of needs. He did this by having a sample of the faculty fill out cards representing document needs as they arose during particular periods of time and having each potential user of the library indicate what was done to satisfy this need. For instance, if a faculty member was reading an article and came across a reference to a document that s/he felt was needed, Line asked the person to fill out a card at that point and then to indicate on the card what was done, if anything, to satisfy that need, such as going to the library, trying to buy a copy, or writing to the author for a reprint. He took a large sample of these faculty members over a reasonable period of time and attempted to study the ability of the Bath University Library to satisfy what he described as the "latent needs" of the users rather than simply their demands.

In determining the probability of a library's being able to satisfy a request for a particular known item, we have identified the factors which affect the probability of success, such as the collection and various factors which affect whether or not the item is on the shelf, and we have discussed some methods used to evaluate these factors. By taking the figure representing the probabilities of these factors occurring, we can determine the probability of success of a known item search. For example, if a user comes into the library looking for a particular known item, a typical probability that the item is owned by the library is 80 percent. There is also, let us say, a 90 percent probability that the item has been cataloged and that the user can find it in the catalog at the time it is needed. In addition, there is a 60 percent probability that the item is on the shelf when it is needed. If we multiply these probabilities together we have a 43 percent probability of success. That is, if the user comes into the library looking for the particular known item, s/he will be successful 43 times out of 100. This is a hypothetical figure but the studies that have been done indicate that it may be fairly representative.

Factual reference service is another area which can benefit from evaluation. Reasonable evaluation of the success of libraries in providing reference service, that is, in answering quick reference inquiries, is quite new. Before six or seven years ago, the most that was done to evaluate reference service was to count the number of reference requests, and not all libraries had good statistics on the number of requests they were handling. More recently, we have had some attempts to evaluate the quality of reference service by using some kind of test set of questions and applying it obtrusively or unobtrusively to a group of libraries.

One technique used by the Institute for the Advancement of Medical Communication, as part of its evaluation of medical libraries, was to devise a set of factual test questions in medicine and to apply it obtrusively to a group of libraries to assess the ability of the library staff to answer these questions completely and accurately. This has the obvious disadvantage that the library staff knows that they are being observed and, in some cases, this means that they perform better than they would normally; in other cases, performances may decline because of the pressure of the situation.

Another technique which was developed and first applied to public libraries by Crowley and by Childers (1971) in New Jersey and has since been applied in at least one university library is to have a test set of questions to which the answer is known, but to apply them unobtrusively by telephone, so the library does not know it is being evaluated. Interestingly enough, whether these tests have been done obtrusively or unobtrusively, or whether they have been done in public or university libraries, the average rate of success is about 50 or 60 percent. Both the Crowley and the Childers studies in New Jersey public libraries revealed an average success rate in answering questions completely and accurately of between 50 and 60 percent. A similar technique applied in the University of Minnesota libraries came out with comparable results. In a Ph.D. dissertation at the University of Illinois, the technique was applied obtrusively and the rate of success was the same as the other studies. The results suggest that when someone calls a library looking for a piece of factual information, he has a 50 to 60 percent probability of receiving the correct answer.

Cost-effectiveness. In an article by Bourne (1965), the main idea concerned the 90 percent library which is highly responsive to the evaluation of library services and the design of improved services. The concept of the 90 percent library is that it is possible to design a library, or some facet of library service, such as reference or document delivery service, which will satisfy a specified proportion of all the demands made upon it at some reasonable expenditure of effort. Thus, it is possible to design a library which can satisfy 90 percent (or 85 percent or 93 percent, whichever level is decided upon) of all the demands. The evaluation of library service is largely concerned with identifying a large homogeneous body of demands, which can be satisfied economically. There is some performance level which can be achieved economically, but to try to raise the performance of the library beyond that requires a disproportionate level of expenditure and effort. It may be that to raise the performance of the library from the 90 percent level to the 95 percent level would require an expenditure of funds equal to the expenditure of funds required to service the first 90 percent. In order to push the performance up 5 percent more would require a greatly disproportionate expenditure of effort because these demands are less homogeneous or less typical of the interests of the majority of users.

Two distributions that have significance for the cost-effectiveness of library service, and are closely related to the idea of the 90 percent library, are the Zipf distribution and the Bradford distribution. The former may be plotted as a curve showing the cumulative percentage of the occurrences of words in texts plotted against the cumulative percentage of the number of words contributing to these occurrences. The Zipf distribution is essentially identical to the Bradford curve which represents the scatter of bibliographic materials over sources. These distributions have extremely important implications for library service because they demonstrate the distribution of the use of library collections, the use of resources of the library over the community of users, as well as the dispersion of citations in journal sources in any subject field. This type of distribution means, for example, that one can reasonably expect that some very high proportion of use of the collection comes from a very low proportion of the total collection and that a very small proportion of all potential users of the library contribute a very high proportion of the total use.

Much of what we are concerned about in the evaluation of libraries is simply identifying at what level of performance we can reasonably operate in terms of the resources available. Where can we best allocate our resources in terms of return on investment? The work that has been done in the last ten years illustrates two things rather clearly. First, evaluation of library service has tended to indicate that librarians have been or are somewhat complacent about their services. There is a strong tendency for librarians to assume that their services are much better than they really are. When they are exposed to reasonably objective evaluation procedures, the results show that if a student or faculty member walks into a major university library there is only about a 40 percent probability of finding needed items on the shelf. When we find that evaluation figures indicate that if somebody calls up a public library with a factual question there is only a 50 to 60 percent probability of getting the correct answer, doubt is raised as to the adequacy of the service. Are we really doing as well as we think we are? Secondly, we must keep in mind the concept of the 90 percent library. We have to forget about designing information services which can satisfy everybody. As long as resources are limited, we cannot continue to say we are trying to serve everyone. We must identify a homogeneous group of interests that can be satisfied reasonably and efficiently with the resources available. A guideline in the design of library services can best be expressed as a paraphrase: "You can serve some of the people all of the time and all of the people some of the time but you cannot serve all of the people all of the time."

REFERENCES

Bourne, C. P. "Some User Requirements Stated Quantitatively in Terms of the 90 Percent Library," in *Electronic Information Handling*, edited by A. Kent and O. E. Taulbee. Washington, DC: Spartan Books, 1965, pp. 93-110.

Buckland, M. K. "An Operations Research Study of a Variable Loan and Duplication Policy at the University of Lancaster." *Library Quarterly* 42 (1972):97-106.

Chen, Ching-chih. *Applications of Operations Research Models to Libraries.* Cambridge, MA: The M.I.T. Press, 1976.

Coale, R. P. "Evaluation of a Research Library Collection: Latin American Colonial History at the Newberry." *Library Quarterly,* 35 (1965):173-184.

Crowley, T., and Childers, T. *Information Service in Public Libraries: Two Studies.* Metuchen, NJ: Scarecrow Press, 1971.

Drucker, P. F. "Managing the Public Service Institution." *The Public Interest* 33 (Fall 1973):43-60.

Fussler, H. H., and Simon, J. L. *Patterns in the Use of Books in Large Research Libraries.* Chicago, IL: University of Chicago Press, 1969.

Hamburg, M., et al. *Library Planning and Decision-Making Systems.* Cambridge, MA: The M.I.T. Press, 1974.

Jain, A. K. *Report on a Statistical Study of Book Use.* Lafayette, IN: School of Industrial Engineering, Purdue University, 1967.

Jain, A. K. "Sampling and Data Collection Methods for a Book-Use Study." *Library Quarterly* 39 (1969):245-252.

Line, M. B. "The Ability of a University Library to Provide Books Wanted by Researchers." *Journal of Librarianship* 5 (1973):37-51.

Lipetz, Ben-Ami. *User Requirements in Identifying Desired Works in a Large Library.* New Haven, CT: Yale University Library, 1970.

Maltby, A. *U. K. Catalogue Use Survey: A Report.* London: Library Association, 1973.

Morse, P. M. *Library Effectiveness: A Systems Approach.* Cambridge, MA: The M.I.T. Press, 1968.

Mostecky, V., ed. *Catalog Use Study.* Chicago, IL: American Library Association, 1958.

Orr, R. H., et al. "Development of Methodologic Tools for Planning and Managing Library Services." *Bulletin of the Medical Library Association* 56 (1968):235-267.

Tagliacozzo, R., et al. "Access and Recognition: From Users' Data to Catalogue Entries." *Journal of Documentation* 26 (1970):230-249.

Tagliacozzo, R., and Kochen, M. "Information-Seeking Behavior of Catalog Users." *Information Storage and Retrieval* 6 (1970):363-381.

Trueswell, R. W. "Determining the Optimal Number of Volumes for a Library's Core Collection." *Libri* 16 (1966):49-60.

Urquhart, J. A., and Schofield, J. L. "Measuring Readers' Failure at the Shelf." *Journal of Documentation* 27 (1971):273-276.

Statistical Methods for Library Management

by Morris Hamburg

In the late 1960s, a research group under my direction at the Wharton School, University of Pennsylvania, undertook a study sponsored by the Library and Information Sciences Research Branch, Bureau of Research of the U.S. Office of Education. Initially, the study was oriented toward investigating the nature of statistical data for and about large public libraries and university libraries, that were published by the U.S. Office of Education and toward making recommendations on how this statistical information could be improved. After a preliminary study, we concluded that these data were not particularly designed for managerial planning and decision-making purposes; consequently, library managers were not using the data for such purposes. Together with our advisory committees we concluded that it would be more interesting and useful to work on a broader study of frameworks for planning and decision-making concerning library operations and resources. We decided to concern ourselves with the design and development of statistical information systems that would provide quantitative information for effective management of university and large public libraries and with the associated problem of planning and decision-making systems. We worked with and received assistance from library directors and librarians at public and university libraries, government officials, officials of library associations, research workers, and others. The results of this research have been reported in Hamburg, M., et al. *Library Planning and Decision-Making Systems*, Cambridge, MA: The M.I.T. Press, (1974), and in doctoral dissertations by M.R.W. Bommer (1971) and R.M. Whitfield (1974).

LIBRARY INFORMATION SYSTEMS

The overall management problems of university and large public libraries have increased tremendously in recent years. The nature of

This paper represents an edited version of a talk given at the Institute.

user demand and expectations has changed considerably. Many trends in higher education and in changing population composition of urban areas have had profound impacts on university and public libraries. Library organizational problems have become increasingly complex as libraries have strained to meet their intensifying problems. There have been expansions in the development of cooperative arrangements among libraries, in centralization of library services, mechanization, computerization, size of collections and in the scope and variety of services offered by librarians.

Logical and systematic frameworks are needed to cope with these problems and developments, and to deal with the economic problem of allocating and controlling limited resources in such a way as to produce maximum benefits. The main elements of such an approach are: (1) a process for planning and decision-making, (2) quantitative information, and (3) analytical tools for analyzing the information. Our research concerned itself with these essential elements of a rational management system.

We took a management science or operations research approach in the study, and began by inquiring into the objectives of libraries. This leads naturally into deriving measures of achievement of these library objectives. The search for this type of a framework for a management information system for libraries is a difficult one. In the private sector of society, the profit-making objective is quite clearly defined. Therefore, a natural framework exists for a management information system in terms of the data required for a profit and loss statement of a company. The balance sheet in terms of assets and liabilities is a similarly useful organizational structure for a component of the data system. On the other hand, no similar natural framework exists for public and university libraries. They do not have a profit-making function nor are their services transmitted in a marketplace of monetary transactions. However, the problem of every library is to allocate and control scarce resources and to manage and control library activities, so as to maximize benefits imparted to society.

Measures of achievement of objectives in the private sector are relatively straightforward. They are usually stated in terms of output per unit input, such as the ratios of profit-to-capital invested or profit-to-cost. In the public sector and in libraries in particular, analogous measures have not generally been used nor are they often constructed. Because of a long standing tradition of accountability, libraries do a conscientious job of measuring inputs (costs), but they typically have done very little either in conceptualizing or in measuring outputs. That is, they rarely attempt to measure in any sophisticated and systematic way the outputs of services that are provided to the public by libraries.

In analyzing what a library tries to accomplish (its objectives), we considered the area of library standards. We concluded that existing library standards tend to be neither objectives nor performance measures, but rather are descriptive rules for "proper" management or are quantitative rules for minimum inputs of materials, personnel, and physical facilities. They represent a static concept pointed toward the evaluation of library resource inputs but do not focus on the outputs of library service.

This presentation will not attempt to make a case for any particular type of measure of library performance. For libraries that have a significant *active* or *promotional* component of library service such as public libraries, measure based on the relationship between benefits (such as exposure to documents) and costs may be appropriate. On the other hand, in certain types of special libraries and university libraries, the users may primarily be sophisticated specialists who are seeking specific materials or information. Such libraries tend to emphasize *reactions* to users and may attribute little importance to the promotion of library use. In such cases, narrower performance measures, such as the proportion of user demands satisfied and document retrieval time, may reflect library performance and may be preferable to measures of document exposure.

Without getting into specifics about how such measures might be derived, it suffices at this point to note that once the objectives of a library or any other organization have been defined, statistical methods can be useful in the measurement of the degree of attainment of the objectives.

STATISTICAL METHODS FOR THE LIBRARY

What, in general, is the motivation for the use of statistical methods in the library or in any other organization? First of all, what do we mean by statistical methods? A rather conventional and somewhat pedestrian definition is the art and science that deals with methods of collection, tabulation, analysis, presentation, and interpretation of numerical data. A more modern definition is that statistics deals with methods for decision-making under uncertainty using incomplete information. Modern statistical inference handles the problems of uncertainty by means of probability theory. Sampling techniques provide a means for obtaining incomplete information (samples), and then drawing inferences about the broader groups (universes or populations) from which the incomplete information has been obtained. In every important decision that one makes in one's personal life, that is essentially what one must do. For example, in one's choice of a lifetime's work, one must make a decision in the face of uncertainty with less than complete information. In choosing a partner with whom to spend a portion of one's lifetime, again we have a decision made under uncertainty with incomplete information.

In the library, managerial decisions can be wisely made only in the light of knowledge of present library use and through the aid of careful estimates of future use. For example, in a public library, the follow-

ing are some questions that must be answered by library boards and
library managers:

1. How should the budget be allocated among costs for personnel,
   the provision of physical facilities, access to documents (selection, acquisition and processing documents and indexes), the
   promotion of library use, etc?
2. How should the annual budget for document acquisitions be
   allocated among the various types of users, such as general
   adults, young adults and children?
3. How much should be spent on documents and how should this
   be allocated among the various types of documents (books,
   periodicals, musical records, etc.)?

Quantitative information about library use and users can certainly
aid in obtaining better answers to such questions and to give guidance
on more effective use of the library.

Furthermore, there are many types of "what is going on" questions that can only be obtained by gathering data. For example, how
do library users differ in their patterns of library use? What percentage of the collection accounts for (say) 90 percent of outside circulation use? Data required to answer such questions can be obtained—
most libraries do not obtain them, largely due to limitations of time
and resources. However, the introduction of data-processing equipment is making it more feasible to collect such data, and librarians
similar to their counterparts in areas such as private industry can learn
to obtain and use these types of data.

The important viewpoint is that the data to be collected are those
needed to assist in planning and decision-making. In government,
industry, and perhaps in libraries, in many situations, much more data
are gathered than are needed for planning and decision-making purposes. Hence, the emphasis should be upon the collection of relevant
data. In that connection, the use of modern techniques of sampling
and probability theory can reduce considerably the cost and time requirements.

A SAMPLING APPLICATION

In a brief conference of this type it is difficult to discuss highly
technical applications and undoubtedly it would not be wise to
attempt to do so. Therefore, this paper will refer to a fairly easily applied technique, statistical sampling. A pertinent warning at the outset
is that although it is often easy to use sampling techniques, analogously it is easy to misuse them as well. Sampling for our purposes means
nothing more than drawing a part (a sample) of a larger group (a population) in order to make inferences about the larger group. A very
simple example might be a sampling study to determine the use of
(say) microform reader equipment in a library. The purpose of such a
study might be to obtain "what is going on" data concerning the fre-

quency of usage of such equipment. The study would be carried out by taking observations at specified time periods on each microform reader to determine whether the equipment was in use. The data thus obtained would provide the basis for conclusions about the total overall use of the equipment. If similar studies were carried out for other pieces of equipment, useful comparisons could be made on relative usage rates of the different types of equipment.

The study would be carried out by breaking a day down into component time periods, as for example, three 20-minute periods in each hour, giving 24 periods in each eight-hour day. Then information could be collected on equipment usage by making observations at specified time points within each 20-minute period. For example, if three observations were made in each period, they could be made at 5, 10, and 15 minutes after the period begins. The investigation would simply note for each piece of equipment whether it was in use. Summary measures could be calculated for each microform reader and for all readers combined in terms of proportions of total possible uses. Many other useful applications of such investigations, usually referred to as work sampling studies, can be made in areas such as usage of staff and equipment time.

A STATISTICAL QUALITY CONTROL APPLICATION

Sampling has been widely applied with considerable success in industry and commerce. For example, the Japanese have attributed a great part of their post-World War II improvement in quality of industrial production to the use of statistical quality control methods, based on sampling. In keeping with Dr. Chen's suggestion that I give some illustrations that are not in the library field, I would like to tell you about an application of statistical quality control in a field far removed from the library. Of course, the motivation is that such ideas when used in a different field might stimulate our imaginations concerning applications in our own fields. I had a consulting assignment a few years ago involving a chain of food supermarkets in which the following problem was posed. Consumers in the stores of this chain had been appearing at the cashiers' booths with articles that were incorrectly priced; hence, heated debates often ensued between customers and cashiers about the prices. The incorrect prices were actually of three types: (1) incorrect price tags or markings, (2) illegible price tags or markings, and (3) no price tag or markings at all. The company's desire was to improve performance in these areas. The firm felt that it was losing considerable amounts of money and goodwill because of customers who had been antagonized by the arguments concerning prices.

After some improvements were made in the equipment and systems by which the prices were placed on product items, the frequency of incorrectly priced items was reduced somewhat. However it was still unacceptably high. At this point, I recommended the use of the types of control charts that are used in process control of manufacturing and administrative operations. For every store in the chain, control charts were set up for each of the aforementioned three categories of incorrect prices, referred to for this purpose as "defective prices." For example, a control chart was established for a particular store for items that had no price tags or price markings at all. This type of chart is depicted in Figure 1. The central line on this chart represented the average experience for the chain as a whole for the past week, as determined from statistical samples of items drawn from each store. Thus in Figure 1, the central line labelled 1.0 percent means that sampling studies had determined that for the chain as a whole 1 percent of the items on store shelves had no price tags or price markings. The number of items sampled in each store was 1,000. The upper and lower lines on the chart defined what is referred to as a "state of statistical control." Hence, the meaning of the lower and upper control lines labelled 0.1 percent and 1.9 percent is the following. In a random sample of 1,000 items drawn in a store on a particular day, if the store as a whole had 1 percent "no price" items, on the basis of chance sampling errors, the percentage in the sample should fall somewhere between 0.1 percent and 1.9 percent. The formulas for computing these (3-sigma) control limits can be found in any basic statistics textbook. Suppose the points for a certain store were as depicted in Figure 1 where for days 6, 7, and 8 they fell above the upper control limit. That is, excessive percentages of "no price" items were found three days in a row. The management by exception principle could be used to seek out the "assignable cause" of this variation and to take appropriate managerial action to remedy the situation. Analogously, if we found a series of points below the lower control line indicating an unusually small percentage of items without price designations, it might indicate that this particular store was "building a better mousetrap." We would like to analyze the reasons for this better performance and to spread these practices throughout the entire chain of supermarkets.

What else does this type of control chart system accomplish? First, it defines what is meant by a state of control throughout a system. Secondly, it enables the detection of deviations from this state of control. Finally, it aids in the discovery of remedies for the departure from a state of control.

A few points may be noted regarding the preceding application. If there were a desired or aimed at standard of performance, that standard rather than some past average of performance, could be used as the central control line. Relatively unskilled people can be used for the sampling and data collection process. In the preceding application, college students carried out these tasks in a most effective manner. Also, this type of control system may be used for other statistical measures than percentages, such as numbers or averages of pertinent characteristics. In the application described above, a substantial reduction in defectiveness of pricing was accomplished throughout the supermarket chain because of the introduction of the control system.

CONTROL CHART FOR THE PERCENTAGE OF ITEMS WITHOUT PRICE TAGS OR PRICE MARKINGS

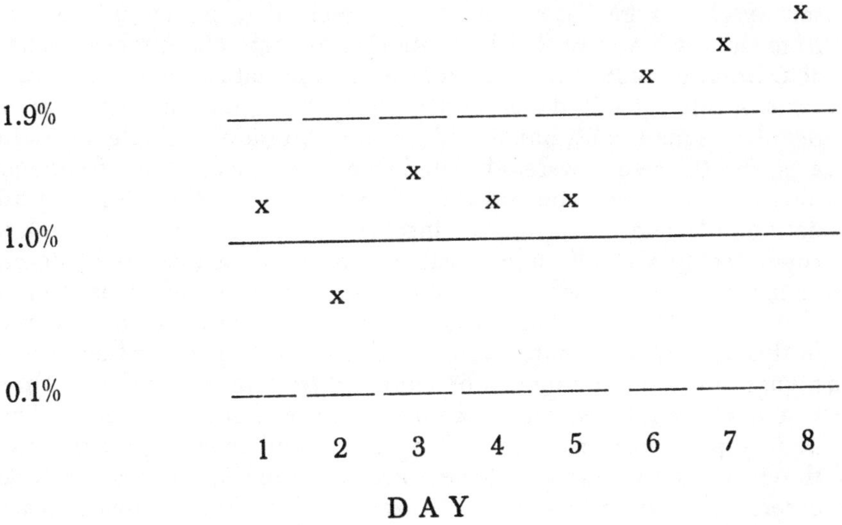

FIGURE 1

This type of control system has been used successfully in manufacturing and in general administrative applications as well as, for example, in the control of computer, clerical and secretarial errors. Many possible analogous applications in the library can easily be constructed for characteristics of interest where instead of sampling items on the shelves of a supermarket, we could sample documents on library shelves or the work activities of library personnel. An important principle is that one should seek out the few important problems for these potential applications as opposed to the many relatively unimportant problems that are present in any system.

SOME CAVEATS

Although sampling applications such as the preceding example are rather easy to construct, some caveats are in order concerning possible misuses of statistical methods. One of the most frequent problems encountered in statistical sampling studies is the presence of *systematic error*, also referred to as *bias*. Systematic errors, as the term implies, cause the conclusion of a statistical investigation to be incorrect in some systematic way. If observations have arisen from a sample drawn from a statistical population, systematic errors persist even when sample size is increased. This is in contrast to *random errors* or *sampling errors*, which arise from the chance variations involved in sampling, and tend to decrease as the sampling size increases.

An example of systematic error or bias occurred when the alumni society of a large Eastern university decided to gather information from the graduates of that institution to determine a number of characteristics, including their current economic status. One of the questions of interest was the amount of last year's gross income, suitably defined. A mail questionnaire was sent to a random sample of graduates, and the results were tabulated from the returns. When frequency distributions were made and averages were calculated by year of graduation, it became clear that the income figures were unusually high as compared to virtually any existing external data that could be examined; in other words the income figures were clearly biased in an upward direction. It is fairly easy in this case to speculate on the causes of this upward systematic error. In this type of mail questionnaire, a higher nonresponse rate can be expected from those graduates whose incomes were relatively low than from those with higher incomes. That is, it appears reasonable and has been found from experience that those with higher incomes have a greater propensity to respond than others. In sampling studies in libraries and in other contexts, biases often arise in much more subtle ways. Considerable care and thought is generally required in the planning stage of an investigation to forestall the possibility of such systematic errors or to set up procedures to adjust for them.

Sometimes the results of a statistical investigation are rather meaningless because the data were obtained from a poorly designed experiment. An amusing example of that idea occurred at the time that fluorescent lighting was first introduced. The suspicion had been aired that exposure to fluorescent lighting could be harmful to human reproductive organs and could result in decreased fertility. An industrial firm decided to carry out a test of this assertion using rats as subjects. One group of rats was placed in a room illuminated by incandescent bulbs while another group was ensconced in a room with fluorescent lighting. After a period of time, it was observed that the rats in the room with incandescent lighting exhibited a normal birth rate for that type of rodent. However, startlingly, the birth rate for the rats in the room with fluorescent lighting was zero! A skeptical reaction to these data resulted in an investigation which found that all of the rats in the room with fluorescent lighting were *male.* Clearly, no matter how sophisticated the subsequent analysis might be, there are situations in which such analysis cannot remedy the deficiencies arising from a faulty design of the investigation.

A PREDICTION MODEL

In library planning and decision-making, predictions are invariably required. No library building can be erected without at least an implicit forecast of future use of this facility. The purchase of books and periodicals involves an implicit forecast about the use of these documents. The entire budgetary process is associated with a large number of forecasts for ensuing time periods.

Our next example pertains to a model for forecasting the demand for a forthcoming new pharmaceutical product. Following that, we will discuss briefly an analogous model developed by a member of the Wharton Research Group for the prediction of circulation demand in a university library.

A pharmaceutical company was interested in predicting the demand for a new ethical drug product, that is, one that is available only through prescription by a physician. The new product had gone through research and development and various stages of screening and evaluation. The company was ready to commercialize the product and to place it on the market. The company wished to obtain a reasonably accurate forecast of the demand for this product during its first year after introduction. An accurate forecast was important because an unsuccessful product had to be recognized quickly and a successful high-volume product similarly had to be discerned. In the past, large losses had been incurred because of faulty forecasts. A chain reaction of decisions would be based on demand forecasts in areas such as marketing, purchasing, production, and finance. Because of the complexity of the phenomena to be predicted, the need for greater accuracy, and the dependency of outcomes on so many different variables, our consulting team recommended the development of a mathematical forecasting model, specifically a multiple regression analysis.

A very elementary, oversimplified example will serve to illustrate the basic nature of a regression equation. Suppose it is desired to estimate the sales of a new product during the first year of its life ("First Year Sales") from information on physician awareness of the product by the third month after introduction ("Awareness"). First Year Sales may be measured in millions of dollars and Awareness in terms of the proportion of physicians who have heard of the product. From such data for all new products placed on the market during the past few years an equation is established relating First Year Sales and Awareness. Assume that this equation was calculated to be

First Year Sales (in $ millions) = 1.2 + (3.0 x Awareness percent)

Then, if 40 percent of the physicians sampled had heard of the product (say) by the third month after introduction, the predicted level of First Year Sales would be:

1.2. + (3.) x 40 percent) = $2.4 million

This would represent a situation in which the forecast of new product sales was made by using information concerning only one other factor. Of course, in any realistic situation, substantially more than one predictor variable would probably be employed. The resulting regression equation would, therefore, reflect the effect of all of the variables and would, of course, be more complex in mathematical form than the one given in the illustration.

In order to construct the regression equation model in the case of the pharmaceutical company, it was necessary to obtain historical data covering not only this company's new products, but all new products introduced in the industry over the past few years for which adequate source data were available. It was from these data that the mathematical relationships subsequently expressed in the model were derived.

Essentially, the technique measured the relationships among many factors expressed in mathematical terms for the purpose of predicting. The underlying rationale was that, if (a) for all new products introduced over a substantial period of time there was a strong relationship between demand levels and the specific variables considered during the early months of a product's life, and if (b) this relationship persisted, then the probable market activity for future new products could be estimated from corresponding early-month variables. Because of the volatile nature of the pharmaceutical market, provision was also made for revising the initial forecasts as additional information became available over time.

An analogous type of model for forecasting circulation demand in a university library was developed by a member of the Wharton Research Group, M.R.W. Bommer (1971). Using the University of Pennsylvania library system, Bommer constructed regression equations by subject area that permitted the prediction of the demand rate for circulation from past circulation use rates, and the teaching and research activity of faculty members. The model also provided for estimates of numbers of unsatisfied demands and for the percentages of new copies in subject areas for which duplicate and multiple copies would be required. This type of model has a distinct advantage over previous models for forecasting circulation in that it not only makes predictions dependent upon past history (Morse, 1968), but also upon the basic determinants of demand such as expected faculty teaching and research activities.

A STATE LEVEL ALLOCATION MODEL

Continuing in the spirit of trying to stimulate thinking on quantitative models that can be of use in library planning and decision-making, I will make a brief reference to another model developed by a member of our research group. The application of statistical techniques and operations research methodology to libraries is a relatively recent phenomenon. Mostly these applications have dealt with individual libraries. On the other hand, R.M. Whitfield developed a model that is useful for library decision-making at the state level (1974). Administrators of library programs at the state level often may feel that they are constrained to follow rigid state-aid formulas that allow little discretion in the use of funds. However, the state-aid formulas can be and should be changed as underlying situations and requirements change. Whitfield's model provided for an "efficient" allocation of funds within a fixed state-aid budget to multi-county systems of public libraries. Criteria were proposed to give meaning to the term "efficiency" in the library context. In addition, a model was constructed that predicted library use as a function of controllable variables.

Turning to some general background, we find that New York was the first major state to develop a substantial state-aid program. Many other states (California, Illinois, Michigan) have similarly patterned their library system structures and aid programs. The basic features of these programs include:

1. Submission of a plan reorganizing public libraries into systems that are legal entities, providing free access to all residents.
2. Establishment of a central headquarters library.
3. Support of the system with local and state taxes.

The Pennsylvania pattern, also followed by Massachusetts, New Jersey, and Rhode Island, features regional and district libraries which form a hierarchy of library service. Local libraries may receive separate aid if they agree to perform certain specified functions. Regional and district libraries receive separate state funding, usually on a per capita basis.

Whitfield's basic construct was a linear programming model that allocates state-aid funds to multi-county systems, maximizing a measure of library usage (exposure counts). The basis for the study was the New York State system. The model included a policy variable that is to be fixed by decision-makers at the state level representing minimal acceptable levels of library service. The model contained constraints regarding local economic resources (underlying tax bases) available to support library services in each system. The objective of maximizing total library usage normally implies that greater state aid would go to the wealthier multi-county units. However, an equity constraint was included to insure that even poorer districts would all receive at least some minimum level of support. A budget constraint placed an overall limit on the total aid that could be distributed.

The output of the model was estimates of the amounts of state aid to be distributed in each library system. This linear programming model was then combined with a regression model that predicted library use as a function of state aid and other variables. Together, the two models can assist in answering questions such as, "What would be the effect on optimal allocation of state aid and on total library service of (1) an increase (or decrease) in the state-aid budget of $1,000,000, (2) an improvement in effectiveness of use state aid by a particular library system, and (3) a change in the prescribed minimal support levels for library usage?"

It is clear that no mathematical decision model will replace a manager or decision-maker. Many variables enter into a decision; some of these variables may be quantifiable, others may not be. However, as

Whitfield notes, a model such as his can be useful to any administrator in a variety of ways. The administrator can process the information from the model along with political and other factors to reach a decision. The models can be used as sounding boards to observe the consequences of alternative allocation decisions. Finally, the administrator can interact with the model. He or she can test various plans to obtain an idea as to their efficacy. Some may be revealed as inferior to others and thus perhaps can be eliminated from further consideration.

CONCLUSION

Quantitative models for library decision-making such as the one just described are still in an embryonic state. However, they possess the potential of becoming valuable aids to decision-making for complex library managerial and administrative problems.

There is that well known adage that you can lead a horse to water, but you cannot make him (or her!) drink. My goal in this talk has been not to make you drink, but to try to make you thirsty.

I would like to conclude with a little story. This is about a minister whose church was far out in the country. One winter Saturday evening there was a tremendous snow blizzard that continued through Sunday morning. It seemed probable to the minister that no one from the congregation would be able to come to church that Sunday morning. Since the minister lived in the rectory next door to the church, he had no difficulty himself in getting there. He trudged through the snow and opened the door to the church to see whether anyone had arrived. As he looked into the church it appeared that no one had been able to attend. The church seemed empty. However, as he stood there a bit and his eyes became accustomed to the darkness, he finally saw one person toward the very rear of the church. So he strode toward the back and found an old farmer sitting there all bundled up, still wearing his overcoat. He seemed as though he was sitting there expectantly. The minister began speaking with him and after a bit said, "You have gone to all this trouble of coming out here and I have spent a good part of this past week preparing my sermon. Even though you are the only one here, would you like me to give my sermon?"

The farmer leaned back in his pew and drawled very slowly, "Well, if I had a load of hay and I went out into the field, and there were a critter out there who looked lonely and hungry, I'd feed him."

"All right," said the minister, "I get the point. I'll deliver the sermon."

So he strolled up to the pulpit and proceeded to deliver the longest, most boring sermon ever given. After a seemingly interminable period, he stepped down from the pulpit and walked to the back of the church. He approached the farmer and inquired, "How did you like it?"

The farmer leaned back in his pew and again drawled very slowly. "Well, back there a couple of hours ago, when I said I would feed that critter, I didn't say I would give him the whole dang load!"

The point of this story is supposed to be that you have not gotten the whole dang load on statistical methods for library management. However, I hope that as a result of attending this Institute you will want to sample some of the remainder of the load.

REFERENCES

Bommer, Michael R.W. *The Development of a Management System for Effective Decision-Making and Planning in a University Library.* Ph.D. dissertation, University of Pennsylvania, Philadelphia, PA, 1971.

Hamburg, M.; Clelland, R.C.; Bommer, M.R.W.; Ramist, L.E.; and Whitfield, R.M. *Library Planning and Decision-Making Systems.* Cambridge, MA: The M.I.T. Press, 1974.

Morse, Philip M. *Library Effectiveness: A Systems Approach.* Cambridge, MA: The M.I.T. Press, 1968.

Whitfield, Ronald M. *The Efficient Allocation of Resources by the State to Systems of Public Libraries.* Ph.D. dissertation, University of Pennsylvania, Philadelphia, PA, 1974.

Systems Approaches to Library Management

by F. F. Leimkuhler

Operations research and management science were developed as deliberate attempts to bridge the gap between the world of science and the world of human affairs. They use the methods of science to develop techniques for organizing and managing many kinds of human activities, including certain aspects of management itself. Because their purpose goes beyond study and speculation to action and involvement they are not pure science, and because they are concerned with only the explicit, rational aspects of human behavior they are not pure management. Marshall McLuhan calls them prime examples of his "mixture principle" whereby the clasp of cultural forces in society releases a creative hybrid energy. Operations research began in England during World War II as an expedient way to mobilize the scientific manpower to help make better military decisions. Its success led to its emulation in the United States and eventually to its adaptation to non-military applications in government and in industry. Today it is an emerging academic discipline and a new profession with an extensive literature.

OPERATIONS

While there are many views on the nature of operations research and management science, the literature shows a consistent pattern in developing methodologies for the analysis and control of many management functions or operations. Such operations include the allocation of scarce resources among alternative beneficial uses, the scheduling of the flow of materials and information through processing networks, the management of raw material, in-process, and finished product inventories, the transportation, distribution, and marketing of products and services, financing and investment management, decision-making, planning, and the design, location, and reliability of production and service facilities. The operations research literature concentrates on those aspects of management operations that are amenable to systematic analysis and comparison across many areas of application in industry, government, and public systems.

Operations research has led to the development of specialized methods of analysis including such optimization techniques as linear, nonlinear, dynamic, discrete, stochastic, and combinatorial programming, all of which are aimed at finding the "best" mathematical solution to complex problems involving a variety of structural relationships and limitations on the choice of solutions. Other methodologies include utility theory and decision analysis, game theory, stochastic processes and simulation. The latter two techniques are aimed at describing the behavior of dynamic, time-dependent systems which are subject to probabilistic influences, as for example in a library where customers arrive at random and make random demands for service which may or may not be available because of the demand and availability patterns in previous time periods.

The concern for developing a better understanding of basic managerial operations, and developing techniques for their analysis, includes a concern with the organizational environments in which the operations take place. Environments such as that of the military, industry, government, or public service all have special characteristics which influence how things are done and should be done. Some key considerations here are identifying who the decision-makers are, what options they have, what objectives they pursue, what information they have available to them, what the possible outcomes of their decisions will be, and how these outcomes relate to their objectives. Such questions often are not easy to answer and may not be possible to answer in a clear and explicit manner. A careful study of isolated operations in an organization may imply something about the environment in which it operates and it may permit considerable improvement in the internal efficiency with which that operation is performed, but of itself it cannot determine its external effectiveness in fulfilling a role in the organization. Information of this kind not only throws light on the value of the operation but also on the value of subjecting the operation to careful analytic study.

MODELS

The operations research and management science literature is not very informative about the benefits which particular organizations have achieved through the application of this methodology. The continued growth of these fields and their support by many organizations is perhaps sufficient testimony of their usefulness. The approach taken in the literature is to focus on the logical validity of the methodology. The operations which are studied are described in terms of models, i.e., logical representations, usually mathematical, of the significant factors in an operation and how these factors combine and interact to produce outcomes. For example, the operation of a reference desk in a library might be described in terms of a flow of customers arriving with some predictable frequency pattern and requesting service which takes some predictable pattern of service times. By making appropriate assumptions about the arrival and service patterns, it is possible to develop mathematical equations which will predict such outcomes as the average waiting time for a customer, the probability that a customer will get immediate attention, and the probability that a customer will have to wait for some specified number of minutes. Models of this kind could be used to indicate the need for additional reference librarians or for the need to modify user patterns or service procedures.

The operations research model necessarily is a gross simplification of an actual operation. The factors and relationships which are represented by symbols in the model are selectively chosen from the many attributes that are present in the real world. They are chosen because the analyst thinks they are significant and because they are amenable to analysis. The research normally begins with the simplest possible model which will represent some important feature of the operation. This is done so that the analyst can be as precise as possible in making assumptions about the interrelationships of the factors, and as precise as possible about the logical consequences of these assumptions. Once the internal logical validity of a simple model is established, the analyst can turn his or her attention to how well the model describes the real world operation. In order to make the model more realistic, it may be necessary to change assumptions or to add new factors that require further assumptions and the verification of the more complex logical relationships. Proceeding in this way the researcher develops more realistic and more complex models which are hopefully more useful in the management of real operations.

Because of the extensive literature on the subject, the analyst has available the experience of prior research in inventing and extending models of common processes. This is particularly helpful in regard to the logical structure and mathematical implications of models. The applicability of a model to a particular situation may require considerable experimentation and a good judgement, as well as considerable patience and knowledge about the intricacies of the arguments given in the literature. This literature tends to follow the pattern of science in exploring every logical nuance of a new idea, so that the practical analyst must be selective about what s/he takes from the literature as well as from the real world.

SYSTEMS

The practical importance of developing a logic of operations is most readily seen when models are used as blueprints in the design of systems. Unlike modeling which is essentially a speculative process, systems analysis and design is oriented towards action and control. A system is a logically efficient way to accomplish some preconceived purpose by defining all of the necessary steps to be taken, including the alternative paths that might be followed. The various subsidiary functions of a system are organized into logical components or subsystems, each with its stated purpose and allowable range of operation. The behavior of each component must be fully understood and related to the performance of the system as a whole. The necessary controls for regulating the system are part of a special subsystem, the managerial component, which monitors the performance of the system in its environment and makes adjustments according to some prescribed standard.

The physical construction of a system is a special art of its own requiring an enormous amount of detailed knowledge about the technology available, the mission to be accomplished, and the environment in which it must operate. New developments in all of these areas contribute to the obsolescence of existing systems, and the designer must strive to anticipate these changes. By building more comprehensive models beforehand it is possible to build more reliable and adaptable systems, but at some point a practical compromise must be struck between available knowledge and the need for action. Existing systems become part of the structural environment in which operations take place and thus become significant factors in the subsequent modeling of operations.

As an example of systems design, an analysis of the congestion problems at a library reference desk could lead to appropriate queueing models that are used to specify the number of service stations needed to handle requests over periods of light and heavy demand for service. Staffing schedules could be determined to control the number of servers on duty, priority rules could be established for handling different kinds of requests, and procedures and standards for service can be worked out. The systemization of service operations in this way will hopefully have beneficial effects on the participants in the operations and on the community in which these operations take place. Identifying the benefits and the costs and striking the appropriate balance between them is no easy task. Furthermore there is a continuing need to monitor this performance as factors change which can affect both user and server behavior.

MANAGEMENT

The decision to develop, install, or modify systems depends on both the logical feasibility of such a project and the net benefits it can provide the organization. Recognition of the need for action and making decisions that modify the structure and behavior of an organization is the preeminent task of management. Operations research models can help greatly in this respect by uncovering options which are available to management and identifying measurable factors which should be considered in evaluating the need for managerial intervention. If action is called for, systems analysis and design can reduce much of the uncertainty in anticipating the concrete effects of a structural change. Ideally if all factors influencing a decision can be reduced to a single, explicit and logically consistent measure of effectiveness, decision-making itself becomes just another component of an autonomous system.

In practice, of course, management cannot be reduced to a set of simple calculations, since it is essentially a complex human activity that defies a totally logical explanation. It is an activity that includes such elements as creativity, compassion, persuasion, conviction, agreement, leadership, loyalty, beliefs, desires, etc. which have an important bearing on actual decisions. As long as systems are ultimately under the control of humans, the essential nature of management must also be human. This is not to say that much of what is done by managers cannot be improved upon through systematic analysis.

Management science focuses on the decision-making activities of managers when they have the opportunity to choose among several courses of action in order to accomplish some goal or set of goals. It seeks to develop techniques for identifying all feasible alternatives and predicting their outcomes relative to the manager's goals. It tries to develop appropriate measures of how effective the alternatives are in accomplishing the goals, and how sensitive these measures are to the information available including the way in which the problem is formulated. Furthermore, it tries to establish some correspondence between the analytic conclusions and the actual performance of managers in comparable situations. Thus, the management scientist is trying to make explicit all of the factors that are implicitly present in actual management decision-making. While there is still much to learn, it is clear that it is this aspect of the managerial function that is most relevant to operations research.

METHODS

Operations research begins with the study of the people who make decisions in an organization and seeks to make more explicit the alternatives they face and their reasons for making choices. There are four major steps: formulation of the decision problem, construction of a model of the decision problem, analysis and design of a system for solving the problem, and incorporation of the system in the organization. The total process is a cyclical one, that is, the research team begins with an elementary formulation of the problem and the construction of as simple a model as is possible to capture the essential features. This leads to a solution system that can be used experimentally in the organization to see how it affects the original problem situation. This usually leads to a much better clarification of the problem, enrichment of the model, refinement of the system, and a new round of experimentation in the organization. The process is intended to continue in this way to evolve into a fully satisfactory control of the operations under study, and to lead to higher levels of management decision-making.

The four step process shown in Figure 1, is augmented by the available analytical tools and experience of other researchers in many

STEPS IN THE OPERATIONS RESEARCH PROCESS

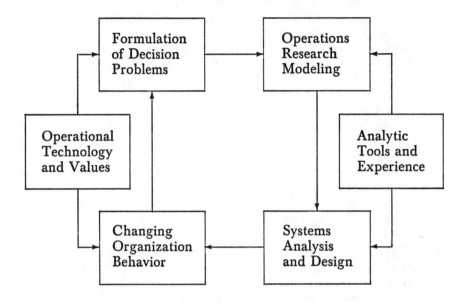

FIGURE 1

different areas of application. Indeed a great advantage of modeling and systems analysis is the connection it can establish between a particular problem and the current state-of-the-art. A second important source of information is the existing operational technology and value structure associated with the particular operations under study. For example, in library studies a comprehensive knowledge of the library environment including its professional principles and standards of practice is needed in order to produce meaningful recommendations. For this reason, operations research is frequently initiated by interdisciplinary teams of experts including analysts and those familiar with the operations and the organizational environment in which they function.

When decision problems can be formulated in a theoretical manner, it is relatively easy to move on to the next steps of building analytic models and designing systems for applying the results of the models. In practice, of course, it is not easy to formulate problems so neatly, and it is always helpful to do this with a view towards how the formulations will lead to models and systems. For this reason, experience with the modeling process is useful in formulating problems. A considerable amount of interaction between the modeling and the problem formulation steps is needed in order to capture all of the essential elements in the problem situation and to formulate it in a manner that will make best use of the analytic tools and experience available.

Problem formulation includes the following steps:
1. Choose the objective; specify its dimensions and value;
2. Isolate all of the variables that are pertinent to the attainment of the objective value;
3. Develop the relationships that exist between the variables;
4. Distinguish controllable variables from those which are not controllable, and classify the latter as to whether they are random or due to competitive strategies;
5. Develop forecasts and predictions of random variables; determine how stable and reliable the forecasts are;
6. Develop the function that relates the variables to the measure of effectiveness in attaining the objective;
7. Identify the restrictions that limit possible values of the controllable variables;
8. Choose those values of the controllable variables that will maximize the degree of attainment of the objective within the limits set by the restrictions.

The goodness of a model is related to the ease with which it can be made to correspond to reality, its sensitivity to the assumptions made, its flexibility in application, its richness in deductive possibilities, its computability, and its plausibility to decision-makers. By experimenting with assumptions about the various factors that influence the variable elements in the model, the analyst can search for the combinations that will yield the optimal benefits. Thus, the operations research model serves the same purpose that a laboratory does for the basic scientist. The major difficulties are in specifying and measuring the "benefits" in a decision, being certain that all useful alternative courses of action have been considered, and predicting the changes in environmental factors that will affect the appropriateness of a model and its solution. Some characteristics of good models are:
1. Relatedness to other OR models;
2. Ease of interpretation or intuitiveness;
3. Lack of sensitivity to special assumptions;
4. Richness in deductive possibilities;
5. Ease of enrichment and modifications;
6. Accuracy in representing the real world;
7. Applicability to different problems;
8. Ease of computation and interpretation of results;
9. Usefulness and ease of application;
10. Cost of set up and use.

Operations research has made it possible and not uncommon to find extremely powerful mathematical methods being used to solve problems with a degree of scientific certitude that is out of proportion to the assumptions and conditions which made it possible to formulate the problem in the first place. As this approach is extended to encompass situations of much larger scale and complexity, the analytic techniques often falter and the role of subjective judgment becomes more apparent. Indeed, it has been argued that operations research methods are only valid at the suboptimal level, i.e., within an arbitrary framework of values and restrictions. Ackoff (1971) has pointed out that the real benefits of systems planning in an organization are not derived by "following a plan" but by the organization engaging directly in the planning process itself as an ongoing activity. "Effective planning cannot be done to or for an organization; it must be done by it," Ackoff says. "Therefore, the role of the professional planner is not to plan, but to provide everyone who can be affected by planning with an opportunity to participate in it, and to provide those engaged in it with information, instructions, questions, and answers that enable them to plan better than professional planners can alone."

The application of operations research models in the planning and control of an organization requires a considerable effort in collecting experimental data and testing the model for its applicability to a given situation. Furthermore, the actual use of such models on a day-to-day basis requires the input of reliable data on a regular basis. For this reason, operations research work often leads to substantial revisions in the way information is processed in an organization. In industry, this development is evidenced by the large management information systems that have become commonplace features in large corporations. Because such systems are designed for decision-making purposes and not historical recordkeeping, they tend to place a high priority on timeliness as well as accuracy, and often require the use of computers and telecommunication equipment. The development of such a system can have profound effects on the organization since it makes possible a different distribution of responsibility and authority. In general, the effect is to enable top managers to delegate decision-making powers to subordinates within certain guidelines, and thus allow more decentralization, flexibility, and local autonomy to exist. The trend is to attach more importance to the process of decision-making and planning as it is practiced throughout the organization, and to give less weight to the development of master plans and policies.

LIBRARY STUDIES

The history of the application of operations research to the problems of libraries is surprisingly long. Many of the early pioneers in operations research, notably Bernal (1949) in England and Bush (1945) in America, were concerned about the deficiencies they observed in conventional methods of scientific communication. They were convinced that the journal was already obsolete and were impatient to see the development of new computer-based methods of storing, retrieving, and transferring information. They argued that scientific communication is the key to the successful application of scientific methods to societal problems, since communication takes the place of administration in guiding and coordinating work in the scientific community. Their dream of new kinds of electronic devices that would replace the book, the journal, and the library still remains a dream for the most part, but one that continues to capture the imagination of many scientists.

Their approach to library problems, the development of a totally new system technology, was well described by one of their contemporaries, the librarian Rider (1944), who had made many studies and experiments on library storage problems at Wesleyan University and came to the conclusion that "no emendations of present library method alone were going to provide a sufficient solution to our growth problem." With remarkable anticipation of what is now called the systems approach, Rider said:

> And the reason for our failure to integrate what were really facets of one single problem was that we were blinded by the *status quo*. We insisted on continuing to accept as library axioms, unalterable and unquestionable, certain assumptions which no longer had validity, such dicta, for instance, as: libraries are collections of books; books are stored on shelves; library materials have to be cataloged; catalogs have to be made on cards; books must be arranged by their call numbers, etc., etc., etc. It is not until we have looked behind and beyond every one of these—and many other—supposedly basic axioms of library method, and have seriously questioned their validity as axioms, that we begin to make any real progress.

When he did this, Rider came to a new synthesis based on the microform card. More recently and in the same vein, Licklider (1965) argued that: "One must be prepared to reject not only the schema of the physical library, which is essentially a response to books and their proliferation, but the schema of the book itself, and even that of the printed page as a long term storage device, if one is to discover the kinds of procognitive systems needed in the future."

More in keeping with the traditions of operations research is the work of Morse (1968) who studied library problems partly because of his genuine interest and concern in this area, and partly because the university library was a convenient and rich laboratory for his students at M.I.T. Similar reasons, along with financial support from the National Science Foundation's Office of Science Information Service, prompted several other university-based operations research groups to give special attention to library problems. Some of these early studies were headed by Roy (1968) at Johns Hopkins, Ackoff (1960) at Case-Western, Churchman (1972) at Berkeley, Leimkuhler (1968) at Purdue, and Mackenzie (1972) at the University of Lancaster in England. The participants in these studies and their work have spread to many other institutions, and have merged with the efforts of two other groups, those concerned primarily with the development of new kinds of information systems and those concerned primarily with the development of the field of information science. The former group is more in line with the ideas of Bush and is computer oriented. The latter group is more concerned with the mathematical and logical description of basic phenomena in information processes.

The practical motivation on the part of library managers for operations research studies is the pressure to economize and expand activities by means of computers. Operations Research is seen as the best way to conduct exploratory studies before making costly commitments for new computerized systems. As Morse says, the need is for logical models of the library that can be experimented with in order to see what is most useful and what data are needed to make a new synthesis of libraries and computers work most effectively. One needs to anticipate the management problems of new systems in order to design the appropriate feedback and control devices. The initial task is to model the library as it functions today and then to experiment with new systems. The preoccupation with existing systems is necessary to form a sound basis for predicting the effects and guiding the development of innovations.

DOCUMENT USAGE

Operations research models that have been developed within library settings tend to focus on the library as a document storage and retrieval center. The majority of information in a library continues to be stored in book form. As Morse (1964) notes,

> A book is a remarkably compact and accessible means of information storage. The usual book contains ten million bits of information in nearly as condensed form as the magnetic tape reels of the modern computer which can hold the equivalent of two to ten books per reel. But the information in the book is much more accessible than that which is on the tape. A book can be opened to any page; it can be read nearly anywhere and from nearly any posture. Before we decide to replace books with something else, hopefully more compact, or even before we decide to store the books in a more compact or differently organized way, we should know in detail how the books are used at present.

The key model in Morse's study is one in which book usage over time can be predicted to follow a known mathematical form, settling down to a steady-state pattern after an initial period of popularity. The model is used to detect some interesting differences in the usage patterns of books in different subject fields, although the data are admittedly skimpy. The model is then used to make policy recommendations for such activities as book acquisition, circulation, retirement, and storage, in the light of the data obtained in the M.I.T. Libraries. Morse warns that these recommendations are carrying the theory well beyond the available facts, but he notes that: "Accuracy is not often important in reaching policy decisions; order of magnitude figures are far better than nothing." Elsewhere, he says:

> But as the library becomes more mechanized or computerized these data will become enormously easier to collect *if the computer system is designed to gather the needed data* . . . what is needed before computer designs are frozen are the models

of the sort developed in this book to be played with, to see which of them could be useful and to see what data are needed and in what form, in order that both models and computers can be used most effectively by the librarian.

Many other studies of the patterns of the use of books and other materials in libraries have been made, as seen in the bibliography by Jain and DeWeese (*LQ,* 1969). A notable early study by Fussler and Simon (1969) at the University of Chicago provides considerable insight into the qualitative aspects of such data. Cole's (1963) study of the pattern of journal usage in a petroleum library led to the development of a relatively simple exponential or geometric model of information obsolescence that has been used many times in subsequent applications. Jain (1969) made a very thorough comparative analysis of different usage models and proposed a model which combined the best features of previous models and gave a more accurate prediction of book use. His data are taken from the Purdue University Libraries. An important corollary development in such work has been the perfection of statistical sampling techniques for gathering and analyzing usage data (*LQ,* 1969). More recently, the study by Morse and Chen (1975) demonstrates how it is possible to analyze data from different kinds of circulation systems in a rigorous and meaningful way.

STORAGE PROBLEMS

Many library usage studies were motivated by the search for more efficient methods of storing library materials that would minimize the inconvenience to users by discarding little used materials or storing them in less accessible locations. The use of a depository for little used material was the subject of a major study by Trueswell (1969) at Northwestern University. Jain's study of usage at Purdue was related to another study by Lister (1967) who developed several least-cost decision rules for the selection of library materials for compact storage. Two types of rules developed from these studies: one using age since publication or acquisition as the determining factor, and the other using some measure of current activity as the selection criterion. Leimkuhler and Cooper (1971) show that when a simple exponential growth model is combined with the exponential obsolescence model then the total circulation of a collection will increase proportionally to the size of the collection, depending on the growth and obsolescence rates. In this way, it is possible to predict how much circulation demand will be generated by a depository collection where age is the determining factor. They were also able to use this model to show how the average cost of circulation might be minimized by use of a book depository. These studies helped to demonstrate the need for and the methods that might be used to make a better determination of the costs of holding materials in libraries. Mann's (1971) study of storage problems is a good mathematical treatment of the subject.

More directly concerned with the physical attributes of book storage systems were the studies by Leimkuhler and Cox (1964) of efficient methods of storing books by size. This model was based on the traditional library practice of using special storage procedures for items of unusually small and large dimensions. By describing the dimensional characteristics of a collection in a mathematical manner, the model shows how to determine the gain in storage capacity by using size as criterion for shelving. This study led to other studies such as those of Gupta and Ravindran (1974) who perfected the mathematical techniques, and by O'Neill (1964) and Saxena (1967) who perfected the statistical methods used in studying the dimensional characteristics of book collections. In general, such studies are able to demonstrate the extent to which improvement in shelving capacity might be gained by using such methods, which is rather limited for many collections but could be very important in large depositories. In addition to their reinforcement of the need for better cost data and other statistical information about libraries, these models also opened the way for demonstrating the applicability of the optimization techniques used in operations research. They also serve to bring into sharper focus the real material handling problems in document systems. Models of this kind are also applicable to other kinds of information storage systems using computers and miniaturization, and possibly to guidelines and procedures for converting information from one kind of medium to the other. The paper by Korfhage (1972) shows how basic concepts in graph theory can be used to model networks of storage and retrieval centers.

AVAILABILITY

The main thrust in Morse's studies at M.I.T. was to provide methods for measuring the effectiveness of various library policies in providing better access to the documents sought by users. Better access means that the document is more likely to be available at the time and place it is sought either as a specific request or as part of a larger search for information. The decision problems which Morse addressed include: the amount and allocation of book and periodical budgets, the purchase of duplicate copies, the placement of books in open shelves, stacks, and reserve collections, changes in loan policies, control of losses, limitations on shelf space, and the use of storage areas. The approach taken was to estimate how many users would be inconvenienced as a result of changes in retirement, duplication, circulation, reshelving, and replacement of lost books, and then to compare these various measures of effectiveness with the dollar cost of making improvements.

One of the best examples of applying this approach in a library is the study at the University of Lancaster by Buckland (1975) and others. The proportion of books having various levels of demand for use was estimated using a model similar to that proposed by Morse but modified to take explicit account of multiple copies of some items. The effect on satisfaction level, i.e., the probability of a book being on the shelf when requested, was calculated for various combinations of loan period, number of copies, amount of in-library use, and the probability that a reader will ask that a book be recalled or reserved. These calculations were made by means of a computer simulation model and showed that the overall satisfaction level was about 60 percent. A new policy of variable loan periods and selective duplication was established whereby the most popular 10 percent of the collection is subject to a one-week loan period and carefully monitored for the need of duplicate copies. The new policy led to a surprisingly large increase in the amount of books borrowed which later subsided. It is believed that the initial improvement in satisfaction level led to increased demand which, in turn, acted to reduce the satisfaction level to a more stable level.

Buckland (1975) points out that the absence of books from the shelves can have a large effect on the success of users who browse for information and must depend on what is immediately available. He concludes that the shelves will tend to be systematically biased towards the less useful materials, since only about half of the 10 percent most popular items are likely to be present. Morse (1970) notes that browsing appears to be at least as popular as catalog searching as a method of finding books and periodicals, and he believes that factual studies of browsing patterns are needed in order to improve the design and control of libraries. By employing techniques that were developed initially for guiding the search for submarines, Morse shows how the expected success of a library browser can be measured in terms of search time and an estimate of the potential relevance of the collection for the user's needs. He uses this measure to show how a browser might best distribute his or her time in different parts of a collection, and how a library might reorganize its collection to enhance its browsability. He also considers the question of whether to retire little used items from the shelves by means of an age or usage criterion. Bookstein and Swanson (1973) have developed models for monitoring the accuracy with which books are shelved according to their designated order.

REFERENCE SCATTERING

Attempts to formulate rules for the selective acquisition of library materials through the use of mathematical models have been usually associated with journal collections. The seminal work in this area is that of Bradford (1948) as expressed in his "Law of Scattering," which held that when journals are ranked according to their productivity of relevant articles to a particular subject the productivity diminishes in an approximately logarithmic manner. More precise formulations of the Law have been made by Vickery (1948), Brookes (1968), Leimkuhler (1967), and recently, Wilkinson (1972) clarified their arguments. Kendall (1960) studied the literature of operations research from this standpoint and showed the relation between Bradford's Law and Zipf's Law in linguistics, as later confirmed in a paper by Kozachkov and Khursin (1968). In a review of the subject, Buckland and Hindle (1969) note that while most of the formal studies are based on citation data, studies by Kilgour (1969) and others show that similar patterns have been found in document usage data.

Brookes (1970) showed how Bradford's Law can be used to estimate the total number of papers that will be found if a complete search is made of the literature, as well as the total number of journals that will contain at least one relevant article. Leimkuhler (1977) used the Law to show that by partially ordering or classifying a file of journals according to their productivity, the expected time it takes to search for a particular piece of information can be greatly reduced. In particular, the benefits from a two or three stage search procedure are relatively very large when compared to the advantages of more exhaustive classification schemes. Buckland and Woodburn (1968) combine Bradford's Law with Cole's exponential model of the obsolescence of document usefulness to show how a library with limited space could determine how many titles to acquire and how long they should be retained. Alternatively, they show how a library could best allocate a limited budget between the acquisition of new titles and their retention in storage. The criterion in these studies is the satisfaction of user demand as predicted by the scattering and obsolescence models.

Kraft and Hill (*Management Science*, 1973) formulated the journal selection problem as a multiple choice model in which one seeks to determine the optimal allocation of present and future (expected) funds for purchasing journals, using a criterion based on expected usage as a measure of journal value. By employing various mathematical programming techniques, they were able to find several methods for finding an approximately optimal solution to this problem. In a subsequent study, Glover and Klingman (1972) proposed an alternative mathematical formulation that has advantages in revealing the implications of the model, and in making it possible to use different solution approaches. Their approach makes it possible to introduce more realistic assumptions about how budgets might be adjusted to accommodate variations in expenditure patterns, and how the model can be made to adapt to the appearance of new journals in future periods. It is unlikely that many libraries could justify using such sophisticated techniques as day-to-day decision aids, but these models provide the basis for developing such tools and making it possible to coordinate journal selection decisions more closely with other managerial decisions and policies.

Newhouse and Alexander (1972) developed a book selection model for a public library which attempts to maximize the benefit the library provides to the community for a given book budget. Benefit is measured by estimating the circulation of a book and the present dollar value of the circulations. The dollar value is based on the price of the book, the proportion of borrowers who would otherwise buy the book, and the benefit of borrowing expressed as a fraction of the purchase price. The product of these factors is discounted over the life of the book in order to determine the equivalent lifetime benefit of a book in terms of present dollars. By combining this measure with the cost of acquisition to form a benefit/cost ratio, the library can determine a rank ordering of the relative advantage of purchasing different classes of books. Newhouse and Alexander found that benefits probably exceed costs for most classes of books, sometimes greatly, and therefore indicate that book budgets should be increased.

TOTAL SYSTEM MODELS

Operations research studies of the kind described previously tend to isolate individual functions in an organization and examine them independently, to the extent possible, of other related functions. Such suboptimization is often necessary in order to make a rigorous analysis of the individual functions as parts of a larger and more complex system. However, there is the danger that a comprehensive and balanced view of the entire system will fail to emerge from the mere accumulation of many small scale studies. For this reason, it is desirable that some early attempts are made to define the larger system within which the various subsystems operate, even though the larger models tend to be less rigorous and less immediately useful for pressing decision problems. Models of this kind for libraries are most commonly found in the schematic diagrams used for automation programs, where large areas of library activity and even entire libraries are viewed as subsystems of computerized information systems. Such models are highly mechanized descriptions of the flow of information along predetermined paths and according to a well-established decision-making structure. They are of more limited usefulness in analyzing alternative routings, unless they can be made to include a great number of variable characteristics. Often, this is too cumbersome a method of modeling for detailed analysis and it is difficult to establish limits and stable characteristics for the output from such models.

At Purdue University, Baker (1970) developed a behavioral model for a library based on a simplified characterization of the objectives of three groups: users, funders, and librarians, and the various interactions of these parties in a library environment. This model revealed the need for librarians to take the initiative in creating a better understanding of the benefits and costs of the services they offer in order to offset the tendency for users to rely on previous experience and possible misconceptions, and to distort the image of the library in the eyes of the funders. Nance (1970) used this approach to model the behavior of a university branch library by means of computer simulation techniques that have been used for industrial and urban planning studies. He was able to show the possible long-range effects of different managerial attitudes and policies on the behavior of library patrons. Rzasa and Baker (1972) studied the problems of goal setting and the measurement of performance by library managers.

At M.I.T., Raffel and Shishko (1969) made a systematic study of user preferences for reallocation of library budgets and the improvement of different services. They found that the library spends more on space for people than space for books and concluded that it would be better to promote outside usage through duplication techniques, paperbacks, and loan policies, than to spend money for economizing on book storage space. Twenty alternative proposals for changing library facilities and services by increasing or decreasing the budget were presented to a representative group of users for their opinions. The results showed that three major campus groups differ markedly in the kinds of changes they would favor. Undergraduates would reduce services to researchers and increase reserve book facilities. Graduate students would cut study space, reduce photocopying costs, and improve catalog and reference services. The faculty are most willing to change storage and cataloging practices in order to preserve and develop departmental libraries.

At the University of Pennsylvania, a major study of library objectives and performance measures was conducted by Hamburg (1974) and his associates. They found that the many verbal statements of library objectives found in the literature did not lend themselves to the measurement of library performance in order to determine how proposed plans and alternative decisions may affect performance. Recognizing the primacy of the effect on persons in the society as essential considerations in the measurement of library performance, they propose to evaluate the "exposure of individuals to documents of recorded human experience." They propose several methods of measuring exposure, including one suggested by Meier (1961) of counting the item-use days generated by each library transaction, and another in which just total user exposure time is measured for all activities. When coupled with an accrual method of matching costs and exposure to the appropriate operating time periods, it is possible to develop performance measures based on either the ratio of exposure to cost or the difference (profit) between the value of exposure and the cost, where the value of exposure might be based on an overall assumed benefit/cost ratio. In this way, the effect of change in policies can be evaluated in terms of their effect on the exposure per dollar ratio measure or on the net gain in the value of exposure less cost.

Another approach to modeling a library as a total system is taken by Black (1967) in his economic model of library operation. The library is conceived as primarily a producer of "circulation." The librarian chooses the division of his revenues between expenditures on wages and salaries, books and other materials, and the purchase of equipment in such a way as to maximize circulation subject to revenue constraints and demand patterns. Demand is a function of population, income per capita, and the implicit cost of poorer service. Equating demand to supply, Black found the implicit cost of borrowing, and the revenue needed to maintain equilibrium levels of circulation, labor services, and rates of purchase of materials and equipment. Each of these solutions is in terms of population, wage rate, income per capita, and book price. By knowing how these variables change over time, it is possible to predict how the library will grow.

From the limited data available to him and by making several assumptions, Black shows that the implicit cost of borrowing grows at a weighted average of the rates of increase of wages and equipment costs. Revenue grows proportional with population, per capita income, and the implicit cost of borrowing. Circulation also increases with population and per capita income, but decreases with the implicit cost of borrowing, i.e., unit circulation cost. Data on U.S. public libraries for the period 1954-62 indicate a growth of about 5 percent per year in circulation, 7 percent in expenditures, 2.8 percent in book stock, and 2.6 percent in library staff. Expenditures grew rapidly because of a 3.5 to 4 percent increase in book prices and wage rates. The implicit rate of increase in the cost of borrowing was 2 percent per year. There was also an apparent increase in productivity of about 1.5 percent per year, i.e., more effective utilization of books and staff to provide circulations.

In the near future it is expected that considerably more research will be done on the economics of libraries and the supply and demand markets in which they operate, adding to the variety of scientific expertise available to operations research studies. At the same time, increasing attention must be given to the social, psychological, and political aspects of libraries.

HUMAN FACTORS

Mackenzie (1973) argues that O.R. and systems analysis are of much more basic importance to the library than a prelude to library automation.

> The library has advanced a long way from the time when it was merely a collection of books, with a relatively small number of users, each knowing his or her way about its shelves. With the expansion of higher education and advances in technology, it has become much more a precise instrument for transfer of information from the author to a large number of users—often in a very short space of time, because of the numbers involved—who need a great deal of guidance and help. The library manager is a relatively new concept. . . . The professional skills and techniques are essential, but to them is being added the realization that a library, if it is to perform its full function, calls for the study of cost-effectiveness and similar concepts drawn from industry.

Mackenzie notes that despite the numerous theoretical studies reported in the literature, there is very little evidence of such studies being used to make any major changes in operational library systems. He is concerned that librarians may be ignoring the potential merits in such studies.

The slowness with which fundamental changes in library methods have emerged over the last several decades is due to several factors beyond antipathy on the part of librarians to make use of operations research techniques. Few libraries find it possible to finance research activities of this kind, and support at regional or national levels is exceedingly limited. Training in systems analysis methods is being introduced in library schools and eventually this should have a salutary effect. But, of greater significance is the scope and complexity of the task of making fundamental changes in library methods. Because of the impossibility of isolating any single library from the regional, national, and even international environment in which it operates, the scale of any major innovation is immediately very large. The study of any single major operation in a library quickly brings the analyst into confrontation with system constraints beyond his or her control. The whole economic viability of the library depends on such interactions with other libraries and other institutions. Furthermore, the library is saddled with a past which it cannot disregard and a commitment to the future which knows few limits. For these reasons it seems likely that major innovations will have to be fostered at the interlibrary level of operation; however, they will need a fundamental understanding of the library itself.

The greatest obstacle to the use of operations research methods in libraries is the human element. Churchman (1968) points out that the user must be the most important consideration in the design of libraries and information systems. He is critical of efforts to measure library performance in purely physical or monetary terms. He says that the true benefit of such systems must be measured in terms of the meaning of information for the user. "People are not better just because they process information more rapidly or more coherently," he says. "People are better because they are better in a moral or aesthetic sense." The argument raises insurmountable problems for building the kind of model person which is needed in order to study information systems in such a way. Even a speculative or dialectic information system which could examine its own premises and argue from different points of view would not escape the spectre of dehumanization which Churchman finds implicit in the systems approach. Nevertheless, this does not deter his advocacy of the need for using such an approach as an inadequate but necessary technique. Fromm (1970) contends that "man is a system that can be studied like any other system" and "that only to the extent that managers or, in general, people who try to understand society or a large enterprise, take the System Man as seriously as they take the system economics, the system technology, and so on, can they meaningfully talk about *human* ends in relation to the aims and ends of the managerial process." He believes that the development of non-bureaucratic, humanistic work systems is possible and no more difficult than space travel, and that "economic and social planning is blind if the Science of Man is not integrated into the science of management and social planning."

Wilson (1968) in his study of bibliographic control gives a proof of the impossibility of building a "universal bibliographic machine," without ruling out the possibility of machines of lesser power. He argues that bibliographic control is much more than simply locating items of information. Rather, it is a kind of knowledge *about* knowledge; and, since knowledge is a kind of power, bibliographic control is a kind of power *over* power. "This mastery," he says, "is not the knowledge of the contents of texts; it is knowledge of all uses to which texts can be put, by all possible users in all possible circumstances. We shall never in this world have such control, but the idea is an intelligible one." Wilson recognizes the need for economic and technical considerations in the design of information systems, but he insists on the primacy of political considerations in the final analysis. "We can have no more bibliographic control then we can afford," he says, "but how much we *can* afford, on whom it shall be spent, and in what proportions are never purely economic questions." Requests or demands for power, including the power of bibliographic control, are political requests, and they raise the issue of the rights of individuals for access to information services.

Despite these admonitions, no serious attempt has been made to develop analytic models of libraries that can take full account of the political and human considerations inherent in such systems. Only recently has there been a shift away from emphasis on the purely technical aspects of information systems development in the research programs sponsored by the National Science Foundation. In a recent announcement, the Office of Science Information Service (National Science Foundation, 1974) focuses attention on managerial, organizational, and economic aspects of the dissemination of scientific and technical information, but still falls short of the eventual need for a more comprehensive understanding of the political issues involved. The limitations here are in the methods themselves. In practice, all operations research is really suboptimization, and it is unlikely that the resources available to the study of libraries and similar systems are sufficient to overcome this deficiency in the near future. However, the thrust of even small scale studies must be towards the eventual solution of a harmonious, total system understanding. The best hope for achieving this goal is to develop subsystem models that are rigorous in their logic and consistent with the objectives and policies at the next higher level of system specification. In this way, more comprehensive models can evolve, as assumptions have to be modified or objectives are changed. There is the risk that the preoccupation with small scale models may never lead to the development of satisfactory large scale models, but this risk can be minimized if the implementation of analytic results is vigorously pursued, and in fact, as Wagner (1969) says, begins on the first day of an operations research study.

EXAMPLE

A simple example of modeling comes from the library operations study at Purdue which looked at the shelving requirement for a large collection of books. Considering book height as the only attribute of interest, one can make the diagram shown in Figure 2 which represents the theoretical profile of a collection if all of the books were arranged on a single shelf according to their height. The simple rectangle enclosing this profile represents the total area of shelf space required to house this collection if all of the shelves are of the same height. As an alternative consider Figure 3, in which a portion of the smaller books are put on shelves of a smaller height, which results in the saving of the space which is represented by the shaded portion of the diagram. One could also consider using three sizes of shelves and saving even more space as in Figure 4. These figures represent the elements of a relatively simple mathematical model of the space requirements for a library collection.

By representing the library shelving problem in a simple two dimensional graph much of the reality of book shelving has been omitted but many of the essential features have been retained. Furthermore, the idealized model makes it possible to do things that would normally not be possible with a real system. For example, it is unlikely that all of the books of any sizeable collection could be arranged by size in a single array as shown in the figures. In Figure 2 where two sizes of shelves are used, the interesting optimization problem is the choice of the height for the second shelf. In the figure it is apparent that one could systematically try all of the different book heights, compute the savings in space as shown by the shaded portion, and then choose that height which gives the greatest savings. At the outset considerable effort was expended in finding efficient ways to determine the optimum shelf height for any profile of book heights and for any arbitrary number of height divisions.

It was also necessary to develop efficient ways to determine the height profiles for large collections of books by statistical sampling techniques. Such studies led to difficult and interesting problems of sampling and data collection. In doing this, data was collected that suggested that there were significant relationships between book heights and other dimensions of books including their age and subject classification. When representative data of the book heights in the Purdue collection were used to determine optimal shelf height classifications, the results were like those shown in Table I, indicating that size classification is relatively most effective when it is confined to three or four classifications, and that this results in about a 50 percent increase in storage capacity. Going to more classifications, as has been done in some storage libraries, does not save very much additional space and leads to more complicated location controls.

ALL SHELVES THE SAME HEIGHT

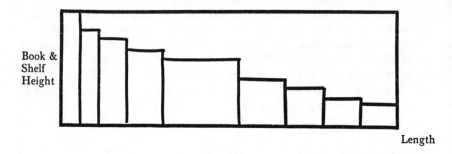

FIGURE 2

SAVINGS WITH TWO SIZES OF SHELVES

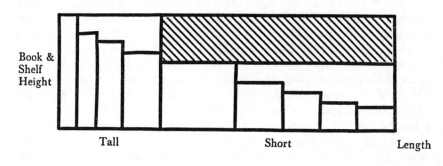

FIGURE 3

SAVINGS WITH THREE SIZES OF SHELVES

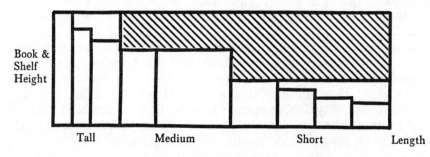

FIGURE 4

TABLE I
EFFICIENCY OF STORAGE BY SIZE

Number of Shelf Heights Used	Percent Increase in Capacity
1	0%
2	38
3	47
4	51
5	53
. . .	. . .
10	58

An interesting subsequent study was an attempt to compute and compare the storage efficiency of three branch libraries with the idealized storage patterns developed by a computer using the optimization algorithms. The initial results indicated that the libraries were storing books even more efficiently than was theoretically possible, because they were flipping the tallest books over onto their fore edge. The computer program was revised to also permit flipping and to take this into account when computing optimal shelving rules. The interesting result is that with flipping it is possible to achieve most of the potential savings in space with only two size classifications. Whether or not size classifications in libraries are of practical importance depends on other considerations, although many libraries do practice some form of shelving by size. The obvious application is in remote storage areas where space is of greater relative importance than is the convenience of user access.

Another interesting subsequent application of the model in a library context was to the storage of MARC bibliographic records in computer-based files. In this application the length of each record was the counterpart of book height and the length of a block of space provided for each record was the counterpart of shelf height. By applying the same optimization techniques developed for book storage, it is possible to find the optimal block sizes for the tape records if they are classified into two or more standard block sizes. The relative efficiency of doing this can be determined. Furthermore, by using special coding techniques which compress the length of records but require later decoding, one can evaluate how this affects the optimal block lengths in much the same manner as the flipping of books affected the choice of optimal shelf sizes.

EXTENSIONS

An important benefit from the book shelving model was that it led to related studies of other library operations. By looking at a spatial classification problem in which relationships could be verified in a directly measurable way, it was possible to establish a credible mathematical approach to library organization. The mathematical exercises associated with the study helped establish valuable connections within theoretical operations research. For example, the book shelving model has been reformulated in several different ways to make it amenable to different optimization techniques such as dynamic programming and graph theory. Because of its more likely application to book depositories, shelving by size led to further studies of the optimal methods for selecting books for such depositories on a basis of age and usage. This in turn led to the study of larger questions of library organization, performance measures, and appropriate techniques for the large scale evaluation of libraries.

A problem of continuing interest is how to classify and organize resource materials for more efficient search and retrieval by users. Libraries have always attempted to classify, select, and organize materials into core groupings which are then recommended to users as the most appropriate place to begin a search. The analyst asks how systematic this procedure is, whether it can be modeled, and whether the models can help to evaluate and improve the procedure. Of particular interest to this investigation is the work of the great librarian S. C. Bradford (1948; Leimkuhler, 1967). Bradford studied the productivity of journal titles in several areas and this led him to propose his famous law of information scattering. He said that if journal titles are ranked in the order of their productivity and then grouped into successive zones of equal total productivity, then the size of these zones increases as the power of some constant. He also showed that a plot of the cumulative productivity was almost a straight line when plotted against the logarithm of the rank.

Bradford's purpose in doing this was not to pursue esoteric research, but to develop a practical rule for deciding just how many journal titles are needed in a specialized core collection. His data led him to conclude, for example, that a library could expect to contain about two-thirds of the total productivity in a field if it held 20 or 25 percent of the most productive titles in the field. In order to cover more of a field, the library would have to be prepared to acquire an increasing number of peripheral journals which are relevant but of relatively low productivity. Bradford's law does not answer the question of what is the optimal size of a core collection, but it provides some valuable information for arriving at such an answer.

One way to approach the core size problem is to consider it in the context of a user who is searching for a particular item of interest in a collection of sources. If the user has no prior knowledge about the relative productivity of these sources, and if it is assumed that the item is somewhere in the collection, then according to the laws of probability that person can expect a search through half of the collection before locating the item of interest. If on the other hand, the collection is divided into two groups so that all items in the first group have a greater productivity than those in the second group and if the user searches the more productive group first, s/he can expect on the average to search through less than half of the collection before finding the item. How much less depends on the profile of productivity in the collection and on the size of the core collection. If the core collection is too small, it will be more likely that it won't satisfy the individual's needs, and if it is too large, it will lose much of its selective value as a core collection.

    This problem is depicted graphically in Figure 5 where the curved line represents the percentage increase in productivity that is contained in an increasing portion of a collection whose members are ranked according to their productivity. If the members of this collection were not in rank order but were randomly arranged then the user hasn't any reason to expect any one member to have greater or less productivity than any other. This is equivalent to saying that the accumulative productivity curve is like the diagonal straight line in Figure

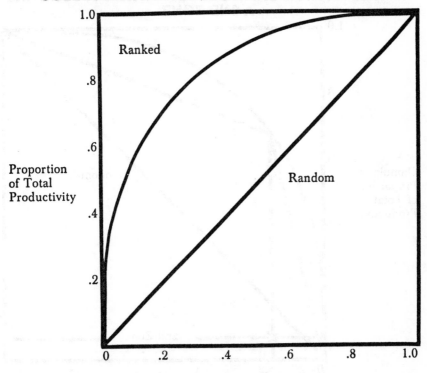

COMPARISON OF CUMULATIVE PRODUCTIVITY FOR A COLLECTION IN RANKED AND RANDOM ORDER

FIGURE 5

6. So in an operational sense, Figure 5 represents two collections, one of which is perfectly ordered while the other has no order at all.

It can be shown by the laws of probability that the area above the curved line in Figure 5, and within the one-by-one rectangle, is equal to the expected proportion of the collection which would have to be searched to find the item of interest. The area above the diagonal line is equal to one-half as mentioned above and implies that with random ordering the average search covers half of the collection. However, with perfect ordering, the average search effort is less than a half, and the area between the curve and the diagonal measures the reduction in search effort obtained by prior ordering of the collection. The exact amount depends on the shape of the curve.

Perfect ordering of a collection according to its potential productivity for a given user or class of user may not be a practical way to run a library. It is more plausible that the library could do a reasonable job in identifying that portion of a collection that is more productive for a given purpose, but within the core, the items are arranged randomly.

CLASSIFICATION OF A COLLECTION INTO A CORE AND A 2ND ZONE

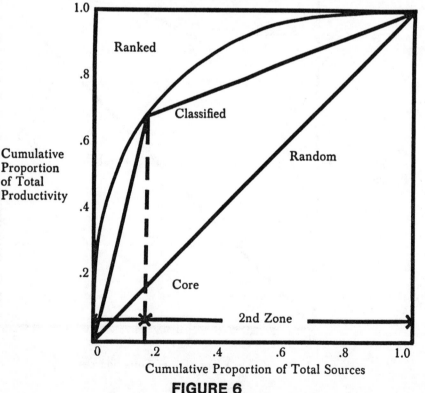

FIGURE 6

This is commonly done in all libraries, both in selecting items for acquisition and classifying items by subject. The graphical representation of the division of a collection into a core and a noncore group is shown in Figure 6. The broken straight line between the diagonal and curve represents the search profile of the subdivided collection. Again the area above the curves and lines represents the search effort. The triangular area between the broken line and the diagonal is of particular interest because it represents the reduction in search effort which is obtained by going from a perfectly random collection to one with a core collection. In the model, it can be seen that the amount of improvement depends on the shape of the curve and size of the core collection.

It is a fairly straightforward mathematical procedure to find the optimum size of a core collection as defined by the model if one knows the equation for the curved line in Figures 5 and 6. Furthermore, the model can be extended to include several zones of decreasing productivity for which the optimal zones can be determined along with the relative improvement in expected search effort. As might be expected, the greatest improvement is obtained by making the first classification of a core zone. The division of a collection into more than three or four zones appears to have relatively little effect on the search effort. All of this kind of analysis depends on the form of the productivity profile for the collection, and the ability to enumerate such a curve. The results to some preliminary studies (1972) along these lines indicate that the optimal core collection should contain approximately 20 percent of the total number of journal titles which contain references on a topic. This core would be approximately two-thirds of the total references on the subject and include all titles with more than four or five references. Whether or not such criteria should be used in the actual planning of special collections needs to be verified by much more detailed analysis and experimentation.

APPLICATIONS

The applicability of mathematical models to library operations is still highly debatable, i.e., there is a very limited body of organized scientific opinion to support the argument that certain library activities follow mathematical "laws." The number of people who are able to devote much of their time to such discoveries are very few, and probably will remain so as support for pure research dwindles. Basic research of this kind should be encouraged within the library profession, but it is not necessary for libraries to await such developments before engaging in serious systems development. In the practical work of systems design, the goal is to find *better* methods for delivering library services—not finding *the one best method.* Optimization to the systems scientist has a very precise mathematical meaning, while to the systems practitioner it represents a general direction for which to aim. It is more like a point of view. The validity of systems models in practical work is the degree of belief they muster in persons of authority, and not something to be demonstrated in a refereed journal. This is not to say that theory and practice are to be kept in airtight compartments, but that there should be recognition of the important difference in their viewpoint.

As libraries make more use of mathematical models and computers in their normal operations, they must necessarily change the level of knowledge about these techniques that is expected of the professional members of the organization. This is not to say that every librarian will eventually need extensive formal training in mathematics and computer science. It does mean that every librarian affected by the new methods needs to be made aware of the extent and source of this influence on his or her work. It is not possible to keep such knowledge confined to a small group of staff analysts.

All persons whose authority and responsibilities could be enhanced or compromised by the development of new systems within the organization must be given access to the planning processes governing these developments. This will necessitate an increase in their conversational literacy among numerical methods. Experience at Purdue University has shown that it is not difficult to achieve such awareness in a library staff if they are given a meaningful and regular opportunity to develop and practice such skills.

In the Purdue experiment, the staff met weekly with administrators and analysts in a series of presentations and critiques of systems analysis and operations research studies of library problems. Within a relatively short time, there was little difficulty in achieving meaningful open dialogue about fairly sophisticated systems concepts. The depth to which any one technique could be explored varied considerably, to be sure; but the significance of these techniques in a particular application could be freely explored at great length to the edification of all participants.

Because the top administrators of the organization attended these meetings regularly, there was little question about the importance of these discussions. It provided an opportunity for all persons to discuss common problems in a free and professional manner. The often oblique and sometimes naive arguments of the analysts had the beneficial effect of making room for other points of view. That this did not always lead to a convergence of arguments was more a measure of the complexity of the problems than the intransigence of their positions.

Mathematical and computer methods did not become a major stumbling block in these deliberations. In fact, there was little concern with limiting the range of sophisticated techniques that might be discussed. Always these were introduced from an applied or ad hoc viewpoint. Criticism was focused on the insights gained from the technique about the library problems under study, and not on the technique itself. The presence of other analysts and the side discussions among them gave sufficient attention to purely technical questions.

While this approach to systems analysis is not easy to start and maintain, there is good reason to believe it is absolutely essential to extensive systems development in a library organization. Historically, it is a logical extension of the team concept in early operations research and systems analysis studies. This approach was justified initially by the need for interdisciplinary approaches and for the close involvement of analytic and operational viewpoints in developing promising alternatives to urgent problems. With the development of very large projects with clear technical missions—such as exploration of the moon—hierarchical staffs of systems specialists could be justified. Highly technical organizations can make good use of systems specialists in a selective, consultive manner; but, as systems methods are applied to situations with a high "human content," participative planning must be deliberately cultivated as a crucial element in systems development for the long run.

REFERENCES

Ackoff, R. A. "Some Notes on Planning." Presentation at a meeting of American Association for the Advancement of Science, Philadelphia, PA, December, 1971.

Baker, N. R. "Optimal User Search Sequences and Implications for Information System Operation." *American Documentation* 20 (1969):203.

Baker, N. R. and Nance, R. E. "Organizational Analysis and Simulation Studies of University Libraries: A Methodological Overview." *Information Storage and Retrieval* 5 (1970):153.

_____. "The Use of Simulation in Studying Information Storage and Retrieval Systems." *American Documentation* 19 (1968):363.

Bernal, J. D. *The Social Function of Science.* Cambridge, MA: The M.I.T. Press, 1965.

_____. *The Freedom of Necessity.* London, 1949.

Blackett, P. M. S. "Operational Research: Recollections of Problems Studied, 1940-1945." In *The Armed Forces Yearbook 1953 (Brassey's Annual).* London: Wm. Clowes and Sons, 1954, pp. 88-106.

Bookstein, A. "Implications for Library Education." *Library Quarterly* 42 (1972):140.

_____. "Models for Shelf Reading." *Library Quarterly* 43 (1973):126.

Bookstein, A., and Swanson, D. R. "A Stochastic Shelf Reading Model." *Library Quarterly* 43 (1973):138.

Bradford, S. C. *Documentation.* London: Crosby Lockwood and Son, 1948.

Brookes, B. C. "The Complete Bradford-Zipf Bibliograph." *Journal of Documentation* 25 (1969):58.

_____. "The Derivation and Application of the Bradford-Zipf Distribution." *Journal of Documentation* 24 (1968):247.

_____. "The Growth, Utility, and Obsolescence of Scientific Periodical Literature." *Journal of Documentation* 26 (1970):283.

Brophy, P.; Ford, G.; Hindle, A.; and Mackenzie, A. G. *A Library Management Game: Report on a Research Project.* Occasional Paper No. 7. Lancaster, Eng.: University of Lancaster Library, 1972.

Buckland, M. K. *Book Availability and the Library User.* New York: Pergamon Press, 1975.

_____. "An Operations Research Study of a Variable Loan and Duplication Policy at the University of Lancaster." *Library Quarterly* 42 (1972):97.

Buckland, M. K., and Hindle, A. "Library Zipf: Zipf's Law in Libraries and Information Science." *Journal of Documentation* 25 (1969):52.

Buckland, M. K.; Hindle, A.; Mackenzie, A. G.; and Woodburn, I. *Systems Analysis of a University Library: Final Report on a Research Project.* Lancaster, Eng., 1970.

Buckland, M. K., and Woodburn, I. *Some Implications for Library Management of Scattering and Obsolescence.* Occasional Paper No. 1. Lancaster, Eng.: University of Lancaster Library, 1968.

Burkhalter, B. R., ed. *Case Studies in Systems Analysis in a University Library.* Metuchen, NJ: Scarecrow Press, 1963.

Burns, R. W. "A Generalized Methodology for Library Systems Analysis." *College and Research Libraries* 32 (1971):295.

Bush, G. C.; Galliher, H. P.; and Morse, P. M. "Attendance and Use of the Science Library at M.I.T." *American Documentation* 7 (1956):87.

Bush, V. "As We May Think." *Atlantic Monthly* 176 (1945):101.

Case Institute of Technology, Operations Research Group. "An Operations Research Study of the Dissemination and Use of Recorded Scientific Knowledge." Cleveland, OH, 1960. NTIS PB 171 503.

Chen, C.-c. *Applications of Operations Research Models to Libraries: A Case Study of the Use of Monographs in the Francis A. Countway Library of Medicine, Harvard University.* Cambridge, MA: The M.I.T. Press, 1976.

Churchman, C. W. "Operations Research Prospects for Libraries." *Library Quarterly* 42 (1972):6.

_____. *The Systems Approach.* New York: Dell, 1968.

Coblans, H. "The Communication of Information." In *Society and Science,* edited by M. Goldsmith and A. Mackay. New York: Simon and Schuster, 1964, pp. 93-101.

Cole, P. F. "Journal Usage Versus Age of Journal." *Journal of Documentation* 19 (1963):1.

_____. "A New Look at Reference Scattering." *Journal of Documentation* 18 (1962):58.

Cooper, M. D. "A Cost Model for Evaluating Information Retrieval Systems." *Journal of American Society for Information Science* 23 (1972):306.

Dougherty, R. M., and Heinritz, F. J. *Scientific Management of Library Operations.* Metuchen, NJ: Scarecrow Press, 1966.

Elton, M., and Vickery, B. C. "The Scope for Operational Research in the Library and Information Field." *Aslib Proceedings* 25 (1973):305.

Flood, M. M. "The Systems Approach to Library Planning." *Library Quarterly* 34 (1964):326.

Ford, M. G. "Research in User Behavior in University Libraries." *Journal of Documentation* 29 (1973):85.

Fromm, E. "Thoughts on Bureaucracy." *Management Science* 168 (1970):699.

Fussler, H. H., and Simon, J. L. *Patterns in the Use of Books in a Large Research Library.* Chicago, IL: University of Chicago Press, 1969.

Glover, F., and Klingman, D. "Mathematical Programming Models and Methods for the Journal Selection Problem." *Library Quarterly* 42 (1972):43.

Goffman, W. "A Mathematical Method for Analyzing the Growth of a Scientific Discipline." *Journal of the Association of Computing Machinery* 18 (1971):173.

Goyal, S. K. "Application of Operational Research to Problems of Determining Appropriate Loan Periods for Periodicals." *Libri* 20 (1970):94.

Gupta, S. M., and Ravindran, A. "Optimal Storage of Books by Size: An Operations Research Approach." *Journal of the American Society for Information Science* 25 (1974):354.

Halbert, M., and Ackoff, R. "An Operations Research Study of the Dissemination of Scientific Information." Cleveland, OH: Case Institute of Technology, n.d. NTIS PB 144 328.

Hamburg, M.; Clelland, R. C.; Bommer, M. R. W.; Ramist, L. E.; and Whitfield, R. M. *Library Planning and Decision-Making Systems.* Cambridge, MA: The M.I.T. Press, 1974.

Hamburg, M.; Ramist, L. E.; and Bommer, M. R. W. "Library Objectives and Performance Measures and Their Use in Decision-Making." *Library Quarterly* 42 (1972):107.

Hayes, R. M. "Library Systems Analysis." In *Data Processing in Public and University Libraries,* edited by J. Harvey. Washington, DC: Spartan Books, 1966.

Heinritz, F. J. "Quantitative Management in Libraries." *College and Research Libraries* 31 (1970):232.

Jain, A. K. "Sampling and Data Collection Methods for a Book Use Study." *Library Quarterly* 39 (1969):245.

Jain, A. K.; Leimkuhler, F. F.; and Anderson, V. L. "A Statistical Model of Book Use and Its Application to the Book Storage Problem." *Journal of the American Statistical Association* 64 (1969):1211.

Johns Hopkins University. "An Operations Research and Systems Engineering Study of a University Library." Baltimore, MD, 1968. ERIC ED 027 926; NTIS PB 168 137, PB 182 834.

Kendall, M. G. "The Bibliograph of Operational Research." *Operational Research Quarterly* 11 (1960):31.

Kilgour, F. G. "Recorded Use of Books in the Yale Medical Library." *American Documentation* 12 (1969):266.

Kochen, M., and Segur, B. "Effects of Catalog Volume at the Library of Congress on the Total Catalog Costs of American Research Libraries." *Journal of the American Society for Information Science* 21 (1970):133.

Korfhage, R. R.; Bhat, V. N.; and Nance, R. E. "Graph Models for Library Information Networks." *Library Quarterly* 42 (1972):31.

Kozachkov, L. S., and Khursin, L. A. "The Basic Probability Distribution in Information Flow Systems." *Nauchno-Technicheskaya Informatsiya*, ser. 2 (1968):3.

Kraft, D. H. "A Comment on the Morse-Elston Model of Probabilistic Obsolescence." *Operations Research* 18 (1970):1228.

Kraft, D. H., and Hill, T. W., Jr. "A Journal Selection Model and Its Implications for Librarians." *Information Storage and Retrieval* 9 (1973):1.

_____. "The Journal Selection Problem in a University Library System." *Management Science* 19 (1973):613.

Lancaster, F. W., ed. "Systems Design and Analysis for Libraries." *Library Trends* 21 (1973).

Leimkuhler, F. F. "The Bradford Distribution." *Journal of Documentation* 23 (1967):197.

_____. "Library Operations Research." *Library Quarterly* 42 (1972):84.

_____. "A Literature Search and File Organization Model." *American Documentation* 19 (1968):131.

_____. "Operational Analysis of Library Systems." *Information Processing and Management* 13 (1977):79.

Leimkuhler, F. F., and Cox, J. G. "Compact Book Storage in Libraries." *Operations Research* 12 (1964):419.

Leimkuhler, F. F., and Cooper, M. D. "Analytical Models for Library Planning." *Journal of the American Society for Information Science* 22 (1971).

Licklider, J. C. R. *Libraries of the Future.* Cambridge, MA: The M.I.T. Press, 1965.

Linvill, W. K. "The Changes in System Modeling Required by Societal Systems Analysis." In *Proceedings of the International Symposium on Systems Engineering and Analysis,* vol. 1. Lafayette, IN: Purdue University, 1972.

Lister, W. C. "Least Cost Decision Rules for the Selection of Library Materials." Ph.D. Dissertation, Purdue University, 1967. ERIC ED 027 196.

Lutz, R. P. "Costing Information Services." *Bulletin of the Medical Library Association* 59 (1971):254.

Mackenzie, A. G. "Systems Analysis as a Decision-Making Tool for the Library Manager." *Library Trends* 21 (1973):493.

Mackenzie, A. G., and Buckland, M. K. "Operational Research." In *British Librarianship and Information Science,* edited by A. H. Whatley. London: Library Association, 1972.

Mann, S. H. "Least Cost Decision Rules for Dynamic Library Management." *Information Storage and Retrieval* 7 (1971):111.

Martyn, J., and Vickery, B. C. "The Complexity of Modeling of Information Systems." *Journal of Documentation* 26 (1970):204.

Mathematica. *On the Economics of Library Operation.* Report to the U.S. National Advisory Commission on Libraries, Princeton, NJ, 1967.

McLuhan, M. *Understanding Media: The Extension of Man.* New York: McGraw Hill, 1964.

Meier, R. L. "Efficiency Criteria for the Operation of Large Libraries." *Library Quarterly* 31 (1961):215.

Miller, D. W., and Starr, M. K. *The Structure of Human Decisions.* Englewood Cliffs, NJ: Prentice-Hall, 1967.

Morley, R. M. "Maximizing the Benefit from Library Resources." In University of Lancaster Library Occasional Paper, No. 3. Lancaster, Eng., 1969.

Morse, P. M. *Library Effectiveness: A Systems Approach.* Cambridge, MA: The M.I.T. Press, 1968.

_____. "Measures of Library Effectiveness." *Library Quarterly* 42 (1972):15.

_____. "Optimal Linear Ordering of Information Items." *Operations Research* 20 (1972):741.

_____. "Probabilistic Models for Library Operations." In *Minutes of the 63rd Meeting,* Association of Research Libraries, 1964, pp. 9-19.

_____. "Search Theory and Browsing." *Library Quarterly* 40 (1970):391.

Morse, P. M., and Chen, C. c. "Using Circulation Desk Data to Obtain Unbiased Estimates of Book Use." *Library Quarterly* 45 (1975):179.

Nance, R. E. "An Analytical Model of a Library Network." *Journal of the American Society for Information Science* 21 (1970):58.

Nance, R. E., and Baker, N. R. "The Use of Simulation in Studying Information Storage and Retrieval." *American Documentation* 19 (1968):363.

Naranan, S. "Power Law Relations in Science Bibliography—A Self-consistent Interpretation." *Journal of Documentation* 27 (1971):83.

Newhouse, J. P., and Alexander, A. J. "An Economic Analysis of Public Library Service." Santa Monica, CA: Rand Corporation, 1972.

Oliver, M. R. "The Effect of Growth on the Obsolescence of Semiconductor Physics Literature." *Journal of Documentation* 27 (1971):11.

O'Neill, E. T. "Sampling University Library Collections." *College and Research Libraries* 27 (1964):450.

Orr, R. H. "Measuring the Goodness of Library Services: A General Framework for Considering Quantitative Measures." *Journal of Documentation* 24 (1973):315.

Pratt, L. "Analysis of Library Systems: A Bibliography." *Special Libraries* 55 (1964):688.

Raffel, J. A., and Shishko, R. *Systematic Analysis of University Libraries: An Application of Cost-Benefit Analysis to the M.I.T. Libraries.* Cambridge, MA: The M.I.T. Press, 1969.

Rider, F. *The Scholar and the Future of the Research Library.* New York: Hadham Press, 1944.

Rouse, W. B. "Applications of Operations Research Techniques in Tufts University Libraries." Boston, MA: Tufts University College of Engineering, 1973.

Rouse, W. B., and Rouse, S. H. "Uses of a Librarian/Consultant Team to Study Library Operations." *College and Research Libraries* 34 (1973):242.

Rzasa, P. V., and Baker, N. R. "Measures of Effectiveness for a University Library." *Journal of the American Society for Information Science* 23 (1972):248.

Saracevic, T., ed. *Introduction to Information Science.* New York: R. R. Bowker, 1970.

Saxena, S. K. "Compact Storage of Books in Open-Shelf Libraries Where Book Height Follows a Compound Type of Truncated Double Exponential Distribution." *Opsearch* 3 (1967):157.

Sinha, B. K., and Clelland, R. C. "Modeling for the Management of Library Collections." *Management Science* 22 (1976):547.

Slamecka, V. "A Selective Bibliography on Library Operations Research." *Library Quarterly* 42 (1972):152.

Solberg, J. J. "Principles of System Modeling." In *Proceedings of the International Symposium on Systems Engineering and Analysis,* vol. 1. Lafayette, IN: Purdue University, 1972.

Trueswell, R. W. "Article Use and Its Relation to Individual User Satisfaction." *College and Research Libraries* 31 (1970):239.

_____. "User Circulation Satisfaction vs. Size of Holdings at Three Academic Libraries." *College and Research Libraries* 30 (1969):204.

Vickery, B. C. "Bradford's Law of Scattering." *Journal of Documentation* 4 (1948):198.

_____. "Statistics of Scientific and Technical Articles." *Journal of Documentation* 26 (1970):53.

Wagner, H. M. *Principles of Operations Research.* Englewood Cliffs, NJ: Prentice-Hall, 1969.

Webster, D. "Planning Aids for the University Library." Office of Management Studies Occasional Paper No. 1. Washington, DC: Association for Research Libraries, 1971.

_____. "Library Policies: Analysis, Formulation and Use in Academic Institutions." Office of Management Studies Occasional Paper No. 2. Washington, DC: Association for Research Libraries, 1972.

Weinberg, C. B. "The University Library: Analysis and Proposals." *Management Science* 21 (1974):130.

Wilkinson, E. A. "The Ambiguity of Bradford's Law." *Journal of Documentation* 28 (1972):122.

Wilson, P. C. *Two Kinds of Power: An Essay on Bibliographic Control.* Berkeley, CA: University of California Press, 1968.

PRACTICAL LIBRARY
STATISTICAL STUDIES

Quantification of Reference Services at the Wayland, Massachusetts Public Library

by Melissa Chait

It is well documented in the library literature that many librarians treat the whole issue of quantifying reference service as a can of worms that they would rather not open. However, as Samuel Rothstein suggests in his *Library Trends* article written in 1964, without quantification of service, reference work runs the risk of being undervalued or ignored. "A harsh fact of library life seems to be if it cannot be counted, it doesn't count."[1] Though there is no one standard method of counting reference services (one of the major problems for anyone who sets out to quantify in this area), many methods have been tried with a variety of partial success. Certainly, librarians should concern themselves with this issue and base more of their decision-making and budget requests on the kind of substantial information that such fact gathering can provide.

It is likely that the problems with which we were faced at the Wayland, Massachusetts Public Library toward the end of 1976, are not unusual ones for public libraries. (The Wayland Free Public Library is located in a suburb west of Boston, population about 13,000, book collection about 50,000 divided between one main library and one branch.) At that time we were faced with dropping circulation statistics—something which hadn't happened for some years. As was true in most libraries, the Wayland Library circulation increased during the period of economic recession and the period of do-it-yourself projects and back-to-the-land philosophy. Circulation built steadily through the sixties and early seventies, peaking in 1975 at 181,307 for the year. However, when the figures were added for 1976 we found a total of 177,775—a drop of 3,532 from the previous year. Because these were the only statistics kept by the library on a regular basis, the trustees usually studied them carefully and the town finance board also expressed interest in the figures from time to time. Of course a dramatic drop such as the one which we experienced was quickly noticed and questioned.

---

[1]Samuel Rothstein, "The Measurement and Evaluation of Reference Service," *Library Trends*, 12 (January, 1964): 456-472.

As far as the library staff felt, it seemed that things were just as busy if not busier at the desk, but we had no statistics to reflect our work other than those circulation statistics. Unfortunately, many times the people who run town government are not library users and often only understand a statistical approach. We did *feel* intuitively that the role of the library was changing—that people were using the library more as an information center rather than as a resource for loaning books, that with the improving economic situation, more people (especially women) were working, and fewer people had a lot of time to read. It was also well documented that the school age population was dropping and that this was affecting our circulation heavily.

At this time, we decided that we had to take some positive and concrete steps to develop some new statistics to better define our library services. Perhaps we would be able to prove the changing role of the library in the community, by beginning to quantify the reference/information services that the library was offering, and prove that we continued to be an important and necessary town department in this time of ruthless budget cutting. Participation in the 1976-1977 Simmons College School of Library Science Institute on Quantitative Measurement and Dynamic Library Service, directed by Dr. Ching-chih Chen provided an excellent opportunity to undertake this statistical project.

A survey of the literature revealed many methodologies which had been tried by all types of libraries in the past. Some used only simple tally sheets with check marks for each patron-staff encounter; some made detailed categories of kinds of questions asked. Others used more detailed query sheets or computer cards which allowed one sheet per encounter and thoroughly analyzed the service given in every way from time spent to age of patron to time of day and type of material used to answer the question. Other libraries, rather than keep track of all encounters on a single, daily, weekly, or monthly basis, did sampling at random times. A few libraries also were interested in how well they did in providing service and actually asked the patron on a questionnaire. These are all examples of quantifying "direct" service or service which involves both a patron and a staff member. "Indirect" service, or those times when the patron helps himself without staff assistance, are much more elusive and difficult to count. Dr. Chen is well-known for her study of the use of periodicals at M.I.T. by counting volumes left on tables after the students had left the library. This is a method used when desiring some quantification of "indirect" service. All of these methods have their merits—none is completely satisfactory—all take staff time both to implement and to analyze data.

At the Wayland Library we decided to adopt the tally sheet format with some simple changes. (See Figure 1) The sheet has a space for indicating which area of the library is being surveyed—children's room, adult desk, or branch. We also designated the time span of one week for each survey sheet. By putting out a new sheet each Monday, the Sunday or weekend staff would not have to remember to change

TALLY SHEET OF REFERENCE STATISTICS

REFERENCE STATISTICS FOR WEEK OF	CHECK APPROPRIATE BOX
TO (Mon.) (Sun.) RETURN TO MAIN LIBRARY	Children's room_____ Main desk up_____ Coch. branch_____

TELEPHONE CALLS One check each call		SINGLE MATERIAL OR DIREC-TIONAL One check each time	
SUBJECT REQUEST	OUTCOME (x-no answer)	SUBJECT REQUEST	OUTCOME (x-no answer)
1.		22.	
2.		23.	
3.		24.	
4.		25.	
5.		26.	
6.		27.	
7.		28.	
8.		29.	
9.		30.	
10.		31.	
11.		32.	
12.		33.	
13.		34.	
14.		35.	
15.		36.	
16.		37.	
17.		38.	
18.		39.	
19.		40.	
20.		41.	
21.		42.	

FIGURE 1

the sheet and the regular staff has this responsibility. The tally method was used to count telephone calls, an aspect of our service which we suspected would be an impressive total (and in fact has turned out to be). The two other areas of the sheet, single step directional and subject reference questions, were broken down by types of queries. A single step or directional question is exactly that: do you have this title or where is the card catalog, bathroom, copy machine, etc. This would be any question not taking much time to answer and having a fairly direct simple answer. The other category, subject requests, involves more effort on the part of staff members. This would be a request which requires some time to answer, perhaps some explanation of reference tools to the patron or some telephone calls to make referrals, etc. In this section staff are expected to write a brief description of the request and to indicate whether they were able to answer the question to any degree of satisfaction. An X after the question designates a significant failure to satisfy.

This form was deliberately designed to be very simple in order to encourage the staff to comply with it. Often the circulation staff is also the reference staff and when things get busy, any extra task or pressure is not appreciated. (As time has gone on, one of the major problems with the form is that staff do get so busy that they forget to keep count. We know at this point that our gross figures, however impressive, are probably not accurate and fall far below what is actually happening.) Before the sheet was put into operation in January 1977, all staff discussed and approved of the form, and before any changes would be made in the current form, the staff would again be consulted for suggestions.

After a full year of collecting some gross statistics and doing some simple analysis, the overall results have been very illuminating and encouraging for the entire staff. (In fact the circulation supervisor has begun collecting some other statistics, such as how many reserve book requests we handle!) We have learned a lot of information about things which we did not anticipate and most of the information has contributed a great deal to better decision-making in the library. We have also succeeded in impressing the Board of Trustees and the Town Finance Committee with the sheer quantity of reference services that we provide each month.

Eventually I hope that we will be able to do more sophisticated analysis than we are doing at the present time, but I think a brief description of some of the things we have done so far is important to the discussion. First, we have numerical evidence that the main adult desk is the busiest area of the library in terms of reference service requests. This certainly has implications in terms of budget dispersal; for example, the director approved a request to earmark and set aside one quarter of the total book budget at the beginning of each fiscal year for reference purchases only. (In the past, reference was purchased on a "here again there again" basis.) Second, we are able to

REFERENCE STATISTICS—
JAN. 1, 1977 THROUGH DEC. 31, 1977

	Telephone	Single Step	Subject
Jan.	986	901	485
Feb.	719	550	386
Mar.	869	553	428
April	522	355	283
May	526	421	293
June	614	395	240
July	441	227	112
Aug.	417	210	154
Sept.	420	256	236
Oct.	480	327	341
Nov.	496	320	254
Dec.	650	355	301
TOTALS	7140	4870	3513

FIGURE 2

answer a *lot* of our patron's questions to some degree of satisfaction. We really have relatively few X's on each sheet—the average is about 15 percent unsatisfied patrons to 85 percent who have obtained some type of satisfaction. It must be kept in mind, however, that each staff member makes a subjective decision about his/her success and the patron is not given any input into the calculation of the satisfaction percentage.

The third and perhaps most important thing that we have been able to do as a result of the reference tabulations is a *qualitative analysis* of our book collection and acquisition and weeding policies. We have been able to fill in our collection nicely by listing X questions and keeping them handy as we make purchase decisions. For example, we discovered that the branch library needed more books on cancer and the adult room didn't have any books on stage lighting and theater craft. (The sheets make fascinating reading—almost a kind of daily log of what kinds of information people are looking for.) We have also been able to identify problems in the card catalog subject headings— sometimes an X question was answerable once the cataloger had added the proper headings or cross-references that had been missing before. In another case, the staff member might have an X question that he or she just didn't know HOW to answer; for example, when a patron wanted a play criticism from 1955, the staff member didn't know that the proper heading in Reader's Guide was Drama-Criticism. Many of these X questions turned out to be learning experiences for everyone and staff development was greatly stimulated from discussing the contents of the sheets at regular in-house workshops. (This is still continuing though not as frequently as before.)

Clearly there is a great deal more to be done with this type of quantification. Hopefully we will become more sophisticated both in our methods of tabulation and analysis. If we can develop these statistics historically, we may be able to perceive patterns of activity from year to year as we have been able to do in the past with circulation statistics. In conclusion, this project has been worthwhile and will continue in the future as a valuable indication of library activities and patrons' needs.

BIBLIOGRAPHY

Altman, Ellen; DeProspo, Ernest; Clark, Philip; and Clark, Ellen. *A Data Gathering and Instructional Manual for Performance Measures in Public Libraries.* Chicago, IL: Cleadon, 1976.

Cameron, Dee Birch. "Public and Academic Library Reference Questions." *RQ* 16 (Winter, 1976):130-132.

Ciucki, Marcella. "Recording of Reference/Information Service Activities: A Study of Forms Currently Used." *RQ* 16 (Summer, 1977):273-283.

Emerson, Katherine. "A Report." *Symposium on Measure of Reference. RQ* 14 (Fall, 1974):7-9.

Hawley, Mary. "Reference Statistics." *RQ* 10 (Winter, 1970):143-147.

Howell, Benita; Reeves, Edward; and Van Willigen, John. "Fleeting Encounters—A Role Analysis of Reference Patron Interaction." *RQ* 16 (Winter, 1976):124-129.

Lancaster, F. W. *The Measurement and Evaluation of Library Services.* Washington, DC: Information Resources Press, 1977.

Pings, Vern. "Reference Services Accountability and Measurement." *RQ* 16 (Winter, 1976):120-123.

Quinn, Karen. "This Works for Us: Capturing Elusive Statistics." *Special Libraries* 63 (September, 1972):404-406.

Rothstein, Samuel. "The Measurement and Evaluation of Reference Service." *Library Trends* 12 (January, 1964):456-472.

Runyon, Robert. "The Library Administrator's Need for Measures of Reference." *Symposium on Measurement of Reference. RQ* 14 (Fall, 1974):9-11.

Spicer, Caroline. "Measuring Reference Service: A Look at the Cornell University Libraries Reference Question Recording System." *Bookmark* 24 (Jan./Feb., 1972):79-81.

Weech, Terry L. "Evaluation of Adult Reference Service." *Library Trends* 22 (January, 1974):315-335.

Quantitative Measurement for Space Utilization in a Medium-Sized Public Library

by Leila-Jane Roberts

INTRODUCTION

It became necessary to study how space in the Winchester Public Library was being utilized in order to plan for change and renovations as part of a town-wide five-year Capital Outlay Plan. It was clear that there would be no possibility of money for adding space because the town had just finished paying for an addition finished in 1966 and bonded over a ten-year period. Since the many town departments were competing for funds, much back-up information was needed to justify our request.

It was felt that better use could be made of a room on the second floor, which was deteriorating, and an area on the main floor which did not have as much use as its central location warranted. Statistical evidence was needed which would serve as proof of the need for the library's request for funding.

PROBLEM

The Winchester Public Library was built in 1931. It was designed in the shape of an inverted T, divided into four areas of approximately the same dimensions. Because of the contour of the land, there were three levels and a balcony extending as indicated by the shaded area in Figure 1.

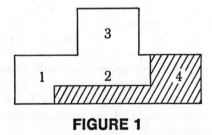

FIGURE 1

level 1		Meeting Room		Passageways
level 2	1	Main Reference	2	Circulation in
level 3		(2 floors high)		Lobby (2 floors)

level 1		Children's Room		3 levels of stacks
level 2	3	Art Gallery with movie	.....4.....	.... Offices
level 3		capability		Downs Room

FIGURE 2

In 1964, after four unsuccessful attempts over twenty years, voters approved an addition. Political means were used to insure that the issue would be put to vote in the year between voting on two separate school building projects. The architects knew that waiting for the removal of a small Victorian house on one side of the building could well lose the battle, so they pragmatically decided to square off one side of the building. This added 8,000 square feet on two levels and a balcony to the existing 12,000 feet.

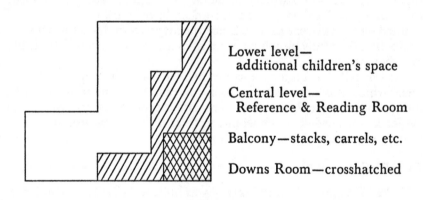

Lower level—
  additional children's space

Central level—
  Reference & Reading Room

Balcony—stacks, carrels, etc.

Downs Room—crosshatched

FIGURE 3

In November 1976, ten years after the original plans were made, shelves were crowded, vandalism problems had arisen, modern safeguards needed to be incorporated, and two additional offices were needed. It was clear that there was no possibility of getting more space, so the use of current space needed to be analyzed. The librarian was asked to submit a long-range plan with alternatives for use of areas. From this the trustees hoped to arrive at a five-year plan for improvements which could be projected by the Town Capital Improvements Planning Committee and incorporated into their long-range plans and budget requests.

METHODOLOGY

To determine what use was being made of auxiliary space, principles of quantitative measurement were applied. Those measures of use which were being counted as part of daily procedures were analyzed. Electric eye counters at the front and back doors were recorded daily, and charts were kept to show the number of people entering and leaving the building by day, by week and by month. A notebook at the adult circulation desk recorded the names of those signing to use the key for access to the Downs Room. Each entry was supposed to include the following information:

Date	Name	Time In	Time Out

There was the circulation count to show the numbers of materials leaving the library. In 1975, the count was broken down into Dewey decimal categories. This meant that usage in 1975 could be compared and contrasted with usage in 1970, the last time nonfiction circulation had been broken down by categories. The other figures did help in reaching other decisions regarding the five-year plan, but because this paper is limited to use of the Downs Room, only the quantitative measurement provided by the notebook will be charted and analyzed.

AREA STUDIED

The Downs Room is that area immediately above the Director's Office which houses the library's collection of books on art and music (700-789 in the Dewey decimal classification).

Originally this area had been a music room. In the 1950's, a hi-fi was built into the special shelving which was custom designed for this room. Books on those shelves related to art and music, including some biographies. Beautiful lounge furniture, including sofas, chairs, leather-covered tables and modern lamps, was purchased with special trust funds. Recorded concerts were presented weekly, complete with program notes.

But times had changed. As part of the renovation that accompanied the building of the addition, the recordings were moved downstairs to the Reference Room to be more accessible to patrons. A listening table strategically placed near the circulation desk allowed for listening with earphones. When the hi-fi equipment broke, it was not replaced because stereo equipment had become a part of most homes.

Because the area was impossible to monitor from the main floor, the furniture was abused with ball point pens, razors and knives. The Downs Room became a favorite spot for forbidden cigarette smoking and burn holes began to appear in the wall to wall carpeting. More bookcases were moved in to replace the vandalized furniture and to allow for shelving more materials in the 700 category, including periodicals which covered the subject categories kept in this room: antiques, photography, interior decoration, and music. At the time it was decided the room had to be locked, a notebook was prepared in which patrons could sign for the key. There were attempts to control who signed, but in moments of stress, it was not possible to check whether a crowd collected with only one person having signed for the key. Clearly some change had to be made involving this area. The notebook would provide one way to measure the use of the room over a period of time.

Since the notebook appeared to be a device which was of interest for only a short period of time, pages were thrown away when it became too crowded; however, the information was still extant for February 1976 and February 1977 so a close study and comparison was made of those two months (Tables IV and V). A count, by month, was made of signatures for the months in between, omitting such illustrious *nom-de-plumes* as Richard Nixon, Ronald Ray Gun, and Jimmy Carter.

ANALYSIS OF DATA

From February 1976 through February 1977, 2,859 people signed to use the room. In this same period, the library had been open 335 days (some were early closings). This use averaged 8.53 people per day which was not heavy traffic for the area. (See Table I.)

The heaviest use was in March 1976 (295) and lightest in July (161). The library was open the most days in March (31) and the

TABLE I
USE OF ROOM BY MONTH

	Key Signed For	Days Open
February 1976	270	27
March	295	31
April	213	25
May	222	25
June	181	24
July	161	21
August	163	22
September	196	24
October	236	25
November	241	29
December	166	28
January 1977	224	28
February	291	26
Total	2,859	335

fewest in July (21). This correlation indicated it was reasonable to average the figures on use. The months when use and number of days opened were approximately the same (see Tables II and III) were March, February 1977, April and May, June and September, and July and August.

The fact that there is less use of all kinds in the summer months is borne out by other library statistics: fewer open hours, electric eye count, circulation figures. Also this area is not air-conditioned so few people would choose to spend time there in hot weather. The use of this area, therefore, followed the same basic patterns as the rest of the library.

For the two months that were analyzed carefully (February 1976 and 1977), the use of the room by periods of time was studied (see Tables IV, V, and VI). Most library users stayed less than 30 minutes each time. However, approximately one-fifth of the users stayed more than 30 minutes.

TABLE II		TABLE III	
NUMBERS OF USE IN RANK ORDER		DAYS OPEN IN RANK ORDER	
March 1976	295	March 1976	31
February 1976	275	November	29
November	241	December	28
October	236	January 1977	28
February 1977	234	February 1976	27
January 1977	224	February 1977	26
May	222	April	25
April	213	May	25
September	196	October	25
June	181	June	24
December	166	September	24
August	163	August	22
July	161	July	21

RECOMMENDATIONS AND RESULTS

One of the possible alternative uses for this area was to make it the quiet study area. At present, the quiet study area is located in the space designated as "1" in the introductory diagram. Since space on the main floor is prime space, it might be more helpful to library users to have books shelved here and move the study carrels to the upper floor. Use patterns as analyzed by quantitative measurement would

TABLE IV
USE AVERAGED BY TIME SLOTS—FEBRUARY 1976

Average Time in Room (minutes)

Date	Total No. of People Signed	9:30-2	2-5:30	5:30-9
2/4	1	45		
2/5	10	22	31	19
2/6	10	25	40	
2/7	15	11	17	
2/8	7		45	
2/9	9	14	25	
2/10	14	30	35	28
2/11	8	18	15	22
2/12	9	23	42	23
2/13	7	8	21	
2/14	8	60	20	
2/15	7		30	
2/16	0			
2/17	24	13	13	12
2/18	14	12	23	45
2/19	13	16	12	
2/20	5		46	100
2/21	17	33	38	
2/22	4		78	
2/23	15	34	26	32
2/24	18	7	29	34
2/25	17	12	25	28
2/26	13	32	12	16
2/27	11	20	33	
2/28	14	68	30	34

support that use of the Downs Room. The traffic in and out of the room would not be overly distracting. It would be possible to keep most of the same materials in the area.

Rearrangement would have to be extensive to have space in the Downs Room for the eight carrels that are now in the quiet room; but removal of all the lounge furniture and the periodicals now shelved there would eliminate the destruction of furnishings and make the necessary room for study furniture. The problem of supervision of the area would be solved during the times that serious students were there. Placement of an office on the balcony would be one alternative to help solve supervision during hours of low use and our statistical survey shows there are many periods of time when the materials in this room are not being used.

Since the study discussed in this paper was completed, the five-year plan has gone through several stages. The first presentation to the library trustees outlined all the renovations, repairs and innovations

TABLE V
USE AVERAGED BY TIME SLOTS—FEBRUARY 1977

Average Time in Room (minutes)

Date	Total No. of People Signed	9:30-2	2-5:30	5:30-9
2/1	10		5	32
2/2	10	30	25	16
2/3	14	5	26	18
2/4	6	15	6	
2/5	11	14	31	
2/6	9		30	
2/7	9	33	10	5
2/8	14	100	15	12
2/9	13		39	30
2/10	4	102		85
2/11	10		14	
2/12	9	12	7	
2/13	5	40	46	
2/14	5		22	25
2/15	17	18	24	7
2/16	15	12	12	36
2/17	7	130	31	32
2/18	5	23	18	
2/19	20	22	8	
2/20	7	30	51	
2/22	11		13	12
2/23	13	61	31	17
2/24	9	20	45	30
2/25	14	22		
2/26	13	22	53	
2/27	4	16	210	
2/28	20	11	40	
2/29	6	5	72	

TABLE VI
AVERAGE LENGTH OF VISITS TO DOWNS ROOM
(data taken from Tables IV and V)

	Total Times Used	Length Unknown	Over An Hour	30-59 Min.	Under 30 Min.
February 1976	270	54	21	35	160
February 1977	291	80	23	38	150

that were needed to bring up-to-date a building approaching its fiftieth birthday. These improvements were divided into capital improvements (to be included in the town five-year plan) and repairs (to be part of yearly budgets). Then costs were estimated and a five-year division was made that would be roughly even in cost.

The plan was presented next at a meeting of the Capital Improvements Planning Committee, the Town Manager, and the Library Subcommittee of the Finance Committee. The conclusions reached by our analysis of the quantitative measurement statistics backed up by the statistical evidence itself, were presented. There was a satisfactory inclusion of our request for the relocation of the Downs Room in the Town Manager's Capital Improvements section of the annual budget which went before the Town Meeting in May of 1978.

Journal Use-Study in a VA Hospital

by Julia L. Long

Providing adequate shelf space for library collections poses a problem for all librarians. The use of microfilm for backfiles or current subscriptions of journal holdings is an increasingly appealing solution. Microfilm requires approximately 1/10 the linear shelf space of bound volumes. Recent improvements in reader-printer technology have made the production of superior quality, dry-process hard copy easy and satisfactory to most users. In addition, many core biomedical journals are now available on film from commercial producers in 35mm or 16mm format, and in reels or cartridges.

Two medical librarians (Meiboom, 1976; Daghita, 1976) have already documented the conversion of their backfile journal collections to microfilm. Meiboom decided to convert all 10-year back files in an entire collection (160 subscriptions) that were commercially available in a suitable format. Current year, hard copy subscriptions were continued. Daghita used the *Abridged Index Medicus* list for her selection of titles to convert to film. Eighty-three of the one hundred *AIM* titles were commercially available in the format she chose (16mm).

This study focuses on the collection of a medical library in a large (800 bed) general hospital affiliated with two medical schools. When this project was begun, the library had 3500 monographs and 4000 bound volumes. Subscriptions to 175 journal titles included 60 titles with backfiles ranging from 10 to 20 years. A decision had already been made (by a former librarian and the library committee) to convert some of the bound journal collection to film. A reader-printer and work-station had been acquired and funding was available for the purchase of film. The former librarian had recommended titles for conversion to film based upon space (the linear feet of shelf space occupied by a title). Since the purpose of converting to film was to conserve space, the journals occupying the greatest lengths of linear shelf space would be converted to film. Shorter items would remain in hard copy until lack of use dictated their disposal.

Before these recommendations could be acted upon, the librarian assumed another position. The present librarian felt that journal use would be a better indicator of which journals to replace with film. The linear space data could possibly later be compared to the use study to determine if there were any correlations between the two sets of data.

The goal of this study, then, was to determine which backfiles of the bound journal collection (60 titles with backfiles ranging from 10-20 years) should be replaced with microfilm. One limitation was immediately established. Eight backfiles were eliminated because they were judged unsuitable for microfilm. The large number of halftones in these backfiles do not reproduce well on film at this time. The unsuitability of pathology, radiology, and several other individual titles was ascertained from Meiboom's article, from conversation with other medical librarians who have some experience with microfilm, and with assistance from microfilm sales personnel. This limitation left a subset of 52 titles to consider. Since we were planning a gradual conversion rather than converting an entire (or even a large portion of a) collection, a second subset of 27 titles was established. These 27 titles had backfiles at least 15 years old and covered the years 1956-1960, our earliest holdings. A five-year block was decided upon for two reasons. First, the linear measurements of the former librarian had been made in five-year blocks. Second, in Fussler and Simon's study of patterns of use (1961), they examined total use data in a serial for a five-year period. Using five-year blocks would allow us to apply some of the rules they derived from their study.

Each volume (230 in all) of these 27 titles was examined to obtain circulation statistics. In this library, all journals, even the latest issues, circulate. The annual circulation figures are high—20,000 circulations for a collection of 7,000 volumes. Special subsidized photocopy privileges are available in most hospital departments while the library has only a 10¢ coin-operated machine. Hence, users are accustomed to checking out journals even for brief periods of time to make copies. In view of this practice, we felt circulation figures were an adequate indication of use without considering in-house or interlibrary loan demands. Other studies have also indicated that recorded use is a good indication of in-house use or that circulation statistics are sufficient to make predictions about the entire collection (Fussler and Simon, 1961; Kilgour, 1962, 1964).

Since our concern was the recent use of old volumes, circulation for the last five years was recorded for each volume of each title from 1956-1970. In other words, we counted the number of times the 1956 volumes of *American Journal of Medicine* circulated in 1971, 1972, 1973, and so on (see Sample Worksheet, Figure 1). In gathering data, one problem arose. Since bookcards are not retained when used up, it would be possible for the transactions on discarded bookcards to be lost to anyone studying the circulation. However, each bookcard transaction was checked against the data recorded on the date due slips (which have space for more than twice the number of transactions that the bookcards have). Using this method, a full circulation history was usually obtainable.

(Upper number of pair—year of volume; lower number of pair—year of circulation 56/71 means the circulation of 1956 volumes in 1971)

American Journal of Medicine (2 vol/yr) 19"

Totals	56/71	56/72	56/73	56/74	56/75	56/76
10	//	//	//	///	/	
	57/71	57/72	57/73	57/74	57/75	57/76
11	///	/		//	/	//
	58/71	58/72	58/73	58/74	58/75	58/76
10	///	/	/	/	//	//
	59/71	59/72	59/73	59/74	59/75	59/76
14		/	//	//	/	卌 III
	60/71	60/72	60/73	60/74	60/75	60/76
8			/	/	////	//
53						

(4 vol/yrs 1956-58
American Journal of Physiology 2 vol/yr 1959-60) 29½"

Totals	56/71	56/72	56/73	56/74	56/75	56/76
	57/71	57/72	57/73	57/74	57/75	57/76
3	/		//			
	58/71	58/72	58/73	58/74	58/75	58/76
6		/		//		///
	59/71	59/72	59/73	59/74	59/75	59/76
9	/	//	/	/	//	/
	60/71	60/72	60/73	60/74	60/75	60/76
5	//	/	/			
24						

FIGURE 1

All titles reviewed for this study are listed alphabetically in Appendix A (Figure 2). Column one lists the number of volumes per year; column two, the total volumes for 1956-1960; column three, the circulation for these volumes from 1971 to 1976; column four, the average circulation per volume; and column five, the linear shelf space (in inches) that each title occupies. This subset represents 230 volumes, 600 circulations, and 506 inches (or 42.2 feet) of shelf space, more than one double range of shelves.

The titles having the largest circulation (over 23 times) are ranked in Table I (with the last three titles having the same circulation). Seven titles are in common with Table II, the largest journals ranked by size (number of inches). These titles are *British Medical Journal, American Journal of Physiology, Annals of Internal Medicine, New England Journal of Medicine, Lancet, Journal of Urology,* and *Journal of Clinical Investigation.* All titles in Table III (average circulation per volume), with the exception of the *Journal of Neurology, Neurosurgery, and Psychiatry,* appear on Table I, though in different order.

The recommendation for the initial purchase of microfilm would be the twelve titles listed in Table I. High use is felt to be the best criterion for our situation because the collection is an active, circulating one with no intent to provide archival material. The demand (as in

TABLE I

10 LARGEST JOURNALS—RANKED BY USE

Title	Circulation (1956-1960)
1. American Journal of Medicine	53
2. New England Journal of Medicine	45
3. Lancet	42
4. Journal of Clinical Investigation	35
5. Medicine	34
6. Archives of Internal Medicine	33
7. Journal of Urology	30
8. Brain	29
9. Annals of Internal Medicine	25
10. American Journal of Physiology	24*
11. (British Medical Journal)	24*
12. (Neurology)	24*
Total (1-10)	350
Total (1-12)	398

* Three titles showed the same circulation for this period

TABLE II

10 LARGEST JOURNALS—RANKED BY SIZE

Title	Linear Inches (1956-1960)
1. Journal of Biological Chemistry	56
2. British Medical Journal	32
3. Journal of Experimental Medicine	30
4. American Journal of Physiology	29.5
5. Annals of Internal Medicine	28.5
6. New England Journal of Medicine	27
7. Lancet	24
8. Journal of Urology	22
9. Gastroenterology	21
10. Journal of Clinical Investigation	20
Total	290

most hospital libraries) is for current material. The objections usually raised with current volumes on film (that they are not as readily available to users since special equipment is required) does not seem as serious with backfiles.

Although use is high for some titles (5-6 circulations per year), the circulation for this subset of journals is less than 1 percent of the total annual circulation. Upon initial observation, the low percentage of total circulation might be reason to simply discard the entire subset. However, using Fussler and Simon's *a priori* rules (1961) regarding storage of journals, the maximum number of journals we could have stored (those showing no use singly or in pairs from 1971-1976) would have been 7 volumes, an insignificant number in terms of space savings.

The next step in our conversion will be to examine the second subset (52 titles, 1961-1966) in the same way. This data will be compared with the first subset to see if the same journals are most heavily used. It would be interesting at a later time to study current circulation to see if heavily used backfiles could have been predicted on the basis of current use.

Statistical analysis in this particular case is mostly a matter of counting. In a larger library, it would be impossible to examine every circulation record for all journals in a five-year block. More predictions would have to be made on the basis of samplings and formulas. However, many of the results in the more complicated papers listed in the reference section are applicable in this much smaller setting. We plan to continue using the techniques appropriate to our scale.

TABLE III

10 LARGEST JOURNALS—RANKED BY AVERAGE CIRCULATION PER VOLUME

Title	Circ/Vol
1. Journal of Clinical Investigation	7
2. Medicine	6.8
3. Annals of Internal Medicine	5.9
4. American Journal of Medicine	5.3
5. Neurology	4.8
6. New England Journal of Medicine	4.5
7. Lancet	4.2
8. Archives of Internal Medicine	3.3
9. Journal of Urology	3
10. Journal of Neurology, Neurosurgery, & Psychiatry	3

ACKNOWLEDGEMENT:

Special thanks to Dr. Ching-chih Chen for her support and enthusiasm.

REFERENCES

Daghita, Joan M. "A Core Collection of Journals on Microfilm in a Community Teaching Hospital Library." *Bulletin of the Medical Library Association* 64 (1976):240-241.

Fussler, Herman H., and Simon, Julian L. *Patterns in the Use of Books in Large Research Libraries.* Chicago, IL: University of Chicago Press, 1961.

Kilgour, Frederick G. "Moderately and Heavily Used Biomedical Journals." *Bulletin of the Medical Library Association* 52 (1964):234-241.

_____. "Use of Medical and Biological Journals in the Yale Medical Library." *Bulletin of the Medical Library Association* 50 (1962):429-449.

Lancaster, F. W. *The Measurement and Evaluation of Library Services.* Washington, DC: Information Resources Press, 1977.

Meiboom, Esther R. "Conversion of the Periodical Collection in a Teaching Hospital Library to Microfilm Format." *Bulletin of the Medical Library Association* 64 (1976):36-40.

APPENDIX A

Titles Considered for Study	Vol/Yr	Total Vol 1956-60	Circ. 1971-76	Circ/ Vol	Linear 1956-60
American Journal of Medicine	2	10	53	5.3	19
American Journal of Physiology	4:1956-58 2:1959-60	16	24	1.5	29.5
Annals of Internal Medicine	2	10	25	2.5	28.5
Archives of Internal Medicine	2	10	33	3.3	21
Blood	1:1956-59 2:1960	6	11	1.2	16
Brain	1	5	29	5.8	10
British Medical Journal	2	10	24	2.4	32
Clinical Science	1:1956-59 2:1960	6	4	.66	11.5
Gastroenterology	2	10	12	1.2	21
International Journal of Psychoanalysis	1	5	11	1.83	8
Journal/American Psychoanalytic Association	1	5	6	1.2	15
Journal of Applied Physiology	2:1956-58 1:1959-60	8	19	2.37	10
Journal of Biological Chemistry	6:1956-57 4:1958 2:1959-60	24	21	.87	56
Journal of Clinical Endocrinology & Metabolism	1	5	9	1.8	15.5
Journal of Clinical Investigation	1	5	35	7	20
Journal of Experimental Medicine	2	10	5	.5	30
Journal of Laboratory & Clinical Medicine	2	10	17	1.7	21
Journal of Nervous & Mental Disease	2	10	16	1.6	13
Journal of Neurology, Neurosurgery, & Psychiatry	1	5	14	2.8	5.5
Journal of Neurosurgery	1	5	15	3	9.5

APPENDIX A (cont.)

Titles Considered for Study	Vol/Yr	Total Vol 1956-60	Circ. 1971-76	Circ/ Vol	Linear 1956-60
Journal of Urology	2	10	30	3	22
Lancet	2	10	42	4.2	25
Medicine	1	5	34	6.8	8.5
Neurology	1	5	24	4.8	11
New England Journal of Medicine	2	10	45	4.5	27
Physiological Review	1	5	9	1.8	10
Quarterly Journal of Medicine	1	5	11	2.2	11

A Survey of Library User Demands in an Industrial Corporate Library

by Karen Feingold
and Jane Ward

INTRODUCTION

Digital Equipment Corporation (DEC) designs, manufactures, sells and services computer systems and components. Over the past 20 years, the company has grown from modest beginnings in an old mill town in Massachusetts into a widely recognized leader in the area of minicomputer technology. Today the company employs over 30,000 people in the U.S., Canada, Europe, Australia and the Far East.

Originally, as a small company, DEC relied primarily on the libraries of the surrounding universities to provide for its immediate needs. The original DEC library was established about 10 years ago to support technical research. It remained a rather static, loosely defined organization until early 1974. The number of persons to be served and the type of service they needed could no longer be done by nonprofessional librarians. So DEC's Corporate Library was chartered in 1974 to serve the Digital community by providing information in these typical areas: basic library services and information purchasing services. During this time period, 1974 to the present, the staff of the library has grown from two to an operation employing 13 persons in two locations.

PROBLEM DESCRIPTION

The Corporate Library main branch is located at company headquarters in the Mill Complex in Maynard, Massachusetts, with a branch operation in DEC's Marlboro, Massachusetts facility. Recently Digital's phenomenal expansion has been taking place primarily outside of Massachusetts, with development groups moving to New

Hampshire in the very near future. While manufacturing plants have gone up in locations all over the world, it has only been recently that the core development groups have outgrown space in central headquarters and have had to make plans to expand to other locations. In order to continue to meet the needs of these groups, library planners felt that data were needed to answer the following questions clearly:

1) What current services are most requested?
2) What job categories make the requests?
3) Where are the requesters physically located within the corporation?

We hypothesized that: basic library services would be most heavily used in locations where library facilities exist; users in locations without library facilities would make demands on the specialized services offered by the library; and that the heaviest users would be hardware and software developers. While these hypotheses seem obvious, we had no hard numbers from which to make planning projections.

METHODOLOGY

This study was not intended to be a finely tuned statistical study. Its intention was to get a picture for planning purposes of what library services were being provided to whom and at what location. An analysis procedure was decided upon which would illuminate the descriptive information: namely, simple frequency distributions and cross-tabulations. With the results of the analysis, we felt we would be in a better position to make recommendations on which particular library services would be most useful to replicate in the various Digital locations being planned and settled. Therefore, we did not weight the findings in any proportion to the size of the group user population, test for significance, etc. Another straightforward reason why this was not done was that the relative proportion of group to group size in the overall corporation remains in a somewhat constant proportion. Thus, if Development grows 30-45 percent, so, too, will other groups, such as Field Service. So the conclusions we would draw from our data analysis would not suffer from the lack of these statistical refinements. The data analysis was used, then, to provide a basis for a planned expansion of library services to locations remote from central headquarters to maximize useful services on a limited expansion budget.

For the purposes of data analysis, library services were divided into three broad categories:

1) any time crucial requests where responses were needed within 24 hours, e.g., a specific request for information from field service out on a service call;
2) non-critical with respect to time requests for basic library services such as: reference, cataloging, on-line information

retrieval, selective dissemination of information services, reserves, circulation, photocopy, inter-library loan, journal routing, standards, use of microforms, reports, etc;

3) non-critical with respect to time requests for specialized information services provided by the library as a service to the corporation such as: purchase of informational materials and societal memberships for employees world-wide, distribution of engineering notebooks and templates, internal information locator projects, internal library publications, audio/visual training materials and course scheduling, educational catalogs and training information, etc.

These categories were chosen because they represent a reasonable picture of what staff does in the library. Also, since delivering library service is a labor intensive operation, any recommendation for expansion translates into job requisitions with job descriptions. So these categories would ultimately allow library expansion planners to pull various functional jobs within these categories and come up with job descriptions which would be most meaningful both to the service receivers and to budget planners. These categories are summarized in Table I.

TABLE I
DEFINITION OF DATA CATEGORIES USED IN STUDY

	TIME CRITICAL	NOT TIME CRITICAL
BASIC LIBRARY SERVICES	CATEGORY 1	CATEGORY 2
CORPORATE SUPPORT SERVICES	CATEGORY 1	CATEGORY 3

The next dimension of interest was location. The highest concentration of Digital employees is in Maynard with the next highest in Marlboro. As was stated in the "hypothesis" section, we wished to understand in what way and how much location was a factor in the use of all three categories of library service. The analysis of the data produced few surprises in this regard. Table II shows how we labelled the Digital locations for the purposes of analysis.

TABLE II
LOCATION CATEGORIES

Region I   - Maynard, Massachusetts Mill
Region II   - Maynard, Massachusetts Parker St. Complex
Region III   - Other Massachusetts locations: including Marlboro Manufacturing plants and field office and excluding Locations I and II
Region IV   - Other domestic locations: including manufacturing plants and field office (all USA but excluding Locations I, II and III)
Region V   - International locations: including manufacturing plants and field office

User groups were labelled exactly as the corporation labels them. In total there are 14 user groups. While this produced a certain amount of cumbersomeness, it surely increased the accuracy of reporting, for this is how persons in the corporation see themselves. It is also how the corporation would group them in the process of expanding and decentralizing. So this made sense to us. In Table III are the groups whose use of the library was recorded during data gathering periods.*

TABLE III
GROUPS WHICH USED THE LIBRARY

HD   = Hardware Engineering
SD   = Software Engineering
MFG = Manufacturing
MKT = Marketing
SA   = Sales
FS   = Field Service
FI   = Finance
CIS = Corporate Information Systems
ES   = Educational Services
PSL = Personnel
PRC = Purchasing
LE   = Legal
CSS = Computer Special Systems
AS   = Administrative Services (Plant Management, Maintenance, Security, etc.)

---

* There are a few other groups not mentioned here because they either did not use the library, or the group itself was of such a small size that it would not be meaningful to consider it in expansion plans.

DATA COLLECTION

The data collection took place over a 12 week period. For one hour each day for sixty running working days, data were collected. The hour of the day in which data were collected was randomly selected to wash out special effects that time of day and day of the week might have on the data. As it turned out, each hour received a fair representation in the study.

The form in Figure 1 was used to record the data.

DATA COLLECTION FORM

Systems Study

Request Category _____

Group _____ Location _____

Notes: _____

_____

Date: _____

FIGURE 1

TRAINING

All library personnel were trained in data collection procedures. At periodic intervals during the 12 week period in which data were being collected, reminders were distributed. All staff were requested to complete a "system study request form" for each phone call or in-house request during the posted sample period.

DATA ANALYSIS

The 60-hour study yielded a total of 254 forms filled out. This averages to 4.2 requests per hour. (Keep in mind that the study did not measure users' visits to the library which did not result in requests. There are many tasks that are performed by library personnel, such as maintenance of the collection, that are not measured directly by user request behavior. In fact, many persons wander into the library, read the magazines and periodicals and never make requests.) The data were reduced and analyzed in the following way:

1) region by category of service where user groups are collapsed;
2) user group by category of service where region is collapsed;
3) category of service, by region, by user group.

RESULTS

Table IV indicates heavy library usage in regions 1, 2 and 3—locations close to headquarters in the Mill and our branch library in Marlboro (region 3). Sixty-five percent of all region 3 requests were handled by the Marlboro library. The high number of total requests originating in region 3 is attributed to region 3 persons having access to both the Mill and Marlboro libraries.

TABLE IV
REGION BY CATEGORY OF SERVICE
(User Groups Collapsed)

LOCATION	CATEGORY OF SERVICE			TOTAL BY LOCATION
	I	II	III	
1	19	36	18	73
2	22	18	35	75
3	11	55	21	87
4	3	1	12	16
5	1	0	2	3
TOTAL BY CATEGORY	56	110	88	254 TOTAL RESPONSES

TABLE V
USER GROUP BY CATEGORY OF SERVICE
(Region Collapsed)

GROUP	CATEGORY OF SERVICE			TOTAL BY GROUP
	I	II	III	
Hardware Engineering	7	28	10	45
Software Engineering	10	37	14	61
Manufacturing	10	12	7	29
Marketing	4	11	4	19
Sales	3	3	4	10
Field Service	4	4	13	21
Finance	4	3	7	14
Corporate Info. Systems	1	0	5	6
Educational Services	3	3	9	15
Personnel	3	5	6	14
Purchasing	0	0	1	1
Legal	1	1	3	5
Computer Special Systems	4	1	2	7
Administrative Services	2	2	3	7
TOTAL BY CATEGORY	56	110	88	254

REGION BY CATEGORY OF SERVICE

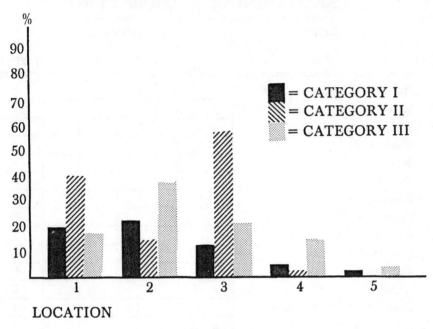

LOCATION

FIGURE 2

Region 3 is serviced by a branch of the Corporate Library located in Marlboro; 65 percent of region 3 responses are contributed by the Marlboro library. Interestingly, there were no category 1 responses for the Marlboro library.

The graph of Table I indicates that regions 4 and 5 use very little of our services. We know of user groups existing in regions 4 and 5 similar to high user groups in regions 1, 2 and 3. This raises the question of user needs not being met in these regions, and a follow-up survey by user type in region 4 is being planned.

CONCLUSIONS AND RECOMMENDATIONS

The conclusions we drew from the data analysis are not surprising. Those persons close to the physical location of the library use all categories of library service more. Those in similar positions but physically removed from the library do not use it in anywhere near the same proportions. We intend to do a follow-up study to ascertain the way in which remote location needs are being met. If local libraries, for example, are filling the gap effectively, an attempt will be made to formalize these relationships, through supporting specialized collections and such.

TABLE VI A
CATEGORY I SERVICE BY GROUP BY REGION

GROUP	REGION					
	1	2	3	4	5	TOTAL
Hardware Engineering	4		3			7
Software Engineering	7	2	1			10
Manufacturing	4		6			10
Marketing	1	3				4
Sales		3				3
Field Service		3			1	4
Finance		4				4
Corporate Info. Systems		1				1
Educational Services		3				3
Personnel		3				3
Purchasing						0
Legal	1					1
Computer Special Systems			1	3		4
Administrative Services	2					2
TOTAL						56

With regard to the needs of those employees outside the United States, region 5 of our study, we have no plan of action other than to send copies of the results of this study to those in positions of influence. The hope would be that these persons would begin to make efforts on behalf of their employees to determine the degree and kind of unmet information needs. However, we believe that any planned delivery of library services should be done in the cultural style of the country in which the DEC facility is located and not planned in corporate head-quarters.

We were surprised by the strong showing of region 2, the Parker Street Complex in Maynard, a few miles removed from the library. Even though the data were collected during one of the coldest winters in decades, the persons at Parker Street came to the library and used it often. Any distance that can't be bridged during a lunch hour, though, causes the use of the library by the removed group to sink dramatically. The manufacturing group in Woburn and Acton (both neighboring towns to Maynard) did not use the library much. We are recommending a bookmobile to cover those locations within striking distance of the Corporate Library.

TABLE VI B
CATEGORY II SERVICE BY GROUP BY REGION

GROUP	REGION					
	1	2	3	4	5	TOTAL
Hardware Engineering	6		22			28
Software Engineering	17	1	19			37
Manufacturing	6		6			12
Marketing		5	6			11
Sales		2		1		3
Field Service		2	2			4
Finance	1	2				3
Corporate Info. Systems						0
Educational Services	2	1				3
Personnel	2	3				5
Purchasing						0
Legal	1					1
Computer Special Systems		1				1
Administrative Services	1	1				2
TOTAL						110

This study has had a few interesting by-products. In the corporation, the study highlighted the role played by the library in meeting the various needs of the company on a very limited budget. We feel more assured that in our planning for the future, it is possible, without being sophisticated researchers, to predict what the needs will be and how to plan best to meet those needs. The corporation, we believe, also feels this.

EPILOGUE

The reader might be interested in what has become of the recommendations made herein to the corporation. This study was done prior to the budget submissions, and in anticipation of them. Most of the actions recommended have been accepted. Starting in January, we will have a bookmobile which will travel to the various sites within a 50-mile radius of Maynard on a weekly or semi-weekly basis. This represents a commitment of resources equal to the amount requested. A general plan has been accepted for expansion of library services to all locations. Detailed plans are being formulated and we feel some level of assurance that the corporation will support these efforts.

TABLE VI C
CATEGORY III SERVICE BY GROUP BY REGION

GROUP   REGION

GROUP	1	2	3	4	5	TOTAL
Hardware Engineering	6		4			10
Software Engineering	5		9			14
Manufacturing	1		5	1		7
Marketing	1	2		1		4
Sales		4				4
Field Service	1	1		9	2	13
Finance		7				7
Corporate Info. Systems		5				5
Educational Services		6	3			9
Personnel	1	5				6
Purchasing		1				1
Legal		3				3
Computer Special Systems		1		1		2
Administrative Services	3					3
TOTAL						88

The Nonresident Borrowers of The Jones Library: A Statistical Study for The Amherst, Massachusetts Public Library

by Anne M. Turner

BACKGROUND

During 1977, The Jones Library at Amherst (and all other public libraries in Massachusetts) conducted seven week-long surveys to determine the number of nonresident borrowers using local library materials. This information was requested by the Massachusetts Board of Library Commissioners, and used to allocate special LSCA Title I funds in the form of one-time grants to compensate libraries which showed "significant" use by nonresidents. Massachusetts law requires that all public libraries grant borrowing privileges to nonresidents if they wish to qualify for the regular program of State Aid to Free Public Libraries. Data collected at The Jones showed that an average of 8 percent of the adult circulation for the weeks surveyed was attributable to nonresidents.

This pattern of use raises several questions about the borrowing habits of nonresidents which would be useful to answer. Do nonresidents rely on The Jones for their recreational reading, or is it the nonfiction collection which draws them to Amherst? If so, which portions of the collection attract them? University and college students are classified as nonresidents (since the 1975 state census excludes them from Amherst residency), and represent a significant proportion of the registered nonresident borrowers. Although these students are also served by fine academic libraries, they are heavy users of The Jones. Do they borrow nonfiction, presumably for course work? Or do they borrow current fiction, records for listening recreation, or older fiction? Data would shed some light on these questions, and might have implications for the collection development policies of The Jones, the smaller public libraries of neighboring towns, and the academic libraries (principally the University of Massachusetts and Amherst College).

Discussion of The Jones Library's continued participation in the State Aid program is also a current issue. Data about borrowers' places of residence and their borrowing patterns would be helpful in resolving this issue.

SUMMARY OF THE QUESTION

What percentage of use is generated by nonresidents? Which types of library materials (fiction, nonfiction, nonbook) do nonresidents of Amherst borrow, and which sections of the collection do they use most heavily? In which towns do registered borrowers reside?

METHODOLOGY

Definitions

Charging System: The Jones Library uses a Gaylord Manual Charging System in which circulation cards from each item checked out are stamped with the patron card number and date due. Patrons are issued borrower cards which list name, address, and expiration date, and include a metal plate bearing the borrower number which is stamped, via the charging machine, on the item's circulation card.

Borrower Registration Records: Two permanent records of borrowers are maintained by the library:

1. A Borrower Registration Book, accessed by borrower card number, which lists the name and address, and indicates if the borrower is a student.
2. A Borrower Registration Card File, accessed alphabetically by patron name, which lists address, occupation, mailing reference of the patron, and the assigned card number.

Borrower Cards: Two types of borrower cards are issued to patrons:

1. 1-Year Cards, with four digit registration numbers, which expired on July 1, 1978, are issued to all new borrowers plus "renewing" borrowers whose previous Jones cards were issued after July 1, 1976.
2. 3-Year Cards, with six digit registration numbers, which expire on July 1, 1980, are issued to all renewing patrons whose previous cards were issued prior to July 1, 1976.

This system was adopted by the Trustees in July, 1977, because of the highly transient nature of much of Amherst's population. All current active borrower cards have been renewed or issued since July 1, 1977. The Jones Library grants borrower cards, free of charge, to any resident of Massachusetts.

Study Period: The survey of nonresident borrowing was conducted during the week of March 13, 1978, through March 18, 1978, Monday through Saturday, during all 62 open hours of the main library. This week was selected because it coincided approximately with the Board of Library Commissioners' March 1977 study week, and one subsidiary purpose of the 1978 study was to verify the original survey data. Surveys in future years will be conducted at approximately the same time in March, since this month is neither a "low" nor a "high" circulation month.

Study Population: All borrowers of The Jones Library who checked out materials from the adult collection.

Sample: All nonresident and resident borrowers checking out material from the adult collection during the study period.

Subgroups of the Sample:

Students: All borrowers, regardless of town of residence, 17 years or older who list "student" as occupation at the time of initial registration. Students living in Amherst are thus regarded as nonresidents and included in the subgroup of the sample.

Other Nonresidents: Borrowers residing in towns other than Amherst who are not students.

Amherst Residents: Borrowers residing in the Town of Amherst who are not students.

PROCEDURE

1. During the Study Period (62 open hours), staff at the adult circulation desk checked the borrower card of every patron checking out library material to determine place of residence. If a nonAmherst address was listed, the circulation card for the item was segregated. If an academic address in Amherst (such as a dormitory) was listed, the circulation card was also segregated. On the second day of the study it became apparent that Amherst students living off campus (as a significant number are known to do) were not being picked up by the study. As a consequence a sign was placed on the circulation desk stating, "We are conducting a study of our nonresident and student borrowers. If you are a full-time student and wish to be included in the study, please tell the Desk Attendant." The number of students included significantly increased, and several asked to be informed of the results of the study.

2. At the close of each day (or the following morning), the circulation cards representing the nonresident borrowers were counted, and index cards made representing each item. The index card listed the borrower card number, the call number of the item checked out, and the length of circulation time. (Books which are less than six months old circulate for fourteen days, and books older than six months circu-

late for 30 days.) Circulation cards for nonresidents were returned to the circulation desk for standard filing.

3. The index cards were then sorted by sequential borrower card number. Each card was checked in the Borrower Registration Book to determine the town of residence and student status of the patron. This information was noted on the index card.

4. The cards were then sorted by students and other nonresidents, and tabulated by one-year or three-year card designation, town of residence (number of borrowers and number of items), classification category or type of material borrowed (Dewey numbers 100 through 900, fiction including subcategories for mysteries and science fiction, periodicals, recordings, and other nonbook items).

5. The daily *total* circulation figure for all adult circulation was tabulated as usual and entered on the same sheet for comparative purposes. The totals for nonresidents were subtracted from these figures to establish the number of circulations attributable to Amherst residents.

6. Subsequent tabulations were made of the data collected in this fashion and are described below.

FINDINGS OF THE STUDY

1. Data collected are exhibited in Appendix A. Figure 1 illustrates the daily pattern of circulation. A total of 162 nonresidents, making 168 visits, borrowed material from The Jones Library during the week of March 13 through 18, 1978. Of this number, 64 (39.5 percent) were students who lived in or outside Amherst, and 98 (60.5 percent) were other nonresidents. These two subgroups borrowed 451 items (35.03 percent by students and 64.97 percent by other nonresidents). This represents 14.88 percent of the total adult circulation of 3,031 for the week. Because of the limitations of the manual charging system, no comparative figures on the number of Amherst resident borrowers who checked out materials during the study week are available. But the number of adult items circulated to Amherst residents was 2,530, or 85.12 percent of the total.

The rate of nonresident use is a significant finding when it is compared with data from the Board of Library Commissioners study conducted during seven selected weeks in 1977. During the week of March 21 through 27, 1977, for example, 408 items were checked out by nonresidents from both the adult and juvenile collections, accounting for 8.8 percent of the total circulation of 4,629 items for the two collections. The total adult and juvenile circulation for the current study period (1978) was 4,316, but no nonresident borrowing data for the juvenile collection were gathered. The significant difference in the percentage of circulation figures (14.88 percent in 1978 and 8.8 percent in 1977) suggests at the very least that the device for eliciting borrowing information from students (the sign on the circulation desk

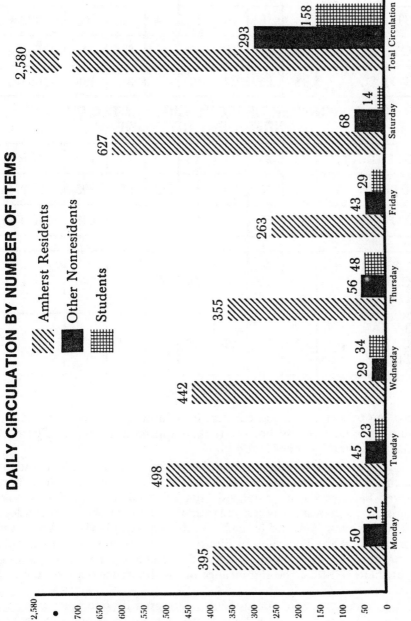

DAILY CIRCULATION BY NUMBER OF ITEMS

Amherst Residents
Other Nonresidents
Students

FIGURE 1

NUMBER OF VISITS BY NONRESIDENT BORROWERS

	3/13	3/14	3/15	3/16	3/17	3/18	Total	% of Total
STUDENT	4	8	10	20	14	8	64	39.5%
OTHER	14	17	12	20	10	31	104	60.5%
TOTAL	18	25	22	40	24	39	168	100.0%

NUMBER OF ITEMS CIRCULATED BY NONRESIDENT BORROWERS

STUDENT	12	23	34	46	29	14	158	35.03%
OTHER	50	45	29	58	43	68	293	64.97%
TOTAL	62	68	63	104	72	82	451	100.00%
1-YEAR CARD ITEMS	31	49	44	56	44	56	280	69.14%
3-YEAR CARD ITEMS	31	19	19	48	28	26	171	30.86%

FIGURE 2

inviting participation) was effective in obtaining a truer picture of the number of nonresident borrowers than appeared during the Board of Library Commissioners' study.[1]

2. The mean number of items borrowed by an individual student during a *visit* to the library was 2.43. The mean number of items borrowed per visit by other nonresidents was 2.82. The standard deviations for these means suggest that about 68 percent of the nonresident visitors borrowed five or fewer books during a single visit. The curves for this data are illustrated in Figure 3. The medians for both sample subgroups fell between one book and two books per visit, suggesting that there is little or no significance in the difference between the two means.

3. The number of nonresident borrowers with one-year cards was 112, or 69.14 percent of the total nonresidents. This subgroup checked

[1]Beginning March 14, 1978, all new and renewing borrower cards issued to other nonresident or student borrowers contain the symbol NR in the upper right corner, thus ensuring easier data collection for future studies of this nature.

NUMBER OF ITEMS BORROWED PER VISIT
BY SAMPLE SUBGROUPS

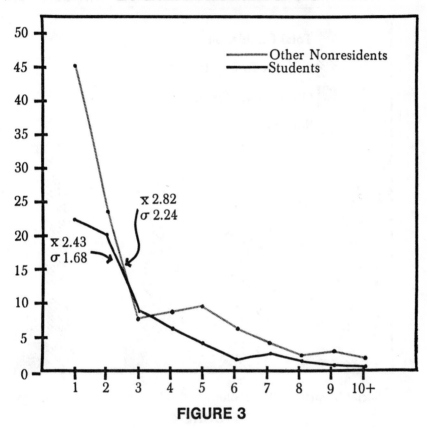

FIGURE 3

out 62.08 percent of the items borrowed by nonresidents. A surprising 12 percent of the 50 three-year card holders were students. There is a significant difference between the number of borrowers with one-year cards in the two subgroups of the sample and the proportion of one-year cards issued by The Jones Library since July 1, 1977. On March 1, 1978, 57.25 percent of all adult cards issued were of the one-year type. This indicates that adopting the one-year card system has been a successful means of putting most of the highly transient student borrowers on a one year status. While a majority of nonresidents (69 percent) are relatively "new" borrowers, a significant number are long time users of the library. One-year card holders borrowed an average of 2.47 items per visit, whereas three-year card holders borrowed 3.11 items per visit.

4. There is no significant difference in the choice of material by students, other nonresidents, and Amherst residents. The four most frequently used categories were social sciences (300s), technology (600s), the arts (700s), and phonograph recordings. Figure 4 illustrates

COMPARATIVE CIRCULATION IN FOUR MOST POPULAR CATEGORIES, AS PERCENT OF TOTAL CIRCULATION

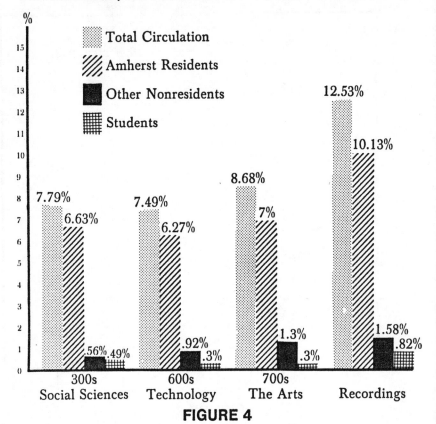

FIGURE 4

the circulation for each of the sample subgroups as a percentage of the total circulation for the week. Curves drawn on this graph would be roughly parallel.

5. If total circulations by broad section of the collection (fiction, nonfiction, and nonbook) are compared, the results indicate some differences. Amherst residents accounted for 88.22 percent of the fiction circulation, other nonresidents 6.62 percent, and students 5.16 percent. However, Amherst residents accounted for only 83.93 percent of the nonfiction circulation, while other nonresidents borrowed 10.48 percent and students 4.93 percent. It is interesting to note that the comparative circulations as a percentage of the collection category circulation does not appear significant until the section totals for nonfiction, fiction, and nonbook are compared. This difference suggests that while the smaller libraries of neighboring communities may be able to meet the fiction reading needs of their residents, the strength of The Jones collections in nonfiction and nonbook items is a significant

drawing factor. These categories of materials are, of course, the most expensive to purchase, for an individual or a library. The pattern of use also verifies the strength of the Jones Library collection as compared to smaller libraries. The same pattern can be observed by comparing the fiction, nonfiction, and nonbook circulations as percentages of each subgroup's total circulation. 44.3 percent of the students' circulation was in nonfiction items, 52.9 percent of the other nonresidents', and 45.5 percent of the Amherst residents'. The data for fiction and nonbook categories are also illustrated in Figure 5.

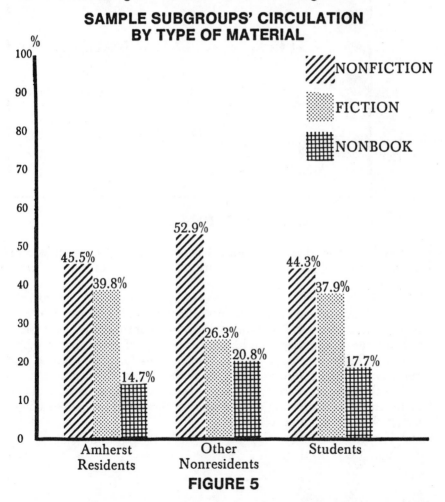

FIGURE 5

6. In only one category, the 300s, is there a significant difference between other nonresidents and students in terms of the age of material they borrow. Unfortunately, no data could be collected on the age selection pattern of Amherst residents. Figure 6 illustrates that in the 600s and 700s the difference in the percentage of newer

AGE OF MATERIAL IN SELECTED CATEGORIES AS PERCENT OF SUBGROUPS' CATEGORY CIRCULATION

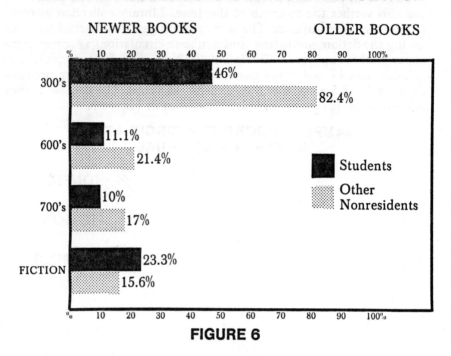

FIGURE 6

materials borrowed is only about 3 percent when the two categories are compared. Students borrow more new fiction than other nonresidents.

In the 300s (social sciences), however, 46 percent of the material borrowed by students is less than six months old, compared to 82.4 percent of the material borrowed by other nonresidents. Because of this difference, and the much higher proportion of newer material borrowed by both subgroups, all 300s circulations for both students and other nonresidents were re-examined to determine which subject areas within the category were most heavily used. It was speculated that students might be borrowing older materials they need for course assignments. The data are as follows:

SELECTION BY SUBJECT IN THE 300s

	Books Less Than Six Months Old		Books More Than Six Months Old		Totals
STUDENTS					
	Women	4	Women	2	
	Slavery	2	Economics	2	
	Adoption	1	Politics	4	
	Total	7	Total	8	15
OTHER NONRESIDENTS					
	Women	6	Women	2	
	Minorities	1	Folklore	1	
	Folklore	2			
	Politics	4			
	Total	14	Total	3	17
TOTAL BOTH SUBGROUPS		21		11	32

The numbers indicate that 14 of the total circulations in the 300s were books about women. Of these, 10 were books less than six months old, of which students checked out four and other nonresidents six. The balance of the circulation in the 300s is varied as to subject. It is interesting to note that four of the newer books checked out by other nonresidents concerned politics, whereas students were interested in older books on this subject. Three of the four politics books checked out by students were copyrighted between 1959 and 1969, although the titles revealed no other evidence of intended use.

7. Table A shows the data for the nonresident subgroups of the sample population organized by place of residence. The data have been grouped geographically, in order to determine the pattern of use. 42.5 percent of the use by nonresidents, whether they are students or

TABLE A
BORROWERS BY PLACE OF RESIDENCE
( ) = Students included in total

	No. of Borrowers	% of Total Nonresidents (162)[1]	No. of Items	% of Total Nonresident Items (451)	% of Total Circulation (3,031)
GROUP I: Towns Contiguous to Amherst					
Belchertown	22 (6)		70		
Hadley	19 (3)		48		
Leverett	9 —		24		
Shutesbury	7 (4)		24		
Sunderland	7 —		19		
Pelham	6 —		27		
TOTAL	69	42.6%	212	47.00%	6.99%

TABLE A (cont.)

	No. of Borrowers	% of Total Nonresidents (162)[1]	No. of Items	% of Total Nonresident Items (451)	% of Total Circulation (3,031)
GROUP II: West, 10+ miles					
Northampton	15 (4)		30		
Easthampton	1 (1)		1		
Florence	1 —		1		
Haydenville	1 —		6		
Hatfield	•1 —		8		
Huntington	1 —		1		
Leeds	1 —		3		
TOTAL	21	12.9%	50	11.09%	1.65%
GROUP III: North & Northwest, 15+ miles					
Greenfield	1 —		1		
Montague	1 (1)		8		
Turner's Falls	1 —		4		
Deerfield(s)	3 —		5		
Shelburne Falls	•3 —		5		
Conway	2 —		4		
Petersham	1 —		9		
TOTAL	12	7.4%	36	7.98%	1.19%
GROUP IV: Northeast, 20+ miles					
New Salem	3 —		11		
Orange	3 —		7		
Erving	1 —		5		
Wendell	2 —		11		
TOTAL	9	5.6%	34	7.54%	1.12%
GROUP V: East, beyond Quabbin Reservoir					
Ware	1 —	0.62%	1	0.22%	0.03%
GROUP VI: South, beyond Holyoke Range, 20+ miles					
Holyoke	1 —		1		
W. Springfield	1 —		2		
S. Hadley	•3 (1)		4		
Longmeadow	1 —		2		
TOTAL	6	3.7%	9	2.00%	0.3%
AMHERST RESIDENT STUDENTS	44	27.2%	109	24.17%	3.6%

•One nonresident Amherst employee
[1]Based on actual number of borrowers, not number of visits to library

not, comes from people who live in towns contiguous to Amherst. While Amherst resident students account for 27.5 percent of the borrowers, Groups II through VI account for the balance at a steadily declining rate. It is important to note that among the groups, the geophysical barriers of the Holyoke Range to the South and Quabbin Reservoir to the East are apparently significant. This supports the contention of the Lower Pioneer Valley Regional Planning Commission that the Holyoke Range is a major east-west dividing line in the Connecticut River Valley, whereas the River itself (where it is bridged) is not.

One explanation for use of The Jones Library by such a significant number of people who live beyond ten miles might be that they are employed in Amherst. Consequently the 48 individual borrowers in Groups II through VI, were checked in the Borrower Registration Card File to determine place of employment. Only three, or 6.3 percent of the 48, are employed in Amherst. It is assumed that a higher proportion of the borrowers in Group I, the towns contiguous to Amherst, are employed here, since this is a known demographic characteristic of the town.

Therefore, some other explanation for the use of The Jones Library must be found. The borrowers in Group II are more proximately served by the Forbes Public Library of Northampton, which is a Western Regional Public Library System subregional center, and has a larger collection than The Jones. The probable explanation for heavy Amherst use by Group II people (other than those who live in Northampton) is the Forbes policy regarding borrower cards for non-residents of Northampton. The Forbes requires nonresident patrons to verify (via forms which must be secured from the Forbes and then signed by the local librarian) that they are borrowers in good standing in their own communities before it will issue a Forbes card. The Jones Library, on the other hand, gives borrower cards to any Massachusetts resident, regardless of their local library status.

No such easy explanation can be found for Jones use by the residents of Group III. Greenfield, the largest town in that area, has a public library which, although smaller than The Jones, is certainly widely known as adequate.

As for the residents of Group IV, the towns in that area are quite small, and it is reasonable to assume that their residents combine visits to The Jones Library with other errands (shopping for example) in Amherst. In Group VI, one of the South Hadley-resident borrowers is employed in Amherst, and another is a student (perhaps a commuter to the University of Massachusetts). This reduces the number of "beyond the Holyoke Range" borrowers for which there is no apparent explanation to four.

RECOMMENDATIONS

This study was undertaken in order to develop detailed knowledge of the pattern of borrowing by nonresidents of Amherst, and to test some commonly held assumptions about them. The data do not support the development of specific recommendations for action, but do provide a factual basis for future discussion.

The study has produced some hard statistics which will be useful in future general descriptions of The Jones Library users. For example, it is known that more than 14 percent of the total adult use of The

Jones is by nonresidents. While generally speaking the use by nonresidents is the same as the use by residents, it is now known that nonresidents rely on The Jones most heavily for nonfiction, phonograph recordings, and back issues of periodicals.

The study also provides new insight into an issue of increasing importance to Massachusetts public libraries. In order to qualify for the State Aid to Free Public Libraries program (as well as LSCA grants), all public libraries have been mandated to institute free borrowing privileges (via reciprocal borrowing agreements between local libraries) to all Massachusetts residents, in stages, with a completion date by 1979. In 1973, The Jones Library Trustees elected to comply with the regulation immediately, and to grant free borrowing privileges to any Massachusetts resident without signing reciprocal borrowing agreements with the resident's hometown library. They did this for two reasons: first, the Trustees believe that a public library should serve all who need it, regardless of their place of residence, and second, because they estimated that the benefit of verifying the library-status of each nonresident would not be worth the cost in either Jones staff time or in citizen goodwill.

Forbes Library in Northampton, on the other hand, has elected to comply on a year-by-year-basis, and has followed the letter of the regulation by insisting upon formal agreements between town libraries. If it is true that this Forbes policy increases nonresident use in Amherst (this would need to be verified by a further study of the Group II borrowers), the Board of Library Commissioners and the Trustees of both The Jones and Forbes should be informed.

The Jones, like all Massachusetts public libraries, is supported by local tax money. The financially hard-pressed Amherst government is increasingly concerned that the compensation Amherst receives in the Direct State Aid program for maintaining a free-access library does not justify the cost of providing the service. Using FY 1977 data (the only complete figures available) compensation can be compared as follows:

	No. of Items Circulated	Dollars Received		Compensation Per Item
NONRESIDENTS	25,296*	$ 9,874	(State Aid)	$0.39
RESIDENTS	185,512	$247,392	(Town & Endowment Income)	$1.33
TOTAL	210,808	$257,266		$1.22

*Estimate based on 12 percent of total circulation, which is a compromise figure between the 9 percent average reported to the Board of Library Commissioners for all circulation during their 1977 survey, and the 14.88 percent use by adults in the current study.

It can be assumed that the cost of circulating an item to a nonresident is the same as it is for a resident, as The Jones uses no special clerical procedures to register nonresidents. Therefore, the Town of Amherst is subsidizing the library use of the taxpayers of other municipalities at the rate of 83¢ per item.

Based upon this fact, it would be my recommendation, as Director of the town library, that the Selectmen of the Town of Amherst and the Library Trustees make every effort to persuade the Legislature of Massachusetts to increase appropriations for the Direct Aid to Free Public Libraries program. I do not believe that free nonresident borrowing should be stopped unless all funding avenues have been exhausted.

APPENDIX A
SUMMARY OF RAW CIRCULATION DATA COLLECTED[1]

	000	100	200	300	400	500	600	700	800	900	910 919	BIO	TOTAL N.F.	TOTAL FIC.	RECS.	PER.	TOTAL NONBK*	TOTAL CIRCULATION
Mon. 3/13 Student	—	—	—	1	—	—	2	—	1	—	7	—	11	1	—	—	—	12
Other	—	5	—	(2)	1	(1)	(2)	5(1)	6	1	—	(1)	24	8	8	10	18	50
All circ.	1	14	3	38	4	16	52	32	33	7	23	14	237	153	51	16	67	457
Amh. circ.	1	9	3	34	4	15	48	26	26	6	16	13	202	144	43	6	49	395
Tues. 3/14 Student	—	—	—	—	—	1	14(3)	(1)(4)	8	(1)	1	—	12	11	—	—	—	23
Other	—	1	—	(2)	1	—	—	—	(1)1	(1)1	13	2	30	11	2	2	4	45
All circ.	7	10	8	34	1	19	59	53	50	32	13	20	306	192	55	13	68	566
Amh. circ.	7	9	8	32	1	18	42	48	40	29	12	18	264	170	53	11	64	498
Wed. 3/15 Student	—	3	—	1	—	2	1	6	—	—	3	—	17	(7)7	3	—	3	34
Other	—	(2)	2	(1)	—	(1)	2	4	(1)	1	2	1	17	6(1)	5	—	5	29
All circ.	6	16	9	50	2	13	28	42	29	7	15	11	228	214	53	8	65	505
Amh. circ.	5	10	7	48	2	10	25	32	28	7	10	10	194	193	45	8	57	442
Thurs. 3/16 Student	—	—	—	7	—	—	(1)	—	2	—	—	—	12	21(2)	12	—	14	48
Other	—	—	—	(4)	—	(1)	—	9(2)	3	—	—	5	24	17(3)	12	—	12	56
All circ.	—	6	3	26	3	3	27	40	36	14	12	9	179	194	80	4	88	459
Amh. circ.	—	6	3	15	3	2	25	28	31	14	12	4	143	151	56	4	62	355
Fri. 3/17 Student	—	(1)	—	2(5)	(1)(1)	(2)(1)	1	2(1)	(1)	(1)	—	2	14	2(4)	9	—	9	29
Other	—	2	—	(1)	—	—	6	5(1)	2	(1)	—	1	25	6(2)	9	—	11	43
All circ.	1	—	1	35	1	5	16	31	13	8	21	11	144	134	42	3	69	335
Amh. circ.	1	1	1	24	—	2	9	22	10	7	21	8	105	120	24	3	49	263
Sat. 3/18 Student	1	—	—	—	—	1	3	—	—	—	—	—	6	4(1)	1	2	3	14
Other	—	3	—	3(3)	—	2	(1)	7(2)	4	3	—	4	33	17(6)	12	—	12	68
All circ.	5	10	6	54	1	14	45	65	32	37	23	14	306	276	99	16	139	709
Amh. circ.	4	7	6	48	1	11	41	56	27	34	23	9	267	248	86	14	124	627
TOTAL ALL CIRC.				336			227	263					1400	1163			497	3031
TOTAL AMHERST CIRC.				201			190	215					1175	1026			416	2580

[1]Circled numbers indicate books which are less than six months old, based on date of acquisition. Books less than six months old circulate for 14 days; books older than six months circulate for 30 days. The non-circled numbers represent the latter category.

*Other nonbook items are included in this total, but not listed separately.

Journal Use in a Community Hospital

by Sheila Newlands Testa

INTRODUCTION

The following is an in-house use-study of health sciences journal titles for both current and back years.

This study was done at Lynn Hospital, a 315 bed acute care facility fifteen miles north of Boston. It is a community hospital which has limited affiliation with Tufts Medical School. The medical and nursing students who comprise part of the user population during the school year were not at the hospital due to the time of the study (June). However, these are only affiliated user groups, not the primary patron groups of the library. The hospital has approximately 1400 employees, of which 315 are registered nurses. There are 170 physicians on the staff.

LIBRARY FACILITY

The library consists of one room which has a seating capacity of ten. There are presently 325 volumes, 125 current journal titles, and 49 titles, 1975 or older. The indexes housed in the library consist of *Cumulative Index Medicus* 1946-56, 1971-72, 1976-77; *Cumulative Abridged Index Medicus* 1973-75; *Cumulative Index to Nursing Literature* 1974-77; *International Nursing Index* 1977; and *Hospital Literature Index* 1972-77. The library is under the direction of one professional librarian, and it has been in operation for one year.

OBJECTIVES

The statistics resulting from this study are valuable in helping to determine:

1) which subscriptions may be dropped due to low utilization;
2) which titles should be bound due to the greater amount of use of one title than another;
3) when to send out journals to be bound due to a lag in use (e.g., possibly due to the slower indexing process); and,
4) which older volumes could be put into storage due to their low use.

METHODOLOGY

The study was conducted during a two-week period (June 13-16 and 20-24, 1977). This time period was chosen because it would provide a better indication of physician use and reflect more of the clinically-oriented readings as the nursing students, lab technician students, etc. were on vacation and use would not be a result of class assignments.

Library policy dictates that journals and books are not to be reshelved by the user. The means of determining in-house use of journals was to collect those journals left on the tables at the end of each day, and then to record the title and year of publication. At the end of the two-week period these titles and dates were categorized.

FINDINGS

Table I lists the number of times a title was used. Both Tables I and II show, as other studies have shown (Chen, 1970; Crawford, 1971; Kamenoff, 1977), that a small number of titles constitute the majority of use; the first nine titles (of the total 66 titles used) account for 54.6 percent of the use (*New England Journal of Medicine, JAMA, Science, Lancet, American Journal of Surgery, American Journal of Nursing, Cancer, British Medical Journal, Annals of Internal Medicine*). These top titles are found to be the same as the top titles found in other studies (Crawford, 1971; Kamenoff, 1977). These top titles should certainly be continually subscribed to; those titles at the lower end of the scale would be the titles to be dropped if the budget limitations required it. If the binding budget had to be limited, money would be used to bind the more frequently used titles. Also, the titles less frequently referred to could be put into storage because of the extreme shortage of space.

TABLE I
FREQUENCY OF JOURNAL USE IN RANKING ORDER

	Title	Total	1977	1973-76	1968-72	Prior to 1968
1	New England Journal of Medicine	47	30	7	8	2
2	Journal of the American Medical Assoc.	37	22	10	4	1
3	Science	29	12	9	8	not applic.
4	Lancet	27	20	5	not applicable ...	
5	American Journal of Surgery	15	10	3	1	1
5	American Journal of Nursing	15	2	13	not applicable ...	

TABLE I (cont.)
FREQUENCY OF JOURNAL USE IN RANKING ORDER

	Title	Total	1977	1973-76	1968-72	Prior to 1968
6	Cancer	11	5	6	not applicable ...	
6	British Medical Journal	11	11	not applicable		
6	Annals of Internal Medicine	11	9	2	0	0
7	Surgery, Gynecology, and Obstetrics	10	5	1	1	3
8	Scientific American	9	9	not applicable		
8	Archives of Surgery	9	3	6	0	0
9	Surgery	8	3	5	0	0
9	Circulation	8	6	1	0	1
9	Annals of Surgery	8	4	0	3	1
10	Nursing	7	1	7	not applicable ...	
10	American Review of Respiratory Disease	7	7	not applicable		
10	RN	7	2	5	not applicable ...	
11	Journal Thoracic and Cardiovascular Surg	5	1	3	1	not applic.
11	Gastroenterology	5	4	1	not applicable ...	
11	Chest	5	5	not applicable		
11	Archives of Internal Medicine	5	4	0	1	0
11	American Journal of Medicine	5	3	2	0	0
12	Medical Letter	4	4	not applicable		
12	Archives of Surgery	4	3	0	1	0
13	Surgical Clinics of North America	3	2	0	1	not applic.
13	Pediatrics	3	2	0	0	1
13	Medical Economics	3	3	not applicable		
13	JOGN	3	3	not applicable		
13	Gut	3	3	not applicable		
14	Radiology	2	2	not applicable		
14	Journal of Urology	2	0	2	0	0
14	Journal of Trauma	2	2	0	0	not applic.
14	International Anesthesiology Clinics	2	2	0	not applicable ...	
14	Hospital Practice	2	2	not applicable		
14	Diseases of the Colon and Rectum	2	1	1	0	not applic.

TABLE 1 (cont.)

	Title	Total	1977	1973-76	1968-72	Prior to 1968
14	British Journal of Urology	2	2	not applicable	. . . .	
14	American Journal of Roentgenology	2	2	not applicable	. . . .	
14	American Journal of Public Health	2	0	2	0	0
14	American Journal of Obstetrics and Gynecology	2	1	0	1	0
14	American Journal of Medical Sciences	2	1	0	1	0
14	American Heart Journal	2	2	not applicable	. . . .	

There are twenty-four titles which had one user per title. See Appendix I for title and date.

not applicable . . . the library does not carry that time period.

TABLE II
CUMULATIVE FREQUENCY OF USE BY RANK

Rank No. of Journals	No. of titles	% of Total Use
1	1	12.6
2	1	22.6
3	1	30.4
4	1	37.6
5	2	45.7
6	3	54.6
7	1	57.3
8	2	62.1
9	3	68.5
10	3	74.2
11	5	80.9
12	2	83.1
13	5	87.1
14	12	93.5
15	24	100.0

Total No. 66

Table III indicates the percentage of the use per year; 1977 (the current year) had the greatest volume, 61 percent of the total use. The greatest amount of use, 88 percent of the total, occurs in the journals' first five years. These figures are valuable in determining which years are to be put into storage. Also, binding could be put off due to heavy use of a title during its early life.

TABLE III
PERCENTAGE OF USE PER YEAR

Use 1977	Use 1973-76	Use 1968-72	Use Pre-1968
61%	27%	8%	2%

88 percent of the use was in the first five years; 96 percent of the use was in the first ten years

LIMITATIONS

As with most studies there are limitations: 1) The short time period covered is a handicap, and the time of year in which the study was done limits the user population due to vacations, school schedules, and the like. To get a better idea of use possibly other periods of time throughout the year should be covered. Plans are underway to do this on a periodic basis. 2) Many of the titles did not have long back runs, and the hospital only had six months worth of titles which were new subscriptions (e.g., *British Medical Journal*) therefore limiting their use. 3) Some use would not be reflected if users reshelved journals themselves. Fortunately, this constitutes an insignificant percentage of total library use.

CONCLUSION

Beyond the obvious conclusions, such as the titles which should be continually subscribed to and bound, are those with the greatest number of times used, the study indicated those titles with the least use (e.g., *Journal of Infectious Diseases*) which the library should consider dropping if the collection budget is tight; journals which are used most frequently during the first five years from their publication date and for which the binding process should be put off until a later date to make them available during the period of the greatest demand; and, those titles five to ten years old which should be available on shelves depending on space as well as those journals which may be put in storage.

REFERENCES

Chen, Ching-chih. "The Use Patterns of Physics Journals in a Large Academic Research Library." *Journal of the American Society for Information Science* 23 (May-June, 1970):254-270.

Crawford, David S. "Periodical Usage." *Bulletin of the Medical Library Association* 59 (July, 1971):516-517.

Jain, A. K. "Sampling and Short-period Usage in the Purdue Library." *College and Research Libraries* 27 (May, 1966):211-218.

Kamenoff, L. "Journal Usage at a Community Hospital Library." *Bulletin of the Medical Library Association* 65 (January, 1977):58-61.

Piternick, Anne B. "Effects of Binding Policy and Other Factors on the Availability of Journal Issues." *Bulletin of the Medical Library Association* 64 (July, 1976):284-292.

APPENDIX I
JOURNALS USED ONLY ONCE DURING THE STUDY
PERIOD

Titles Used Once	Year Used
American Journal of Digestive Diseases	1977
American Journal of Law and Medicine	1975
Anaesthesia	1977
Archives of Neurology	1977
Brain	1977
Bulletin of the American College of Surgeons	1975
CA	1977
Heart Lung	1977
Hospitals	1977
Journal of the American Dietetic Association	1974
Journal of Continuing Education in Nursing	1973
Journal of Infectious Disease	1977
Journal of Nursing Administration	1976
Medicine	1977
Modern Concepts of Cardiovascular Medicine	1977
Modern Healthcare	1976
Nursing Clinics of North America	1974
Nursing Forum	1974
Nursing Outlook	1975
Nursing Research	1976
Pediatric Clinics of North America	1971
Point of View	1977
Postgraduate Medicine	1977
Thorax	1977

Document Exposure Counts in Three Academic Libraries: Circulation and In-Library Use

by Joan Stockard, Mary Ann Griffin,
and Clementine Coblyn

Increasingly, librarians are being held accountable for "knowing" what is happening in their libraries. It is now expected that justification for specific operations as well as evidence of our effectiveness as service organizations be based on documentable information rather than on tradition or experiential knowledge. Among methods for measuring performance that have been discussed in the literature, Morris Hamburg's suggestion, based on document exposure counts, is the most comprehensive and provides a uniform approach to applying quantitative measurement to library operations. Hamburg sees "the exposure of individuals to documents of recorded human experience" as the "most important aspect of all public and university library objectives." (1974)

Recorded circulation transactions provide us with some document exposure data and have traditionally been used as an indicator of library activity. Every librarian, however, is conscious of the fact that a great deal of in-library use occurs that is not reflected in circulation records. The question, then, becomes how to measure in-library use. To get a complete picture of in-library document exposure, incidence of the following types of use would have to be recorded:

1. General collection books and periodicals consulted but not borrowed.
2. Use of non-circulating special collections (maps, rare books, special subject collections, U.S. or foreign government publications, etc.).
3. Reference works used either directly by the client or with a reference librarian as intermediary.

4. Use of documents in microform.
5. Audiovisual "documents" used.

None of these kinds of use is as readily recorded as circulation transactions. However, approximations based on sampling can be employed to give an acceptably accurate figure for in-library use. The tally of in-library use can then be compared in a ratio statement to the tally of circulation use for the sampling period. If the ratio proves relatively stable, circulation figures can be used henceforth as known indexes to in-library use with some assurance of reliability.

It was the aim of this modest preliminary study to test this theory for one of the six types of in-library use in a fashion which would not be unduly burdensome in terms of staff time and effort. General collection materials were chosen for study because they likely comprise the greatest percentage of in-library uses and because documenting such use by tallying materials left on tables, desks, and other surfaces can be accomplished with minimum extra effort when done in conjunction with normal library reshelving procedures. Recognizing that this pick-up method is somewhat simplistic since it cannot account for users reshelving their own material or for the incidence of browsing, the authors nonetheless felt these controversial complicating factors fell outside the scope of this pragmatic and preliminary study.

There is little published literature on in-library use and, in many cases, the reporting of a ratio of in-library to circulation use is so peripheral to the concerns of the author that numbers presented in tables and charts designed for other purposes must be examined to deduce that ratio. There are reports on in-library to circulation ratios differing as widely as 0.4:1 and 11:1. This wide range is explainable to some degree by differing parameters of type of in-library use being measured, but differences are also attributable to factors such as loan policies and duration of loan periods, ease of access to materials, availability of seating, as well as variations in demand characteristics of specific clienteles. With one exception, the published studies were performed in academic libraries; only two found in-library use to exceed circulation use. The methodology used in the studies was predominantly the pick-up method or, less successfully, a questionnaire.

Within the literature of the recent past, Fussler and Simon (1961) were the first to devote some attention to in-library use. Their study, which was a part of a larger management study, was conducted in 1959-60 at the University of Chicago. Its goal was to establish the value of browsing to library users. A random sample of monographs and serials in physics (QC) and general history (D) was equipped with questionnaires. Although expressing reservations about the accuracy of the questionnaire method because of low response rate and possible biases, the authors stated that there were between three and nine times as much browsing as circulation use.

Many of the tabulated browsing encounters resulted in circulation uses. Fussler and Simon established that a predictable correlation exists between the number of in-library uses and the number of circulation uses for individual circulating titles.

In a published report generated by Operations Research studies under Dr. Morse at M.I.T.'s Science Library, Bush et al. (1965) reported on the basis of a five day questionnaire sample survey that there were 92 loans of periodicals and 365 loans of books and reports. They also reported in-library use of 2022 periodicals (exclusive of indexes and abstracts) and 899 report and book uses (exclusive of reference works, items on reserve, and theses). The overall ratio of total in-library use to total circulation was, therefore, 6.4:1 with the rate for books being 2.5:1, and that for periodicals being 21.9:1.

A. K. Jain (1966) reported on a Purdue library use study conducted in June and July 1964 on monographic titles in DDC 330-379. As a sub-unit of the study, a questionnaire tested users' reasons for visiting the library. On-site use was indicated 114 times, while checking out materials for home use was checked 42 times, a ratio of 2.7:1. Concerned over the approximate nature of figures obtained by the pick-up method used for measuring in-library use in the core of the study, Jain published an article in 1972 outlining a more rigorous methodology for such studies. Clearly, his solution is statistically elegant, but the cost in staff time for even the 21,000 volume collection hypothesized by Jain would cause any administrator to reconsider the need for the increased confidence factor.

Morse's monograph (1968) summarizing the Operations Research investigations at M.I.T., refers to an overall ratio of 4 in-library uses to 1 circulation for books. In citing an unpublished paper by Elson which demonstrated that half of the items used at reading tables were reshelved by users and, therefore, not included in pick-up counts, Morse was of the opinion that as long as sampling showed this phenomenon to be constant the reliability of the pick-up method was not affected.

In a study designed to determine what parts of the periodical runs, in the library of Children's Hospital of Michigan, could be stored, Smith (1970) sampled circulation use, in-library use, and interlibrary loan use. In-library use figures were derived from a count of items picked up three or four times a day when tables were cleared. Periodicals, in this study, included serials issued annually or less frequently but not abstracts or indexes. During the survey period, from September 1967 to February 1968, periodicals dating from 1933 to 1968 circulated 632 times and were used in-house 1083 times, a ratio of in-library use to circulation of 1.7:1.

In 1971, McGrath published his results based on studies done by the pick-up method for books at the University of Southwestern Louisiana. Carrying Fussler and Simon a bit farther, McGrath (1971) established that there is a direct correlation between the subject grouping of books used within the library and the subject grouping of books loaned. Within an overall ratio of 1 in-library use to 2 circulation uses, McGrath found circulation use to exceed in-library use, unlike most other studies in the literature. This finding may be explained by the subject scope of the study. McGrath's is one of only two reports which include all academic disciplines. The other studies are science-oriented, with the exception of Fussler and Simon who included history.

Seymour (1972), in an article devoted to reviewing research on collection weeding, refers parenthetically to in-library use studies conducted by the Library Management Research Unit at university libraries in Sussex and Bradford, England. Data were collected on books and periodicals in 1970 and 1971 for periods of two weeks by means of both the pick-up method and questionnaires. At Sussex a ratio of 1.6:1 was determined; in the Engineering and Science Library at Bradford, the ratio reached 11.2:1.

In a study by Saracevic et al. (1977), concerned with user frustrations at Case Western Reserve University, it was found that of the books used in the science/technology/management library during a nine day study period in November 1974, 44 percent were loaned and 55 percent were used in-house for a ratio of 1.3 in-house uses to 1 circulation use. The data, on "known item" user searches only, were gathered by questionnaires distributed at the card catalog.

Most recently, Harris (1977) reported on a study of the use of book stock at Newcastle-upon-Tyne Polytechnic. This study attempted to compare issues (circulations) and recorded in-library uses of specific books. In-library use was sampled in two separate studies to test assumptions concerning the significance of defining "use" in different ways. The first sample (10 percent of the stock) was based on a record of books picked up by the library staff for reshelving between January 1973 and July 1974. Reference works, periodicals, official publications and limited-access collections were excluded. Since it had long been the practice at the Polytechnic to distinctively date-stamp each item during reshelving, it was comparatively easy to gather this large body of data. Feeling, however, that this method gave too low a result for in-library use, Harris designed a second study based on a 20 percent sample in four selected subject areas. The methodology involved putting a slip within each sample item in such a way that any use, no matter how trivial, of the volume would be obvious. Slips were in place from October 31 to December 19, 1974. The hidden slip method is as vulnerable to charges of distortion as is the pick-up system. Results of the pick-up method (A) show 0.4 in-library uses to 1 circulation; results of the more cumbersome hidden slip system (B) show a ratio of 4.7:1.

The data collection method used for the study reported in this paper required circulation desk assistants to keep tallies on work sheets from February 7 through February 20, 1977 (see sample form appended). Personnel engaged in normal reshelving operations recorded the LCC main class letter or DDC class number of each book

TABLE I
SUMMARY OF LITERATURE REVIEW IN
ASCENDING RATIO ORDER

STUDY (DATE)	MATERIAL TYPES	RATIO OF IN-LIBRARY USE TO ONE CIRCULATION USE	DATA COLLECTION METHODS
Harris — A (1977)	Books	0.4	Pick-up
McGrath (1971)	Books (by subjects)	0.5 (0.2-1.1)	Pick-up
Saracevic (1977)	"Known" books	1.3	Questionnaire
Seymour (1972)	Books & periodicals	1.6-11.2	Pick-up & question-naire
Smith (1970)	Periodicals	1.7	Pick-up
Jain (1966)	Books	2.7	Questionnaire
Fussler & Simon (1961)	Books & periodicals	3.0-9.0	Questionnaire
Morse (1968)	Books	4.0	Pick-up
Harris — B (1977)	Books	4.7	Hidden slip
Bush (1965)	Books & periodicals (Books alone) (Periodicals alone)	6.4 (2.5) (21.9)	Questionnaire

and periodical from the general collection which was left on a table, desk, or other surface in reading areas, study areas, photoduplication areas, and in the stacks. Unbound as well as bound periodicals were tallied. For the sake of erring on the side of underestimation, bound periodicals were counted as one use although in some cases the client undoubtedly consulted more than one issue. Likewise, a pile of unbound periodicals of the same title left on a surface were counted as one use on the assumption that in most cases the pile represented a search for one known issue. Use of periodicals on microfilm was tallied in two of the libraries but not in the third since that library has few journals on microfilm and is physically distant from the microfilm storage and reading areas.

The three libraries involved in this study were the Science Library of the Massachusetts Institute of Technology, Wessell Library at Tufts University, and the Margaret Clapp Library of Wellesley College. A comparison of the three environments is displayed as follows:

TABLE II
COMPARISON OF THREE ACADEMIC LIBRARIES

	TYPE	SCOPE	COLLEC-TION SIZE	SEATS	BOOK LOAN PERIOD	CIRCULATION OF PERIODICALS	ANNUAL CIRCULA-TION
M. I. T.	Special subject division	Astronomy and Astrophysics Biology, Chemical engineering, Chemistry, Experimental medicine, Materials science, Mathematics, Nuclear engineering, Nutrition and Food science, Physics, Physiological psychology	90,000 books; 1,700 current period.	200	4 weeks	QA (Math) only (1 week)	74,000
T U F T S	General university	Social science Humanities, Biological and Earth sciences	321,000 volumes; 1,400 current period.	800	2 weeks	No circ.	87,000
W E L L E S L E Y	Women's under graduate	Social science except Psychology, Humanities except Fine arts	380,000 volumes; 2,499 current period.	700	4 weeks	Faculty only	41,800

The wide range of in-library to circulation ratios discovered in the three libraries participating in this study (Figure 1) reinforces the perception gained from the literature search: that any library administrator, desiring to establish a figure to be used in conjunction with circulation counts as an indicator of use, will benefit little from the numbers reported in published studies of other libraries. Factors unique to each library, such as subject focus, characteristics of clientele, holdings, access, seating capacity, and loan policies influence in-library use. "Use" itself remains of uncertain definition with each administrator likely to take a somewhat different philosophical stand.

In the three libraries examined for this study, the ratios for the two libraries emphasizing humanities and social sciences were closest to the ratio established by McGrath, who included all academic disciplines in his study. It will be interesting to see if future studies reinforce—and explain—the deduction from both the literature and this

COMPARISON OF BOOK AND PERIODICAL USE RATIOS

	IN-LIB	CIRC	RATIO
M.I.T.	3510	2037	1.7
Tufts	2950	3842	0.8
Wellesley	1281	2041	0.6

FIGURE 1

project that in-library use is less than circulation use in academic libraries with broad subject scope, while the reverse is true in science oriented libraries.

Additional insight into the variation of the ratios over time was made possible by displaying portions of the data in a different arrangement (Figure 2). Of course, two weeks out of the year are a poor basis for firm conclusions. The display does indicate, however, how more

DAILY TABULATION OF BOOK
AND PERIODICAL USE RATIOS

	M.I.T.			Tufts			Wellesley		
DATE	IN-LIB	CIRC	RATIO	IN-LIB	CIRC	RATIO	IN-LIB	CIRC	RATIO
2-7-77 M	231	60	3.8	218	396	0.6	131	185	0.7
2-8 Tu	240	185	1.3	196	281	0.7	126	197	0.6
2-9 W	250	200	1.2	187	275	0.7	136	140	1.0
2-10 Th	268	159	1.7	162	270	0.6	70	178	0.4
2-11 F	250	162	1.5	63	226	0.3	43	139	0.2
2-12 Sa	398	174	2.3	75	150	0.5	90	78	1.2
2-13 Su	203	57	3.6	347	196	1.8	50	110	0.5
Week subtotal	1840	997	1.8	1497	1794	0.8	646	1027	0.6
2-14 M	147	69	2.1	234	368	0.6	77	171	0.5
2-15 Tu	248	197	1.2	197	365	0.5	128	204	0.6
2-16 W	250	223	1.1	199	382	0.5	135	167	0.8
2-17 Th	357	146	2.4	186	320	0.6	77	136	0.6
2-18 F	287	180	1.6	41	348	0.1	94	147	0.6
2-19 Sa	233	165	1.4	71	165	0.4	62	98	0.6
2-20 Su	148	60	2.5	290	100	2.9	62	91	0.1
Week subtotal	1670	1040	1.0	1453	2048	0.7	635	1014	0.6

FIGURE 2

extensive data tabulated in this fashion might prove useful. Even in libraries where door counts of entering clients are tallied, there is no way to estimate what percentage of clients intend to remain in the building. This type of display, however, could establish indicative patterns. The table also defines the parameters within which the general ratio statement functions.

Following the lead of McGrath, data were collected by classification letter/number in order to plot the ratio pattern from that point of view (Figure 3). A display of this type suggests that librarians should examine some of the independent variables such as circulation policy, seating arrangements, collection development emphases, etc., to see why certain classes of material are more heavily/lightly used in-library. Ratios may be explainable—even desirable—but if not, the effect of experimental change could be monitored by this simple method of measuring in-library use.

CLASSED TABULATION OF BOOK AND PERIODICAL USE RATIOS

Class	M.I.T.			Tufts			Wellesley		
	IN-LIB	CIRC	RATIO	IN-LIB	CIRC	RATIO	IN-LIB	CIRC	RATIO
000							3	4	0.8
100							23	43	0.6
200							25	76	0.4
300							50		0.3
400									
500	60	36	1.6				7	16	0.4
600	18	26	0.7				1	9	0.1
700							6	16	0.4
800									
900							37	116	0.3
A				10	5	2.0	195	2	98.0
B				85	356	0.2	48	108	0.5
C				1	11	0.1	10	12	0.7
D				188	289	0.7	95		0.8
E				93	187	0.5	39	44	0.9
F				25	54	0.5	22	28	0.7
G				26	92	0.3	15	17	0.9
H				260	598	0.4	211	196	1.2
J				69	130	0.5	60	56	0.6
K				51	17	3.0	6	18	0.4
L				71	163	0.4	28	18	1.6
M				5	62	0.1	5	3	1.7
N				17	262	0.1	7	10	0.7
P				667	1188	0.6	287	907	0.3
Q	2568	1581	1.6	124	186	0.7	15	6	3.0

CLASSED TABULATION OF BOOK AND PERIODICAL USE RATIOS (cont.)

	M.I.T.			Tufts			Wellesley		
R	261	91	2.9	63	133	0.5	2	1	2.0
S	22	13	1.7	7	7	1.0			
T	581	290	2.0	49	56	0.9	5	3	1.7
U				8	19	0.4	2	6	0.5
V				0	4	0	1	0	0.0
Z				18	23	0.8	29	7	4.0
*No class				1186	0	—	47	53	0.9

*Tufts: periodicals are unclassed, non-circulating.
Wellesley: a special collection of recreational reading is unclassed.

FIGURE 3

There are, of course, any number of ways data collection sheets can be modified to bring out information significant to the management of specific collections while simultaneously providing the over-all ratios reported in these inter-library comparisons. As an example of the possibilities, the M.I.T. Science Library analyzed book use apart from periodical use to determine ratios for heavily used subclasses in that collection. With few exceptions, as is shown in Figure 4, in-library use matched circulation or was slightly more; the library's over-all ratio, therefore, is uniform within the parameters of 0.7 to 2.1.

A further example of data manipulation is shown in the display in Figure 5 which provides information about daily in-library use of periodicals at M.I.T.'s Science Library. Variations were also explored in the other libraries involved in this study; however, the examples in Figures 4 and 5 are sufficient to suggest the potential usefulness of the simple data collection method employed.

This study served as a useful preliminary step in establishing the ratio of in-library use to circulation use for the three participating libraries. The methodology employed proved simple enough to be applicable in virtually any library without the need for cumbersome and costly studies, unacceptable demands on manpower, or great sophistication in quantitative measurement. If the study is repeated for a statistically valid sample of days within a year, the ratios suggested here can be confirmed or refined. With the qualification that the figures represent only the majority, not the totality, of in-library use of all materials available to clients, the ratios provide administrators with quotable and more nearly accurate measurement of the use of their library's holdings. Breakdowns of the data collected in order to display ratio statements for specific subject areas can be used, for example, in designing library space allocations: more reader spaces should be pro-

M.I.T. SCIENCE LIBRARY — FEB. 7-20, 1977
BOOKS

CLASSES	IN-LIB	CIRC	RATIO
Q	27	13	2.1
QA	514	558	0.9
QB	39	20	2.0
QC	369	361	1.0
QD	270	237	1.1
QH	75	98	0.8
QK-QM	39	35	1.1
QP	140	106	1.3
QR	28	28	1.0
R	118	91	1.3
S	12	13	0.9
T,TJ,TL	68	78	0.9
TA,TN,TS	92	78	1.2
TD,TP,TR	146	114	1.3
TX	27	20	1.4
500	60	36	1.7
600	18	36	0.7
TOTAL	2042	1912	1.1

FIGURE 4

vided where in-library use is heaviest. They are also indicative of which materials might be stored without seriously discommoding users.

When tallied separately for books and periodicals, this kind of measurement can help monitor changes in policy such as extending or restricting loan periods for different materials or for different types of users. Daily tabulation of ratios can suggest which days will see the heaviest in-library use traffic and require, therefore, more reshelving staff on duty.

It is hoped that other investigators will soon address the more difficult problems not within the scope of this study: (1) an acceptable definition of what constitutes legitimate "use"; (2) reasonably accurate, easily applied methods for calculating similar ratio statements for browsing and for materials reshelved by users; (3) the design and testing of reliable measurement techniques for other types of library holdings used in the library; and (4) determination of the relative impor-

IN-LIBRARY USE OF PERIODICALS M.I.T. SCIENCE LIBRARY
FEB. 7-20, 1977

DATE	LC Classification															TOTALS
	Q	*QA	QB	QC	QD	QH	QK-QM	QP	QR	R	S	T TJ-TL	TA TN,TS	TD TP-TR	TX	
2/7/77 M.	4	6	0	5	12	3	3	8	2	5	0	7	1	5	0	61
2/8 Tu.	10	4	0	11	14	6	0	15	8	9	0	5	1	6	5	94
2/9 W.	7	4	0	17	8	9	3	13	6	12	2	5	5	6	3	100
2/10 Th.	14	1	0	37	11	5	0	13	6	5	0	1	2	7	6	108
2/11 F.	5	12	2	20	6	15	4	3	0	10	0	2	2	0	7	88
2/12 Sa.	9	12	3	22	46	15	3	36	3	28	4	14	4	33	4	236
2/13 Su.	13	3	0	4	8	8	2	15	2	5	1	1	3	8	2	75
Week subtotal	62	42	5	116	105	62	15	103	27	74	7	35	18	65	27	762
2/14 M.	6	6	0	2	3	3	0	14	1	5	0	1	0	0	0	42
2/15 Tu.	7	5	0	8	25	27	4	12	0	14	0	1	0	1	2	112
2/16 W.	7	2	0	6	6	7	0	26	0	6	0	4	2	7	1	71
2/17 Th.	9	9	0	18	12	9	2	40	6	8	0	6	2	4	3	136
2/18 F.	12	3	0	7	16	13	0	34	5	14	3	1	9	12	2	125
2/19 Sa.	7	9	1	6	26	8	2	41	3	19	0	2	10	6	15	155
2/20 Su.	3	1	2	8	11	11	0	18	2	3	0	1	0	6	5	65
Week subtotal	51	35	3	55	99	78	8	185	17	69	3	16	23	36	28	706
TOTALS	113	77	8	171	204	139	23	288	44	143	10	51	41	101	55	1468

*Only QA (Math) periodicals circulate, there were 77 in-library uses to 125 circulation uses (ratio of 0.6:1)

FIGURE 5

tance of each of the wide variety of factors which influence in-library use to circulation ratios in specific library environments. Although this modest study is clearly a small step in the evolving process of measuring library service, it confirms that henceforth no discussion of library use is complete without consideration of the in-library component of that use.

REFERENCES

Bush, G. C.; Galliher, H. P.; and Morse, Philip M. "Attendance and Use of the Science Library at M.I.T." *American Documentation* 7 (1965):87-109.

Fussler, Herman H., and Simon, Julian L. *Patterns in the Use of Books in Large Research Libraries.* Chicago, IL: University of Chicago Library, 1961.

Hamburg, Morris et al. *Library Planning and Decision-Making Systems.* Cambridge, MA: The M.I.T. Press, 1974, p. 4.

Harris, C. "A Comparison of Issues and In-Library Use of Books." *Aslib Proceedings* 29 (1977):118-126.

Jain, A. K. "Sampling and Short-period Usage in the Purdue Library." *College and Research Libraries* 27 (1966):211-218.

———. "Sampling In-Library Book Use." *Journal of the American Society for Information Science* 23 (1972):150-155.

McGrath, William E. "Correlating the Subjects of Books Taken Out and Books Used Within an Open-stack Library." *College and Research Libraries* 32 (1971):280-285.

Morse, Philip M. *Library Effectiveness: A Systems Approach.* Cambridge, MA: M.I.T. Press, 1968, pp. 84-85.

Saracevic, T.; Shaw, W. M., Jr.; and Kantor, P. B. "Causes and Dynamics of User Frustration in an Academic Library." *College and Research Libraries* 38 (1977):7-18.

Seymour, Carol A. "Weeding the Collection: A Review of Research on Identifying Obsolete Stock." *Libri* 22 (1972):137-148. (Augmented by working papers SC 32a and SC 32c of the Library Management Research Unit now at Loughborough University, England.)

Smith, Joan M. B. "A Periodical Use Study at Children's Hospital of Michigan." *Bulletin of the Medical Library Association* 58 (1970):65-67.

APPENDIX: SAMPLE DATA COLLECTION SHEET

CLASS	DATE: BOOKS PERIODICALS ALL	DATE: BOOKS PERIODICALS ALL	DATE: BOOKS PERIODICALS ALL	DATE: BOOKS PERIODICALS ALL
000				
100				
200				
300				
400				
500				
600				
700				
800				
900				
A				
B				
C				
D				
E				
F				
G				
H				
J				
K				
L				
M				
N				
P				
Q				
R				
S				
T				
U				
V				
Z				
NO CLASS				
TOTAL				

The Cost-Benefit of a Book Detection System: A Comparative Study

by Donald L. Ungarelli

INTRODUCTION

During the late 1960s and early 1970s, a serious problem confronting academic libraries was the high loss factor of library materials. The social unrest of the times may have contributed to the problem. Unfortunately, the tight financial exigencies facing institutions of higher learning, and the spiralling inflationary trends have further compounded the situation at a deleterious level. Library budgets, too, were drastically cut. In some instances, the budgetary cuts, the inflationary trends, and the high losses have contributed to the difficulties encountered by libraries in developing retrospective and current collections.

Essentially, library administrators must allocate funds to those programs that enhance the over-all effectiveness of the library. It must be determined in advance which programs justify the costs; especially since this is an integral part of managing the business affairs of the library. One particular program which warrants consideration is a book detection system. This paper will attempt to answer the following questions: (1) What are the annual losses in a college library? (2) What are the annual losses in a college library utilizing a book detection system? (3) Are all books lost permanently? and (4) What are the cost-benefits of a book detection system? The answers to these questions are necessary for both the library profession and the library administrator alike. As an integral part of the decision-making process, library administrators must be more cognizant of the cost-benefits of programs—particularly because the inflationary trends and the budgetary cuts will probably continue into the 1980s.

NEED FOR THE FIRST STUDY

Five years after a complete inventory of the entire circulating collection was conducted a search service was developed in the Fall of 1971 to locate materials that could not be found in the bookstacks. The problem was compounded by an open bookstack arrangement, poor exit controls, and classrooms in the library building. In 1972, this search service indicated that one of ten books could not be readily located after repeated searches. Therefore, a plan was designed to conduct an inventory of the 280,000 circulating books by employing the random sampling technique (from this point forward, this shall be known as the first study).

METHODOLOGY AND DESIGN—FIRST STUDY

Based on the search service, it was estimated that the loss factor would be 10 percent. Before the sample was chosen, it was determined that the percent of missing books would be checked against a 95 percent confidence interval, and the lower and upper limits would be obtained.

The sample was obtained from the shelf list rather than the public catalog. The cards were chosen by a set number of inches (three inches) rather than a set number of cards by drawers. At the time of the sample selection, there were 1,816 linear inches in the shelf-list drawers, excluding the reference and rare book collections. The sample finally selected represented 605 cards. The decision to use a set number of inches rather than a set number of cards by drawers was motivated by the fact that some drawers had two to three times as many cards as others. Also, it made the selection process faster because it did not involve counting X number of cards before a card was chosen and it did not bias the sampling. The cards were photocopied on 8½ by 14 paper.

After the completion of the above procedures, the samples were checked in the bookstacks, in circulation or on reserve. Any books that were not located in the bookstacks, in circulation, or on reserve after the third search nine weeks later were designated as lost.

RESULTS—FIRST STUDY

The first search indicated that the percentage of losses were 15 percent, approximately five percent higher than the original estimate. However, after two additional searches nine weeks later, there were 49 books still missing, representing an 8.1 percent loss factor. Checking this loss against a 95 percent confidence interval, the lower limit would be 5.88 percent and the upper limit would be 10.32 percent. The chances were 95 times out of 100 that the missing volumes would be within the lower and upper limits, and that the best possible estimate was 8.1 percent. If the sample was truly random, and if each of the cards from the population had an equal probability of being selected, the sample was unbiased, and the missing volumes would be between the lower and upper limits.

Fussler and Simon stated:

> Past use, where sufficient data are available, was found to be the best single predictor of the future use of a book, and . . . with no records of prior use, the single predictor variable is publication date.[1]

Because the last complete inventory of 1967 had purged all missing volumes, and the collection more than doubled in size between 1967 and 1972, the basic assumptions of this paper are that there is a correlation between loss rate and the publication date of materials, and that there is a correlation between loss rate and the use of materials. Basically, the more recent publications are more susceptible to losses.

It was assumed that the 8.1 percent loss factor was for the entire collection. This assumption was based on the fact that 242 volumes had publication dates prior to 1967. At the end of the search period, nine volumes were missing with publication dates prior to 1967, and forty volumes were missing with publication dates between 1967 and 1972. Table 1 indicates the percent of the sample for each of the categories and the percent of missing volumes by categories. If this assumption is valid, over the six-year period 1.49 percent of losses represents titles prior to 1967, and 6.61 percent represents losses with titles between 1967 and 1972. Therefore, the cumulative loss factor was extrapolated into an average annual loss of 1.35 percent for the six-year period. The 8.1 percent loss factor represented a significant number of assumed missing volumes (.0810 X 280,000 = 22,680). If arbitrarily it was decided to replace all missing volumes, the cost to repurchase would have been $294,484 (excluding searching, reordering, cataloging and processing costs). Based on the results of this survey, a book detection system was recommended to be purchased for installation in January of 1973.

COST ANALYSIS APPLIED TO FIRST STUDY

By purchasing the system, the institution saved approximately $3,635 rather than utilizing the rental/purchasing agreement plan. Once this decision was made, it was necessary to determine the number of detectors to be inserted into the present collection. Trueswell (1965, 1969) suggests that 80 percent of circulation can be satisfied by 20 percent of the library's holdings. Analysis of the circulation records over a four-week interval indicated that 83 percent of circulation could be satisfied by 35 percent of the 280,000 books. However, all new books acquired by the library would be automatically sensitized. Books that were not sensitized during the installation period would be treated with the detectors only if they had been returned from a circulation loan period.

The next question to be raised was: What would be the cost to insert a detector in each book? To estimate this cost, three support

---

[1]Herman H. Fussler and Julian L. Simon. *Patterns in the Use of Books in Large Research Libraries* (Chicago: University of Chicago Press, 1961), 15.

staff members were timed inserting detectors into a group of books. During a one-hour interval, the numbers inserted by each of the three were: 325, 297, 289. The estimated cost to insert one detector in a book was estimated to be approximately 1 cent. The library administrator costs were, therefore, 11 cents per book. Listed in Figure 1 is an analysis of the installation and annual costs:

Set-up Needs		Costs
Equipment:		
one sensing unit		$15,723.00
five book check units		
one locking turnstile		
Installation and delivery		$ 850.00
Detectors (98,000 X .11)		$10,780.00
	TOTAL	$27,353.00

Continuing Needs		Costs
Detectors (25,000 X .11)		$ 2,750.00
Maintenance		$ 420.00
	TOTAL	$ 3,170.00

FIGURE 1

A basic assumption of this paper is that a book detection system must significantly cut losses to justify the costs. If all of these volumes were actually lost, it is assumed that only 35 percent of these volumes would be replaced based on the circulation analysis (.35 X 22,680 = 7,938). This figure represents assumed losses that would have to be replaced, but does not account for volumes that eventually come back. Based on the search service, 7.8 percent of missing volumes show up again. However, because many users do not utilize the service, this figure may be misleading. Bommer and Ford (1974) suggest a return rate of 13 percent while Ayres (1975) suggests a figure of approximately 45 percent after three years. Basically, each library will have to apply different strategies to estimate this percent. As previously noted, this investigator utilized the 7.8 percent figure simply because the search service generated approximately 3,151 requests of known lost books over a four-year interval. These books were checked every semester and only 246 did eventually show up. Thus, the predicted losses are reduced by the above percentage and the cumulative losses would be 7,319.

It is further assumed that losses must be cut by 90 percent for the system to be cost-justified. This assumption is based on the following premises: (1) machines are not 100 percent efficient; (2) only 35 percent of the collection was originally sensitized; (3) normal losses will occur with or without the system; and (4) as collections increase in size and as user demands increase, the more likely it is that materials will be missing.

Therefore, employing at least a 90 percent efficiency rating for the system towards the number of missing volumes, approximately 6,587 volumes would have been protected from losses. It is assumed that because of instructional demands these materials must be replaced. It would cost $140,303 for the six-year period or $23,384 annually to replace these materials. Table II indicates the estimated labor costs of replacing a missing book in 1972; this figure was added to the purchase price of $13.00. This estimated cost is comparatively low considering that Dougherty and Leonard (1970) and Dougherty and Maier (1971) suggest estimated costs between $15.00 and $20.00. The cost calculated for this library assumes that cards for these books are not always pulled and only minor changes may be necessary. Based on the results of this cost analysis for the first study, the second study attempted to test the cost-benefits of the book detection system over a four-year interval.

METHODOLOGY AND DESIGN—SECOND STUDY

The sample was chosen from the shelf list rather than the public catalog. Again, a fixed number of inches (three) was used rather than a fixed number of cards per drawer. The random sample was obtained from books with a publication date of 1973 through 1976 (a four-year period). Since books published in 1977 were probably on the shelves for only one month to twelve months, they were excluded from the sample. However, if some of the items chosen in the sample represented titles purchased within a year with publication dates between 1973 and 1976, the results would be biased. Therefore, it was decided in advance of the sampling procedures to obtain a large enough sample to correct this possible bias. At the time of the sampling selection, there were 2471 linear inches in the shelf-list drawers excluding the reference and rare book collections. Trying to obtain a sample from the approximately 62,568 books cataloged for the circulating collection during the period 1973 through 1976 proved to be a very tedious task. Many times the process involved flipping through hundreds of cards before the appropriate publication dates were located. Eventually, there were 655 items chosen for the sample.

The samples were checked in the bookstacks and any items found or missing were noted. Items that were not located in the bookstacks, in circulation, or on reserve were designated as missing after the third search, two weeks later.

RESULTS—SECOND STUDY

The first search indicated that there were fourteen books missing. This represents a loss of 2.14 percent. After two additional searches were made there were ten books presumed missing. This represented a loss factor of 1.53 percent for a four-year period, or a 0.38 percent average loss annually. Table 3 indicates the number of samples in each year and the percent of missing books.

Solving for the accuracy of the 1.53 percent at the 95 percent confidence interval, the lower limit and the upper limit would be 0.57 percent and 2.49 percent. If the sample was unbiased, the chances were 95 out of 100 that the losses would fall between 0.57 percent and 2.49 percent.

Applying the loss rate to the number of books in the population, the cumulative loss would be 957 books with publication dates between 1973 and 1976. Assuming that, over a period of one year, approximately 7.8 percent of the books return, the cumulative loss would now be 882. In the previous cost analysis study, only 35 percent of the losses would be replaced, and if this application is utilized, the total number of missing books to be replaced would be 309. Utilizing the average price per book during this four-year period ($14.70) and the estimated labor costs from Table II, it would cost approximately $7,107 to replace these materials or, $1,776.75 annually. However, assuming that labor costs increased during the four-year period approximately 20 percent, the annual cost would be $2,132. Therefore, the book detection system has cut annual book loss costs by more than 90 percent ($23,384 versus $2,132).

Unfortunately, if the installation and annual costs over this four-year interval are added to the present cumulative loss costs ($40,033 + $8,528 = $47,140), the book detection system had only begun to pay for itself in the third year of operation. Undoubtedly, as the system is used after X number of years, the cost-benefits become greater. Based on the results of this comparative study, library administrators would do well to consider the cost-benefits of a book detection system as a program that warrants funding and that would contribute to the overall effectiveness of the library.

CONCLUSIONS AND RECOMMENDATIONS

The strategies outlined in this comparative study described methods that may be of value to others in estimating book losses. Although the main intent of this study was to evaluate the cost-benefits of a book detection system, the results presented evidence that the random sampling technique can also be an effective tool in analyzing the rate of loss without entailing the unnecessary expense of doing a complete inventory. However, depending on the methodology and design utilized in the sampling technique, the analysis may indicate which areas of the collection need selective inventories. The decision rule to apply may vary from library to library, but this investigator would recommend rates between 3 percent and 5 percent.

Based on the results of this study, the book detection system cut losses more than 90 percent, thus justifying the installation and annual costs. By extrapolating the cumulative loss rates into cumulative monetary losses and into annual monetary losses, a more cogent depiction was made from which to analyze the cost-benefits. This method enables the administrator to observe what the cost-benefits would be for a system rather than using raw percentages.

Additionally, this study reinforced the concept that library administrators must allocate funds for programs that contribute to the overall effectiveness of the library. The increasing demands for information placed on libraries by users have shown the need for more appropriate planning in establishing the future direction of operations and services. Especially during a period of limited budget allocation, library administrators must make decisions that are cost-effective. Decisions based on intuition and tradition are not effective managerial techniques.

Finally, this study reemphasizes that there is a correlation between loss rate and publication date, and that there is also a correlation between loss rate and the use of materials.

BENEFITS AND IMPLICATIONS OF THE STUDIES

As noted previously, the random sampling techniques can be effectively utilized to evaluate the loss rate without undue expenses of time and energies. The results of this comparative study are potentially applicable to other areas of concern for librarians. For instance, the sampling strategies indicated that four subject areas, i.e., education, literary history and American authors, psychology, and philosophy, have the highest loss rate. Philosophy, however, is not a high volume use area while the others are. Why has this happened? What factors are affecting the loss rate in these areas? Is it the difference in the size of the collections or are there more current materials in these collections than others? Is the curriculum different in these areas? Are there more majors in these subject disciplines? Is there a need to have duplicate copies in these areas? Will duplicate copies alleviate the problem? What are the budget implications? What effect will this have on the collection development policy? There are probably numerous other questions to be raised and whether answers to these questions may be forthcoming will depend on further research. This investigator intends to conduct complete inventories of these four subject areas and analyze the circulation patterns in an attempt to answer some of the questions as well as to determine the factors affecting the loss rate. Chen (1976) succinctly stated:

> But experience has taught us that librarians, in order to present well-grounded budgetary requests and to compete with other programs for limited resources, can no longer present arguments based on their own or their colleagues' judgement and experience. They need hard and cold facts and measurements, knowledge of the effectiveness of their collections, services, and activities, and predicted knowledge of future use and demand.[2]

[2]Ching-chih Chen. *Applications of Operations Research Models to Libraries* (Massachusetts: The M.I.T. Press, 1976), 101.

REFERENCES

Ayres, F. H. "Letter to the Editor." *College and Research Libraries* 36 (March 1975):153.

Bommer, Michael, and Ford, Bernard. "A Cost-benefit Analysis for Determining the Value of an Electronic Security System." *College and Research Libraries* 35 (July 1974):270-79.

Dougherty, Richard M., and Leonard, Lawrence E. *Management and Costs of Technical Processes: A Bibliographical Review, 1876-1969.* Metuchen, NJ: Scarecrow Press, 1970.

Dougherty, Richard M., and Maier, Joan M. *Centralized Processing for Academic Libraries.* Metuchen, NJ: Scarecrow Press, 1971.

Fussler, Herman H., and Simon, Julian L. *Patterns in the Use of Books in Large Research Libraries.* Chicago: University of Chicago Press, 1961.

Trueswell, Richard W. "A Quantitative Measure of User Circulation Requirements and Its Possible Effect on Stack Thinning and Multiple Copy Determination." *American Documentation* 16 (January 1965): 20-25.

Trueswell, Richard W. "Some Behavioral Patterns of Library Users: The 80/20 Rule." *Wilson Library Bulletin* 43 (January 1969):458-461.

APPENDIX TABLE I
SAMPLE RESULTS FOR SIX-YEAR PERIOD

Publication Dates	Number of Volumes by Dates	Number of Volumes Missing	Percent of Volumes by Publication Dates	Missing Percent of Publications
Prior to 1967	242	9	.40	1.49
1967 to 1972	363	40	.60	6.61
TOTAL	605	49	100	8.10

APPENDIX TABLE II
ESTIMATED LABOR COST FACTORS FOR THE REPLACEMENT OF LOST OR MISSING BOOKS

DEPARTMENT	ACTIVITY	RATE X TIME*	INCREMENTAL COST	TOTAL
Circulation	Catalog verification	$0.0333 x 3	$0.10	
	Shelf check	0.0333 x 6	0.20	
	File check	0.0333 x 3	0.10	$0.40
Catalog	Shelf list	0.0333 x 3	0.10	
	Official catalog	0.0333 x 3	0.50	
	Public catalog	0.0333 x 15	0.50	
	Check "Dead File"	0.05 x 6	0.30	1.00
Subject Specialist	Judge to replace	0.0833 x 6	0.50	0.50
Acquisitions	Search	0.0333 x 9	0.30	
	Place order	0.0833 x 18	1.50	
	Receive	0.0833 x 18	1.50	
	Pay Invoice	0.0833 x 12	1.00	4.30
Catalog	Catalog	0.0833 x 12	1.00	
	Process for shelf	0.05 x 6	0.30	
	Adjustment of catalog record	0.05 x 12	0.60	1.90
Circulation	Proofread	0.0833 x 1.2	0.10	
	Shelve	0.0333 x 3	0.10	0.20
			TOTAL	$8.30

*Rate expressed in dollars per minute. Time expressed in minutes. Staff members were actually timed in the procedures of replacing missing books. The hourly rates ($2.00, $3.00 and $5.00) were first converted into rates per minute, and secondly, multiplied by the number of minutes it took to complete the task. Fringe benefits and overhead costs were not included because staff members would have been doing other tasks as well.

APPENDIX TABLE III
SAMPLE RESULTS FOR FOUR-YEAR PERIOD

Publication Dates	Number of Volumes by Publication Date	Number of Volumes Missing	Percent of Volumes by Publication Date	Missing Percent by Year of Publication
1973	240	2	.3664	0.31
1974	199	4	.3038	0.61
1975	122	3	.1863	0.46
1976	94	1	.1435	0.15
TOTAL	655	10	100	1.53

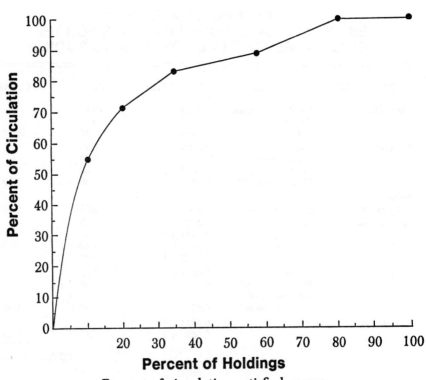

Percent of circulation satisfied versus
percent of holdings satisfied circulation.

APPENDIX FIGURE 1

An Analysis of the Effectiveness and Cost-Benefit of the Checkpoint Mark II Book Detection System Installed in the Library Section of Bristol Community College's Learning Resources Center

by Harvey Varnet

INTRODUCTION AND PROBLEM

This study was done as a companion to Ungarelli's study on the same topic in a large academic library. There are two significant differences in these studies. The first is the size of the libraries. Bristol Community College's Library is relatively small, housing approximately 40,000 volumes. The second significant difference in these two studies is the methodology followed. Ungarelli has used a systematic sampling technique to assess cost benefits, while the technique used at Bristol was an inventory or universal census approach. The universal census approach is one that examines each element in a given population; in this case, the entire book collection was examined.

The decision to install a book detection/security system is an important one. These systems are expensive and it must clearly be shown that they will save money at some point in the near future. For Bristol Community College, the data from our inventories indicated that the loss rate for books was increasing. This trend had enormous economic implications for us, and we decided to investigate the installation of a book detection/security system.

At Bristol Community College, the policy of the Learning Resources Center has always been that the positive aspects of services should be stressed. That is why no fines for overdue books have ever been charged. That is also why a book detection system was not installed earlier than it was, for in effect its mere existence is a negative statement (this point is open to interpretation). For the first ten years of the Library's existence (the college opened in September of 1966), it was felt that a book detection system was not needed. While there were losses, the rate of loss seemed to be acceptable. This, of course, was directly related to our ability to replace missing books. Though funds were not abundant, they were adequate so that most lost or missing books deemed replaceable were indeed replaced.

Funds for library books began to shrink, however, and by Fiscal Year 1976 the ability of the Library to replace lost books was severely hampered. At that point, we started to investigate book detection/security systems. After a year or so of investigation, a Checkpoint Mark II Book Detection System was purchased and installed in October of 1976.

ASSUMPTIONS

Several assumptions were made at the time the system was installed. The vendor had touted an expected reduction in the loss rate of eighty-five percent, and discussions with other librarians indicated that this was likely to occur. Thus, we assumed that the system would work properly and that loss rate would be dramatically reduced.

Another assumption made was that our newer books were those more likely to be used and therefore more likely to be lost or missing. Fussler and Simon (1969), in their study at Chicago, pointed out that age is related to use.[1] If our assumption here was accurate, we were concerned that recent acquisitions would not be available to students and faculty.

Another assumption made was that as our size increased, both in number of books owned and number of students and faculty served, our loss rate would remain constant and/or grow larger unless some type of loss prevention system was installed. A look at the Methodology section of this paper and at Appendix A shows this point to be correct.

HYPOTHESES

Our hypotheses are that the Checkpoint Mark II Book Detection System installed in the Library Section of the Bristol Community College Learning Resources Center is both effective and cost-beneficial. If this is true, then our assumptions are substantially correct, and the decision to install such a system was a good one. Effectiveness was defined as reducing losses eighty-five percent or more. Cost-beneficial was defined as whether or not the costs of the book detection system were less over a period of time than the costs of potentially replacing lost or missing books; in other words, whether or not the book detection system would pay for itself.

METHODOLOGY

It should first be pointed out that sophisticated sampling techniques were not used in this study. The methodology used to test the hypothesis was as follows: Historically, for the past five years, an annual inventory or universal census of the Library's book collection has been conducted. The results of these inventories, for losses, are shown in tabular form as Appendix A. These inventories are supervised by a paraprofessional staff member of the Library, and most of the inventory is performed by student aides reporting directly to this paraprofessional. The procedure for conducting the inventory, though somewhat standard, is very exacting. The Shelf List serves as the master file. Books are matched against the Shelf List. Items checked for each book are: the correct classification number; the title; the author(s); the publisher; the copyright date; and the pagination. Discrepancies occurring between the Shelf List and the book are reported to the paraprofessional in charge, who then supervises the correction of such problems. As a regular part of this process, statistics are kept, by classification, for number of titles and volumes and for number of missing books.

DATA ANALYSIS: EFFECTIVENESS

As Appendix A shows, the first inventory conducted was for the fiscal year 1973. This inventory or universal census served as a record for the first eight years of the Library's losses. Thus, the 2.6% loss rate for eight years translates into an approximate annual loss rate of 0.3 percent. This figure was certainly well within an acceptable range for us.

However, as the succeeding three years' figures show, loss rates rose to 1.3 percent to 1.7 percent. One of the explanations for this increase stems from the fact that in the Spring of 1973 the Library moved from old, very close quarters to a new and spacious building. The new facility allowed for egress in a much more unsupervised manner. Even with an increased loss rate of from .3 percent to 1.3 percent in 1974 and to 1.7 percent in 1975, we were not terribly worried. Our funding was such that we were able to replace most of those books deemed worth replacing (though this task was becoming more difficult).

Then in Fiscal Year 1976, our funding for library materials decreased dramatically, as Table I shows.

TABLE I

LRC'S MATERIALS ACQUISITIONS BUDGET

1971	1972	1973	1974	1975	1976	1977
71,940	79,518	63,015	49,932	50,468	21,586	35,150

With this sudden decrease in funds, our perception as to what was an acceptable loss rate also changed dramatically. The replacement costs for lost books, if replacements continued at the same rate as in previous years (approximately 60 percent of the lost books were being replaced), would place a severe strain on our ability to acquire new titles.

With some thoughts about installing a book detection/security system already in mind, we determined that the inventory following Fiscal Year 1976 would be pivotal in the decision-making process. To provide further information, we added a step to the inventory process to determine what percentage of the collection was satisfying our users' demands. Each book was checked to see whether or not it had ever circulated. This information was collected for each main LC Classification. Appendix B shows in tabular form the percentage of books not having circulated. Appendix C is a graph showing percentage of books used by Library of Congress Classification. While pointing out some interesting aspects concerning distribution of use of the collection, we learned that 61 percent of the collection was circulated. This was matched against our assumption that newer books were more likely to be used and the fact that our inventory results were showing that recent acquisitions were those that were lost or missing (a check of copyright dates on Shelf List cards showed this to be the case).

Given this information, plus the results of the 1976 census, we determined that a book detection/security system was necessary. The Checkpoint Mark II Book Detection System was installed in October of 1976. The data for losses as a result of the Fiscal Year 1977 inventory shows that losses are now at the rate of .2 percent.

DATA ANALYSIS: COST-BENEFITS

In order to determine whether or not the installation of the system has been cost beneficial, the following analysis was completed.

First, the total costs for installing the Checkpoint Mark II Book Detection System were computed. They were:

System Costs	
Library turnstiles	$ 1,450.00
Electronics	4,400.00
Freight/installation	449.00
50,000 labels @ 9.5¢	4,750.00
New library railings	2,560.00
Installation of labels	1,207.50
	$14,816.50

Next, using the average cost per book as reported in *The Bowker Annual,* the loss cost per year was established. These figures are shown as Appendix D. For 1966-1973, the average prices were summed and then divided by eight.

It was also necessary to compute the cost of searching the shelves for a lost book, and then to add to that figure the cost of replacing a missing book. A standardized approach is used once a book is reported lost or missing as a result of the inventory process. This approach is outlined in Table II. The figures given are for the costs incurred by Bristol Community College; they will of course vary from institution to institution.

TABLE II
SEARCH SERVICE

I.	Inventory to discover loss	-separate cost
II.	Catalog Cards pulled	- .075
III.	a. Re-check shelves after 2 weeks	- .06
	b. Re-check shelves after 1 month	- .06
	c. Re-check shelves after 6 months	- .06
IV.	Order/No-order decision (professional)	- 1.80
V.	Ordering costs	- 4.29
VI.	Supervisory costs (10%—an arbitrary figure used by BCC to estimate supervision costs)	
	Total	$6.97

Search Service costs were derived in the following manner. Each function (from II through V in Table II) was analyzed to determine how long it took to complete. Five separate measurements were taken, and the mean of the measurements was used as the standard time needed in order to complete the task. Function II is performed by a library aide. Function III is performed by student aides. Function IV is performed by a professional librarian. Function V is performed by both a semi-professional staff person and student aides. The costs for each function were then computed as a fraction of the performer's salary based on the standard rate of time needed to complete the task.

Using the data from the Fiscal Year 1977 inventory, the following computations were made. Assuming that the pattern of replacement was to continue at 60 percent of the total number of lost books, that number of books was multiplied by the average cost per book. Also factored in was the complete Search Service cost. For the remaining 40 percent of the books lost, steps II through IV, plus supervisory costs (item VI) were computed and added to the other costs. Table III describes the costs incurred as a result of lost books.

TABLE III

COST OF LOST BOOKS PER YEAR

1966-1973	1974	1975	1976	1977
1205.02	6197.32	8930.84	9004.31	1634.88

Noting the difference between 1976 and 1977 replacement costs, the book detection/security system has saved $7,369.43 in its first year of operation.

CONCLUSIONS

It is fair to conclude from the data presented in the data analysis section of this paper that the hypotheses have been verified. If effectiveness is defined as a drop in the loss rate of 85 percent or more, then a drop from 1.7 percent to .2 percent represents an 89 percent drop in the loss rate, thus verifying the hypothesis for effectiveness.

Verifying the cost-benefit portion of the hypothesis has more subjective elements than verifying the effectiveness hypothesis. To determine cost benefits, one has to choose what period of time is acceptable for the installed book security/detection system to pay for itself. If one year is used as a criterion, then the installation of the system at Bristol Community College was not cost beneficial. However, in cases where a one-time capital expenditure is made, it is customary to amortize costs (and thereby denote savings) over a number of years. At the present rate of savings, the book detection system installed at Bristol Community College will have paid for itself in dollars saved on lost books in just a little over two years.

At Bristol, the fact that the book detection system will have saved the amount that it cost in a relatively short time is evidence enough that the decision to install it was correct. However, two other points must also be brought out. The first is that the book detection system's performance has actually meant a healthy percentage increase in funds available for new acquisitions. Less money must now be reserved for replacement of lost or missing titles. In a community college setting, the process of acquiring new and up-to-date titles is extremely important. If use is a function of age in the life of a book (and we believe it is), then with the dollars saved as a result of installing a book detection system we are able to provide the college community with more useful and likely-to-be used books. The second point concerns user satisfaction. With fewer books lost or missing, we are in a much better position to satisfy user demands. This is a difficult area to assess, but our analysis reveals that user satisfaction has indeed increased.

SUMMARY

In summary, we believe that the installation of a book detection/security system at Bristol Community College's Library has provided both an effective method of reducing losses and a successful approach to maximizing already scarce acquisition funds. In a library the size of Bristol's, the inventory or universal census technique appears to be a valid approach to assessing effectiveness and cost benefits. The universal census' main feature is that one can have a high degree of confidence in the data used for analysis. Judgements must still be made, but this technique allows one to make such judgements with a high degree of precision.

A few final comments should be made regarding other benefits derived as a result of this analysis process. The process of determining what part of the collection was meeting the needs of our users presented us with the distribution of use as shown in Appendix C. These figures were somewhat different than what we had assumed to be the case. As a result, an analysis is now being done on our acquisitions patterns. This information is also being correlated with the enrollment figures in the various programs offered by Bristol Community College. Another spin-off as a result of this study is that a collection development policy for the entire Learning Resources Center is being developed. The earlier assumptions we had made concerning use were shown to be incorrect, and this point emphasized even more the necessity for having a written plan for developing the materials collections. Related to the collection development policy, this study also pointed out the difficulty of having a single individual responsible for developing all of the print collection. There are now four staff members involved in this process, each having responsibility along broad subject lines. The size of the collection may be relatively small, but the task of developing it is a complex one requiring the efforts of more than one person. Again, another spin-off of this study has been the realization that a study needs to be made to analyze frequency of circulations for the book collection in order to establish criteria for which books need to be duplicated. As can be readily seen, the process of analyzing the effectiveness and cost benefits of the book detection/security system, while beneficial in and of itself, has led to other data and insights which have proved useful to the overall management of the Learning Resources Center at Bristol Community College.

REFERENCE

Fussler, Herman H., and Simon, Julian L. *Patterns in the Use of Books in Large Research Libraries.* Chicago: University of Chicago Press, 1969.

APPENDIX A
INVENTORY LOSS DATA

Classification	1966-1973	1974	1975	1976	1977
A	3	2	0	2	1
B	20	25	48	71	13
C	0	0	4	0	0
D	52	32	24	37	8
E	41	13	25	33	4
F	15	8	1	12	1
G	41	4	13	2	4
H	101	78	77	65	13
J	26	9	4	11	2
K	20	19	29	37	1
L	37	22	13	3	2
M	19	5	10	0	2
N	42	16	24	15	1
P	164	111	150	117	25
Q	73	18	26	30	6
R	60	44	66	74	8
S	13	4	4	1	1
T	77	25	45	53	10
U	3	0	0	0	0
V	4	1	3	2	0
Z	18	11	23	34	0
Total No. Lost/ Total No. in Collection	829/30,858	447/32,768	589/33,974	599/34,387	102/35,304
Loss Rate/Annual	0.3 (prorated based on 2.6 for 8 yrs.)	1.3%	1.7%	1.7%	.2%
Loss Cost @ 60% Replacement	1205.02 (9640.17/8 yrs)	6197.32	8930.84	9004.31	1634.88

APPENDIX B
VOLUMES REPORTED NOT CIRCULATED
INCLUSIVE TO AUGUST 1976

Classification	No. Volumes in Collection	No. not circulated	% not circulated
A	207	109	53
B	2,539	914	36
C	370	150	41
D	3,434	1,425	41
E	2,125	807	38
F	706	258	37
G	715	144	20
H	4,344	1,216	28
J	1,418	904	64
K	445	196	44
L	1,319	472	36
M	595	251	42
N	889	240	27
P	9,071	4,535	50
Q	2,561	965	37
R	1,374	211	15
S	204	47	23
T	1,183	408	34
U	180	78	43
V	47	14	30
Z	631	211	33
	Total Volumes in Collection	Total Volumes Not Circulated	Percent of Total Volumes Not Circulated
	34,387	13,555	39

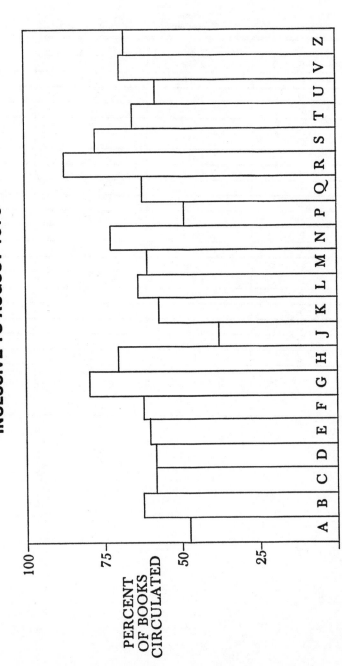

APPENDIX C

DISTRIBUTION OF USE OF PRINT CLASSIFICATION
INCLUSIVE TO AUGUST 1976

APPENDIX D

AVERAGE PRICE PER VOLUME OF A HARD COVER BOOK (ALL CLASSIFICATIONS)

REPORTED IN *THE BOWKER ANNUAL*

Year	Price
1966	$ 7.94
1967	7.99
1968	8.47
1969	8.77
1970	11.66
1971	13.25
1972	12.99
1973	12.20
1974	14.09
1975	16.19
1976	16.32
1977	18.03

Study of the Acquisition Profile — Yale University Library System

by Myra Carbonell

ABSTRACT

This paper presents the results of a study of acquisitions data pertaining to the Yale University Library system extracted from the machine readable files of MATPS-2. Comparisons were made based on different parameters of the acquired materials, such as medium, language, country of origin, vendor and fund. These comparisons, as well as some analyses of parameter fluctuations with respect to time, yielded several interesting results and correlations discussed in the paper.

INTRODUCTION

One of the primary tasks of a library system is the acquisition of new materials. The MATPS-2 (Machine Aided Technical Processing System, version 2) was developed to automate some of the processes and logistics of acquiring new material from many different sources and to aid in the classification and cataloging of newly acquired material. MATPS-2 has been operational since June, 1972 and has processed about 67 percent of the items acquired each year by the entire Yale Library system since 1973. The reason that the percentage is less than 100 percent is that MATPS-2 was basically designed as a monographic system. MATPS-2 includes monographic materials for most (but not all) libraries, newly ordered serials (but not continuing subscriptions), monographs in series when they are cataloged separately, Roman alphabet materials, and Cyrillic and Greek (transliterated) materials. Due to the existence of the MATPS-2 system, much of the relevant data concerning recent acquisitions is stored on disk and magnetic tapes and hence can be readily accessed by computer programs.

The objectives of this study are threefold. First we analyzed the acquisition profile of the Yale Library system with respect to such factors as language of the acquired publication, country of origin, and the vendor who supplied the material. We were interested in creating a clear statistical picture of the library acquisitions pattern and any changes in this pattern that reflect significant trends over the years in which MATPS-2 was active. Our second objective was to analyze fluctuations and correlations among the number of newly acquired volumes as functions of different parameters. Our third and primary objective was to compare acquisition data with circulation data to see if the former reflects the needs and demands of the latter.

We believe it is very important to determine whether the acquisitions of a library system truly reflect the needs of the students and researchers as measured by circulation studies. Furthermore, comparisons of present and future circulation studies with present acquisition patterns should shed considerable light into the problem of determining which of the materials currently being acquired are most needed by the researchers and other people who make use of the extensive collections. Since no statistical circulation studies comparable to our acquisition study have been conducted, we have not been able to fulfill our final objective. We provide, however, data which could easily be used for comparison with a possible future circulation study.

WHAT DATA WERE ANALYZED

The following data were analyzed for the FY 1975-76:

1) Number of items acquired as a function of country in which the items were published;
2) Number of items acquired as a function of the language in which the items were written;
3) Number of items acquired as a function of the medium (e.g. monographs, periodicals, etc.) in which the items were printed;
4) Number of items acquired as a function of the fund which allocated money for their purchase; (This item is probably only of internal interest to the Yale Library.)
5) Number of items acquired as a function of the vendor who supplied the items.

The results of the above analyses for the most significant items appear in graphical representation at the end of this paper. For instance, we graphed only countries which supplied over 500 items a year and vendors which supplied more than 1000 items a year.

In order to determine if there were any significant trends or correlations we analyzed the country and language data as a function of time. Figures 6 and 8 depict the number of items received in each two month period from November 1974 until February 1977 for the eight most significant countries graphed as a function of time. The graphs are presented in two sections for greater readability. Figures 7 and 9 provide the same data, but for the seven most significant languages.

We also conducted cost analyses as functions of several interesting parameters, e.g., country, language, vendor. Unfortunately there was too much noise and missing data to be certain of any possible conclusions. Therefore, these analyses are not included in the present study.

RESULT OF THE ANALYSIS

An interesting result of the breakdown of the total number of items by country and by language is that only 50 percent of all the volumes acquired in FY 1975-76 were written in English and only 39 percent of the total are published in the United States. We suspect that these items account for the bulk of the circulation and reference use. It would be interesting, but logistically complicated, to carry out a circulation study of books as a function of their acquisition parameters (such as language and country of origin). The five countries accounting for the largest number of volumes are in descending order: the United States, Germany, Great Britain, France, and the USSR. The five languages accounting for the five largest number of acquired items are in descending order: English, German, Spanish, French, and Portuguese.

In the breakdown of number of items by their source it is interesting to note that gifts account for more acquired items than any other single source (11 percent of the total number of items acquired). About 3 percent of the items are acquired directly from publishers and the rest are acquired through numerous vendors. It may prove profitable to compare the acquisitions from the vendors accounting for large fractions of the total number of items with the same data for other library systems. This may show that some library systems may not be using a vendor who is popular with other library systems due to discounts, dependability, large selections, or some other compensating qualities.

There were no real surprises in the breakdown of total number of volumes by medium; the vast majority were monographs and serials, as expected, with only 3 percent microfilm. See the chart in Figure 3 for a full breakdown.

Figures 6 through 9 contain a breakdown of the acquisitions from each of the most significant countries and languages as a function of time. There were no net trends towards any given country or language accounting for a larger or smaller percentage of the total acquisitions. In other words, there were no relative increases or decreases of items in one category relative to other categories. The ratio of acquisitions per language to total acquisitions remains constant over the period from November 1974 to February 1977. In a normal distribution about the mean value for each ratio as a function of time, the majority of the data is within one standard deviation of the mean.

The fluctuations in the graphs are not all random noise in the data, however. There is a cyclic 15 percent decline in the total number of volumes received during each September through December period with respect to the yearly average (this is statistically significant; it is a 3 sigma deviation from the norm). The following is a tentative explanation for the cyclic fluctuation. It takes on the average 16 weeks to receive an item after an order has been placed. During the summer months there is an expected decrease in the number of requests for items (there is generally less activity in the university) and library personnel tend to take their vacations during the summer months. Thus one would expect there to be fewer orders placed during the summer months, the effect of which shows up in number of items received about sixteen weeks later (give or take a little), somewhere in the September through December period.

There is a high correlation between the number of items received in certain languages and the number of items received from certain countries. This effect is not at all surprising because, for instance, most items written in Italian are published in Italy. There are, however, some unexpected correlations among the acquisition patterns of certain languages. These same correlations are also manifest in the respective countries. For instance, Figure 9 shows a strong correlation between the number of Portuguese and Italian items acquired, also a strong correlation between the German and French items acquired for each two month period. (The correlation coefficients were .83 and .80 respectively.) We tried to account for these strong correlations by cross-tabulating vendors and languages to see if the same vendors supplied items from both countries. This was not usually the case, at least not sufficiently so as to explain the strong correlations. Thus it remains to be discovered why this interesting effect is present in the acquisition of items in several languages.

There are two sources of error in the data used for this study. First, all the data records were originally entered as punched cards and there were a few errors in mispunching and misspelling country names and vendor names. This error is a small part of the whole and only introduces a small amount of extra noise into the data. Second, about 3 percent of all the items received were rejected and subsequently returned or sold or traded. The 3 percent figure held roughly constant across all major languages, countries, mediums and vendors, hence it is only a constant additive error to each analysis and cancels itself out in comparisons among the analyses.

As a concluding remark we wish to reiterate that the results of this study become much more significant if used as part of a larger study encompassing cross-comparisons among the acquisition patterns of other library systems. We recommend that a circulation study be conducted as a comparison with the results of our acquisition study based on the same parameters. This comparison should tell us which of the newly-acquired material is in circulation and whether a strong demand for some other type of material is not reflected in the acquisition pattern.

Perhaps a sampling method could be devised for conducting an otherwise massive circulation profile study of the different branches of the library system. The ultimate goal of our study is to make acquisitions more responsive to the needs of the library users. Thus, we may establish a statistical feed-back system that enhances the effectiveness of the library system.

INDEX OF ABBREVIATIONS
USED IN THE FIGURES

I) Country	Abbreviation
Argentina	ARG
Australia	AUSL
Brazil	BRAZ
Canada	CAN
Czechoslovakia	CZE
France	FRAN
Germany	GERM
Great Britain	GTBR
Italy	ITAL
Netherlands	NETH
Portugal	PORT
Sweden	SWED
United States	USA
Union of Soviet Socialist Republics	USSR

II) Language	Abbreviation
Czech	CZE
English	ENG
French	FREN
German	GERM
Hebrew	HEBR
Italian	ITAL
Polish	POL
Portuguese	PORT
Russian	RUS
Spanish	SPAN
Swedish	SWED

III) Fund	Abbreviation
African Coll. — Genl. Appropriation	AFRGEN
Cross Campus — Anonymous	ANON68
Automation Project	AUTOM
Bookpool	BKPOOL
Carrie Beinecke Trust	CARBEI
Gift	GIFT
I.P.L. Decision	IPLDEC
Lat. Amer. — Genl. Appropriation	LATGEN
Plain	PLAIN
Slavic Coll. — Genl. Appropriation	SLVGEN
Edward W. Southworth	SOUTHW
Edwin J. & Frederick W. Beinecke	SRLBEI
Serials	SRLPLA
Exchange	XCHANG

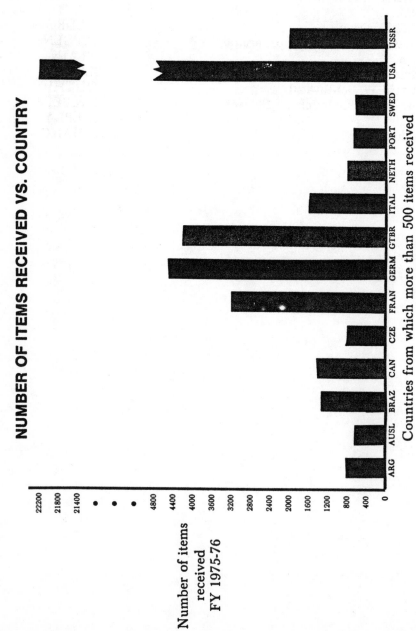

NUMBER OF ITEMS RECEIVED VS. COUNTRY

Number of items received FY 1975-76

Countries from which more than 500 items received

FIGURE 1

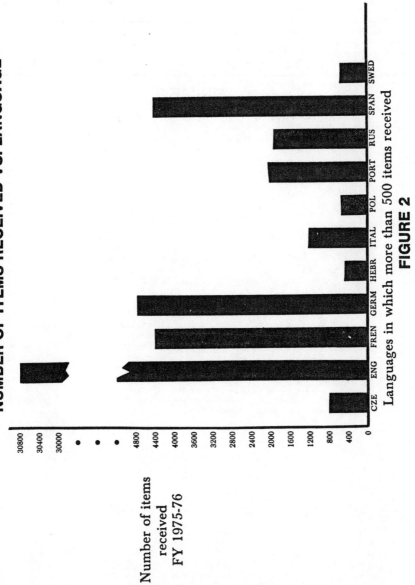

FIGURE 2

NUMBER OF ITEMS RECEIVED BY MEDIUM IN FY 1975-76

MATPS-2

Med Code	Med Type	% of Total	Avg. Cost
0	Books	69%	12.06
1	Periodicals	2%	39.97
2	Microtext	1%	39.29
7	Serials	25%	10.55
8	Monographs in series purchased on standing order	3%	16.59

FIGURE 3

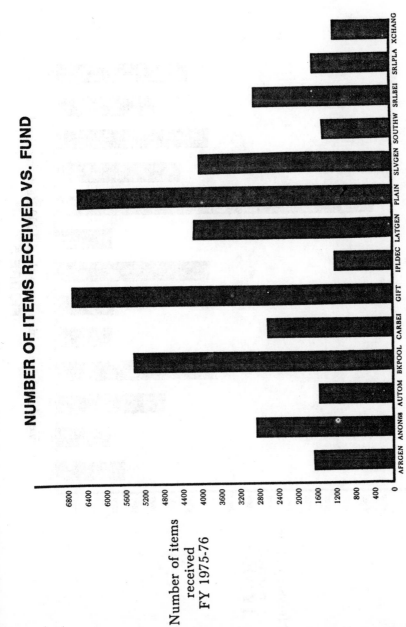

NUMBER OF ITEMS RECEIVED VS. FUND

Number of items
received
FY 1975-76

Funds in which more than 1000 items received

FIGURE 4

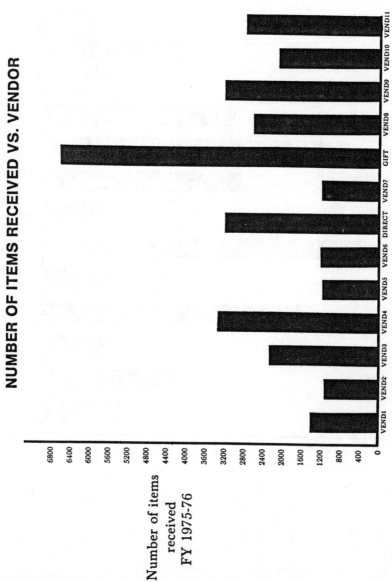

NUMBER OF ITEMS RECEIVED VS. VENDOR

Vendors from which more than 1000 items received

FIGURE 5

NUMBER OF ITEMS RECEIVED VS.
TIME OF RECEIPT
FOR SELECTED COUNTRIES

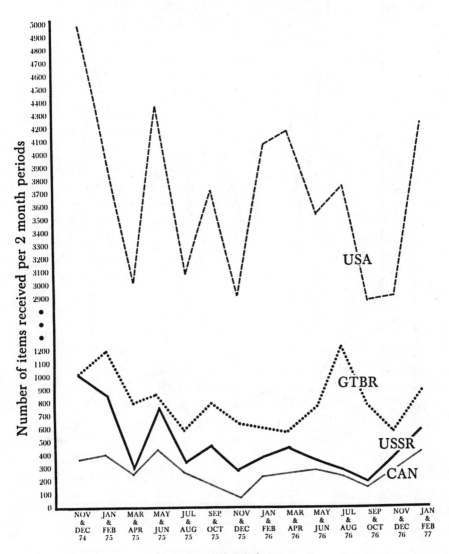

FIGURE 6

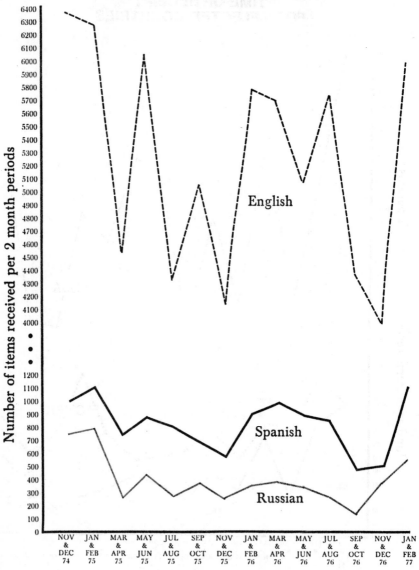

NUMBER OF ITEMS RECEIVED VS.
TIME OF RECEIPT
FOR SELECTED LANGUAGES

Time in 2 month units

FIGURE 7

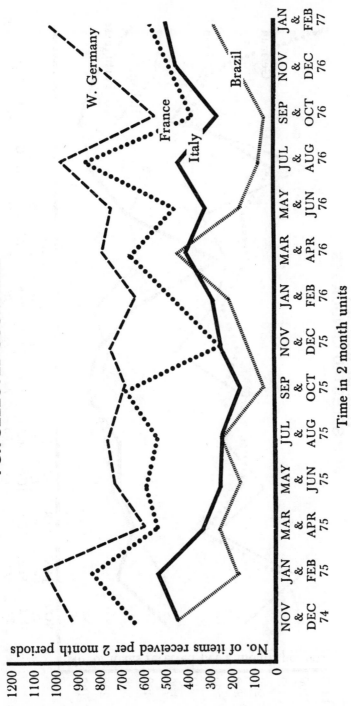

NUMBER OF ITEMS RECEIVED VS.
TIME OF RECEIPT
FOR SELECTED COUNTRIES

W. Germany

France

Italy

Brazil

No. of items received per 2 month periods

1200
1100
1000
900
800
700
600
500
400
300
200
100
0

NOV & DEC 74 — JAN & FEB 75 — MAR & APR 75 — MAY & JUN 75 — JUL & AUG 75 — SEP & OCT 75 — NOV & DEC 75 — JAN & FEB 76 — MAR & APR 76 — MAY & JUN 76 — JUL & AUG 76 — SEP & OCT 76 — NOV & DEC 76 — JAN & FEB 77

Time in 2 month units

FIGURE 8

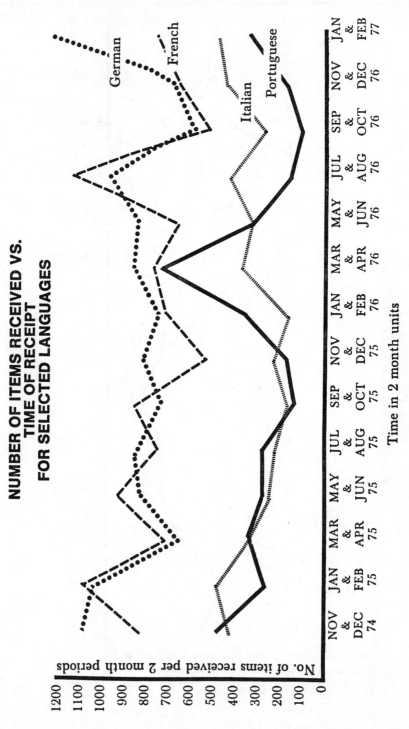

NUMBER OF ITEMS RECEIVED VS.
TIME OF RECEIPT
FOR SELECTED LANGUAGES

FIGURE 9

Survey of a Learning Resources Center: Facilities and Use

by Ethel Apple

INTRODUCTION

The Learning Resources Center (LRC) of a community college provides a combination of materials and a staff of specialists to support the open door philosophy of the institution. This includes all areas and levels of education: transfer, terminal vocational, developmental, and community service programs.

Standards for collections, equipment, and staff are published and easily identified, but statistics on use of the LRC tend to be elusive and vague except for daily circulation counts and head counts of people entering. In these days of pressure for accountability there is a distinct need for more documentation of users and facilities. Provision of curriculum support needs to be evaluated in all areas of operation: public services, technical services and production services.

In 1974 the LRC at Elgin Community College completed a survey in the following areas of public service: title availability; equipment and facilities use; in-library circulation; user characteristics; and, reference service.

The past survey was based on the New Measures of Library Effectiveness utilizing forms and data gathering procedures developed at Rutgers University for the New Measures Pilot Project and adapted by Ellen Altman and William P. Larson for the North Suburban Library System (NSLS). NSLS is a part of the Illinois library network and is headquartered in Wheeling, Illinois. The LRC of Elgin Community College is an affiliate member of the system. Using this background, the 1977 survey took the same categories and completed the first four of them. Forms have been somewhat revised to serve current needs and further analysis, particularly in the user characteristics portion, has been possible with the availability on campus of the Statistical Package for the Social Sciences (SPSS), a "package" of computer programs, for statistical analysis. SPSS development began at Stanford

University in 1965 as an attempt to serve the needs of a select group of users. More recently it has been located at the National Opinion Research Center at the University of Chicago. Currently operating by batch processing methods, plans are being developed for a conversational feature of SPSS. Actual use is much broader than just for areas of social science, and persons without computer experience are able to run SPSS jobs by using a self-instructional manual.

GOALS

This effort to further document the use and performance of the LRC and develop a basis on which to make future management decisions in areas of budgeting, staffing, and ways of providing services to users grew out of our past attempts at performance evaluation and was furthered by the availability of our new computer tool.

The New Measures format covered the areas of materials, staff, and facilities. Our objective was to look at these functions in terms of our service to users, rather than by comparison with operations at other LRC's. The methodology had been developed and tested in a pilot project and further tested by a sizeable number of public libraries and a limited number of academic libraries. Attendance at a workshop for the 1974 survey had provided instruction that was then passed on to other personnel involved in the current data collection.

Ideally, the survey should have been run repeatedly over several days at different times during the week and at various weeks throughout the semester or entire academic year. Limited staff made this approach unrealistic; therefore a day in the middle of the week during a midpoint in the spring semester was chosen for the study. We know from our experience and circulation statistics that the first weeks of the semester are needed for students to get into assignments and that the end of the semester tends to be devoted to exam preparation and review.

TITLE AVAILABILITY SURVEY

Data Gathering Procedure

A sample of 500 cards was drawn from the shelf list by the procedure outlined in Figure 1 and recorded as indicated by Figure 2. In this portion of the survey student workers played the part of users and took pages as identified in Figure 2 and checked the shelf to see if the material was available.

Purpose

This measure is designed to assess a user's chance of obtaining books owned by the library. As originally designed by the North Suburban Library System, a check of the system's union catalog would indicate back-up service provided by interlibrary loan. Because of the time involved, this procedure was done by estimate.

SHELF LIST DISTRIBUTION FORM

Step 1   Take seven different samples from Shelf List and record number of cards per inch in each sample.

Sample 1	91
Sample 2	88
Sample 3	88
Sample 4	87
Sample 5	87
Sample 6	84
Sample 7	89
Sum	614

Step 2   Divide sum above by seven = _____ *88* _____ (Average number of cards/inch)

Step 3   Measure length of shelf list in inches (do not include reference) = _____ *353* _____ (Inches in shelf list)

Step 4   Multiply total inches of shelf list by average number of cards per inch (Step 2 X Step 3) = _____ *31,064* _____ (Total cards in shelf list)

Step 5   Divide total cards in shelf list by 500 (Step 4 ÷ 500) = _____ *62.13* _____ (Number of cards per sample interval)

Step 6   Divide number of cards per sample interval by average number of cards per inch (Step 5 ÷ Step 2) = _____ *.706* _____ (Inches per sample interval in hundredths)

Step 7   Convert inches per interval from "hundredths" to "sixteenths" by means of Index table below = _____ *11/16* _____ (Inches per sample interval in sixteenths)

Index

Hundredths / Sixteenths		Hundredths / Sixteenths	
0.0625 =	1/16	0.5625 =	9/16
.1250 =	2/16	.6250 =	10/16
.1875 =	3/16	.6875 =	11/16
.2500 =	4/16	.7500 =	12/16
.3125 =	5/16	.8125 =	13/16
.3750 =	6/16	.8750 =	14/16
.4375 =	7/16	.9375 =	15/16
.5000 =	8/16	1.0 =	16/16

FIGURE 1

TITLE AVAILABILITY OF 500 SAMPLE TITLES FROM
SHELF LIST
1977

Sample #	Call Number	Author	Title	Date	On shelf

FIGURE 2

Implications

Study findings should have implications for book selection policies, purchase of duplicate copies, reciprocal borrowing arrangements, and interlibrary loan policies.

A relatively high success rate for finding a book on the shelf could give a somewhat false sense of satisfaction to the LRC. Instead the library should examine why the books are on the shelf. Are they out of date? How frequently have they circulated? Do they need repair or replacing? Are they conveniently accessible to the patron?

If the material is not available, can it be obtained on interlibrary loan or by reciprocal borrowing? Should the library purchase additional copies, possibly temporary copies in paperback rather than all hard cover?

In general, how well is the library performing in terms of selecting materials and obtaining information pertinent to the needs of the users?

Analysis

Net results of this survey, Table I, shows that users have a 75 percent chance of finding a needed book on the shelves. Membership in the North Suburban Library System and Illinois Regional Library Council should increase this rate by 10 percent to 15 percent. By comparison with our earlier study the availability percentage has dropped 10 percent. It is possible this is due to increased circulation in specific areas and therefore indicates that the library should examine the possible need for additional copies of books. Because of the size of our library and its relatively recent inception, the practice of purchasing multiple copies has not been extensive. Further manipulations of age and class are possible and it is hopeful we will be able to use SPSS for more detailed analysis.

In a follow up of the Title Availability Survey the computer print out was checked against the listing of books not found on the shelf. Results of this check are found in Table IA. The computer circulation for the survey day showed 33 percent of the books not on the shelf were actually charged out to users. The balance of 67 percent were then misplaced on the shelves, awaiting shelving, or lost.

A further check of the 67 percent missing against the 1976 inventory showed 12 books, or 14 percent missing in this count. This leaves a balance of 53 percent which may be misplaced or awaiting shelving. Completion of inventory in the summer of 1977 will provide further documentation.

TABLE I

Date of Publication	Fiction			000			100			200			300			400			500		
	# Sampled	# On shelf	%	# Sampled	# On shelf	%	# Sampled	# On shelf	%	# Sampled	# On shelf	%	# Sampled	# On shelf	%	# Sampled	# On shelf	%	# Sampled	# On shelf	%
1976	1	1	.002				5	3	.005				2	1	.002						
1975	1	1	.002	2	1	.002	3	3	.006				2	1	.002				2	1	.002
1970-74	9	7	.014	1	1	.002	6	6	.012	2	2	.004	17	15	.03	1	1	.002	10	5	.01
1965-74	6	5	.01	1	1	.002	3	3	.006	4	1	.002	40	37	.074	1	1	.002	14	10	.02
1960-64	5	4	.008				2	2	.004	1	1	.002	29	28	.056	1	1	.002	18	12	.024
1950-59	4	3	.006							1	1	.002	11	8	.014	1	1	.002	3	2	.004
Pre 1950	5	5	.01							2	2	.004	4	4	.008				4	4	.008
Total	31	26	.052	4	3	.006	19	17	.034	10	7	.014	105	94	.138	4	4	.008	51	34	.068

Date of Publication	600			700			800			900			B			AV			Total		
	# Sampled	# On shelf	%	# Sampled	# On shelf	%	# Sampled	# On shelf	%	# Sampled	# On shelf	%	# Sampled	# On shelf	%	# Sampled	# On shelf	%	# Sampled	# On shelf	%
1976	2	2	.004	2	1	.002	1	1	.002	2	2	.004	1	1	.002	3	2	.004	14	11	.022
1975				2	1	.002	3	3	.006	3	2	.004	1	1	.002	3			24	14	.028
1970-74	21	15	.03	16	11	.022	25	17	.034	13	11	.022	4	3	.006	21	7	.014	143	98	.196
1965-69	17	11	.022	9	3	.006	20	15	.03	9	7	.014	6	6	.012	9	3	.006	142	106	.212
1960-64	9	4	.008	11	7	.014	12	11	.022	16	14	.028	3	3	.006				108	88	.176
1950-59	2	1	.002	4	3	.006	3	2	.004	7	6	.012	2	2	.004				40	31	.062
Pre 1950	2	2	.004				4	4	.008	6	4	.008	2	2	.004				29	27	.054
Total	53	35	.07	44	26	.052	68	53	.106	56	46	.092	19	18	.036	36	12	.024	500	375	.75

TABLE IA
STATUS OF BOOKS NOT ON SHELF
TITLE AVAILABILITY SURVEY

Date of Publication	Fiction		000		100		200		300		500		600		700		800		900		B		AV		Total	
	Circulation	Missing	Circulation	Missing	Circulation	Missing	Circulation	Missing	Circulation	Missing	Circulation	Missing	Circulation	Missing	Circulation	Missing	Circulation	Missing	Circulation	Missing	Circulation	Missing	Circulation	Missing	Circulation	Missing
1976										1	1	1				1									1	3	1
1975			1		1	1			1			1	1	1		1	1	1		1				3		8	4
1970-74		1			1	1			2	2	1	4	2	4		5		8	1	1	1		9	2	14	28
1965-69		2					1	2	1	1		4	1	5	1	4	1	4		2			5		12	25
1960-64										2	1	4		4		4		1		2					1	17
1950-59		1							1	2		1		1	1		1	1		1					3	7
Pre 1950																				2						2
Total		4	1		2	3	1	2	3	7	3	14	4	14	2	15	3	14	1	9	1		18	2	41	84
%																									33%	67%

TABLE IB
STATUS OF MISSING BOOKS — 1976 INVENTORY
TITLE AVAILABILITY SURVEY

Date of Publication	200	300	500	700	800	900	Total
1976							
1975							
1970-74				1			1
1965-69	1	1		2	1	1	6
1960-64			1	3		1	5
1950-59							
Pre 1950							
Total	1	1	1	6	1	2	12
%							14%

EQUIPMENT AND FACILITIES USE

Data Gathering Procedure

A count of equipment and facilities usage was taken as indicated in Table II. To gather data for this portion of the survey a list was made of the various kinds and quantity of seating spaces and equipment available for users in the center. Due to staff limitations the study was limited to one day as identified in the goals and objectives. At approx-

TABLE II
EQUIPMENT AND FACILITIES IN USE

Item	No. of Items	Total no. of users	Ave. use per hour	Utilization Factor
Table seats	78	140	10.769	.139
Lounge chairs	21	42	3.231	.154
Carrels	195	190	14.615	.075
Tape player	8	10	.769	.096
Photocopier	1	9	.692	.692
Microform	1	8	.615	.615
TV	2	11	.846	.423
Record player	2	1	.077	.039
Film strip	1	2	.154	.154
Movie	1	2	.154	.154

imately half past each hour from 8:00 A.M. to 9:30 P.M. a count was taken by a staff member moving throughout the room to record use in each category. Average hourly use was determined by dividing the total count by 13, the number of hourly counts made during the day. Utilization factor was determined by dividing the average use per hour by the total number of items available.

Purpose

The purpose of the activity was to calculate utilization of facilities and equipment available. Performance of the LRC should be at least quantitatively indicated by these counts.

Implications

This portion of the study should have implications for future purchasing of equipment, space utilization, and staffing patterns.

This count gives no indication of the number of different persons at any one station during the hour, nor for how long a time they were there. A continuously active station at each count would certainly lead to consideration of purchasing additional equipment or adding more seating space. Total counts also indicate heavy periods of use during the day when more staff could be used to provide service. Unfortunately there was no way in this study to determine what equipment a user might have used if it had been available.

Analysis

From this profile, it would appear that both facilities and equipment are adequate. An important consideration, however, is the fact that these are averages based on a count once every hour. In many instances there are multiple users during the hour. At peak hours of the day, there are always times where users are waiting for the copier, microform reader/printer, television, etc. Though there is always a choice of table or carrel seats, the best areas are not always available. Class assignments dictate to some extent periodically heavy use of microfiche, television and other equipment.

In comparison with the earlier survey, use of table seats remains constant, lounge chairs increased 4 percent, and carrel seats increased 3 percent. Use of the photocopier increased 44 percent. This is always in demand and there was no particular indication of any single influencing factor for the day. Microform reader/printer use has increased by nearly 62 percent. This is to be expected due to increased purchase of software in this area. Television and movie projectors were not in use in the center at the time of the first survey.

A continued watch needs to be kept so that patrons do not encounter undue waits at peak times. Because of the nature of the community college student's schedule, users cannot always return to the LRC during slow demand time for equipment. With two television tape players in the center, the utilization factor was 42 percent. This is a significant figure, considering the fact that no courses taught primarily by television were currently being offered. If and when a course such as "The Ascent of Man" might again be given, there would be an immediate need for additional equipment.

IN-LIBRARY CIRCULATION

Data Gathering Procedure

Student workers were informed not to shelve materials left on tables and carrels. Numerous signs (Figure 3) were placed throughout the center requesting users to also leave materials out for collection. Periodically, these items were collected, recorded, and put away.

The LRC is conducting a survey today. Please do not reshelve any materials — leave them on tables or in carrels for our staff to collect. Thank you

FIGURE 3

Purpose

This portion of the study was designed to provide a more accurate indication of use of materials than a simple record of daily circulation activity. Some kinds of library materials, particularly non-circulating items such as reference books and periodicals are known to be excluded from the daily circulation count. In addition to these it was assumed other items, probably mostly nonfiction, were used on the premises in a "study hall" situation and never removed from the center. Such in-library use is considered to be a valid part of the circulation statistics.

Implications

The publication data and classification of these items gives a profile of library use indicating a need for up-to-date reference sources with a lesser need for old newspapers and periodicals. These findings should provide direction in selecting new materials, determining how long to maintain back files of periodicals, and weeding the collection to make space for materials in demand.

Analysis

Total in-library circulation indicated in Table III was 245 items. The largest number was represented by current newspapers and periodicals. Reference materials and circulating nonfiction far outnumbered fiction. Average daily library circulation was 139 as shown in Table IV. In-library use was approximately 75 percent higher than outside use. Again, this portion of the survey gives a more comprehensive picture of LRC use.

TABLE III
IN-LIBRARY CIRCULATION

Date of Publication	Reference	Fiction	Nonfiction	Newspapers & Periodicals	Total
1977			2	41	43
1976	16		2	29	47
1975	9		4	8	21
1970-74	22	1	33	16	72
1965-69	12	3	17	1	33
1960-64	2		13	1	16
1950-59	2	1	7		10
Pre 1950			3		3
Total	63	5	81	96	245

TABLE IV
OUTSIDE OF LIBRARY CIRCULATION

Month	No. of Days	Total Circulation	Daily Average
August	7	889	127
September	21	3124	149
October	20	3310	166
November	18	2521	140
December	13	1161	89
Total	79	11005	671
Average			139

USER CHARACTERISTICS

Data Gathering Procedure

A questionnaire (Figure 4) was distributed to users entering the LRC. A large poster was at the door telling what was being done and a collection box was placed at the exit door so complete anonymity was maintained. No pressure was exerted on persons not wishing to complete or turn in their questionnaires. By an electronic counter on the door we know that the number of persons who entered the center participated in the survey was about 80 percent.

Purpose

To provide the best possible service it is necessary to have a profile of the user and the amount of time spent taking advantage of the LRC and its services. User reactions are probably the most important.

Implications

Feedback from users helps the staff to take an objective look at their services and themselves. Staffing patterns can be determined by expressing needs of the users. Suggestions and comments can improve existing services and use of the facilities, but a question that arises here is whether users know their needs. If not, how can they know their needs are not being met? If needs are known, can they be adequately expressed?

Analysis

From our past survey we know that users in 1974 were 54 percent male and 46 percent female, mostly part-time students who spent pri-

QUESTIONNAIRE

DIRECTIONS:

Please put an ☒ in the box which best answers each question.
Mark only one box per question.

WHAT IS YOUR STATUS?   **SEX**   **AGE**

Full-time student	☐	Male	☐	18-20	☐
Part-time student	☐	Female	☐	20-24	☐
Faculty/staff	☐			24-30	☐
Other	☐			Over 30	☐

HOW MUCH TIME DID YOU JUST SPEND IN THE LRC?

Under 15 minutes	☐
Approximately 1/2 hour	☐
Approximately 1 hour	☐
Over 1 hour	☐

HOW DID YOU USE THE LRC?   **WHY DID YOU COME TO THE LRC?**

To check out materials	☐
To do research	☐
To read or study	☐
Used listening/viewing center	☐
Used AV production services	☐
Other	☐

Mostly because of assignment.
(Study, research, etc.)   ☐

Mostly for pleasure.
(Read for pleasure, meet
friends, etc.)   ☐

WERE YOU SATISFIED WITH OUR SERVICES?   **DID YOU ASK FOR HELP?**

Yes	☐		Yes	☐
No	☐		No	☐

COMMENTS:

FIGURE 4

marily one hour or less in the library for the purpose of reading or studying. Eighty-six percent of the users were satisfied.

The current profile furnished by the Vice President for Student Affairs gives an enrollment of 5,175 students in 37,383 credit hours. Females outnumbered males 2,687 (52 percent) to 2,488 (48 percent). Of the total students, 1,384 (26 percent) were full time and 3,827 (74 percent) part time. The average age was 27 years and 50 percent are or have been married.

Because of information being collected, nonparametric tests were chosen to test our hypothesis, specifically, the chi square. The chi square statistic was selected as the most appropriate tool for our purposes as it is a procedure to test hypotheses about the relationships between discrete categorical data (nominal measure). By cross-tabulating questionnaire results with the SPSS Package, it is possible to determine whether or not sample data differs significantly from hypothesized statements. Hypothesized statements, of course, can be entirely theoretical or based on previous information and assumptions.

A synthesis of significant cross-tabulation results is shown in Table V. All elements of the questionnaire were examined to determine whether a relationship existed, with the six categories shown in the table indicating significant relationships. Comments for each category are included in the table.

In conclusion, it would seem that our typical user would be a full-time student, 18-20 years old, who uses the LRC to complete a course assignment, is satisfied with the facilities and services, and spends at least one hour in the library.

There are some interesting implications, such as:

1. how to reach those who were not satisfied and did not seek help; and,
2. what were the problems of those few who sought help and were still not satisfied.

Perhaps a manual check should be done for comments made by these users.

SUMMARY

As a result of this study we have identified our users and their known, expressed needs. Further we have examined our collection, equipment and facilities and how they are used. This information should prove valuable as documentation in planning for our future growth as an alert, concerned, user-oriented LRC. Though change is constant, we have identified current strengths and weaknesses in our services. Budget planning to provide continued growth, adequate staffing and facilities is probably one of the best uses for the results of this kind of study.

TABLE V
CROSS TABULATIONS BY SPSS

Categories	Chi Square*	Degree of Freedom	Level of Significance	Comments
Time vs. Status	57.52310	6	<.01	Full-time students are the heaviest users, spending one hour or more.
Time vs. Age	23.82309	9	<.01	Younger students are spending more time, one hour or more.
Status vs. Age	125.83209	6	<.01	Largest volume of use comes from full-time, 18-20 year old student.
Time vs. Purpose	14.75052	3	<.01	76% come because of assignment and are apt to spend over one hour. 24% come for pleasure and are apt to spend a short time.
Status vs. Purpose	8.84513	2	<.05	Mostly full-time student doing assignment (study or research?)
Satisfaction vs. Help	16.83444	3	<.01	94% satisfied and most did not ask for help. 6% were not satisfied and of these, 4% requested help. (What was source of dissatisfaction?)

*See Glossary for definition of Chi Square.

A Study of Life Sciences Book Use in the M.I.T. Science Library: Budgetary Implications

by Sandra Spurlock
and Ellen Yen

THE PROBLEM

Some of the most difficult decisions for librarians to make concern the allocation of funds among monograph and serial accounts when money is scarce and the cost of books is rising. It is desirable to determine which categories of books require the most attention from a budgetary point of view.

In order to most effectively spend budgeted money, librarians try to make budget allocation decisions which will satisfy current and future user needs. In the past, the needs of users have often been estimated on the basis of unsystematic and intuitive criteria. It is difficult to distinguish real user needs from apparent needs which result from a temporarily popular research trend, from well-meant but inaccurate advice from faculty advisors, or from intuitive judgments on the part of librarians.

In order to more accurately measure user needs, a variety of quantitative techniques have been employed by librarians in recent years. These are summarized and reviewed in a recent book by Lancaster (1977). Of particular interest to us are models which allow one to predict the future use of books.

This study addresses the question of how to allocate monograph and serial funds among several accounts in the life sciences. An operations research model is used to measure past use and predict the future use of medical books compared to other books in the life sciences, and the results are used as an aid in making budgetary allocation decisions. It is hoped that the predicted use of books in the collection will accurately reflect future user needs, and that decisions which take into account the measured variables will result in a more effective use of budgeted funds.

OBJECTIVES OF THE STUDY

The objectives of this study are:

1) To measure the past use of books in the life sciences area in the Science Library, and to compare the use of medical books to that of other life sciences books;
2) To predict the future use of medical books as compared to the future use of other books in the life sciences, using the operations research model of book use developed by Philip Morse (1968) and modified by Morse and Chen (1975);
3) To use the measured variables as an aid in deciding whether more monograph money should be allocated for the purchase of medical books in the Science Library;
4) To apply the Morse-Chen model of book use to a selected group of books in the Science Library in order to see how difficult it would be to use this model to evaluate the whole collection in the ways listed above.

HYPOTHESIS

There is a particular need for a study of the use of medical books compared to other life sciences books in the Science Library.

Research in the medical sciences has grown rapidly at M.I.T. in recent years, with 1/3 of the total federally-funded research now being done in the life sciences (*Tech Talk*, March 9, 1977, p. 1). Medical research, as well as programs of study in medically-related fields, is expected to continue to rise in future years. This growth is reflected at M.I.T. by increases in staff, programs of research, and programs of study in the Departments of Biology, Nutrition and Food Science, and Psychology. In addition, a new Cancer Research Center was established at M.I.T. in 1975, and the last two years have seen a proliferation of research and degree programs offered by the joint Health Sciences and Technology Program established between Harvard and M.I.T. Therefore, a measurement of the use of medical and other life sciences materials, and evaluation of the allocation of funds for medical books in order to provide for future use of these materials, are the primary goals of this study.

We anticipate that the results of this study will show:

1) A larger proportion of medical books in the collection are currently used in the Science Library compared to other life sciences books in the collection, and the mean circulation of these medical books is higher;
2) The allocation for medical books from funds for all life sciences books will need to be adjusted in order to provide for future use of medical materials, based upon their current use.

THE M.I.T. SCIENCE LIBRARY COLLECTION

The collection in the Science Library consists of materials in the subject areas of astronomy, biology, chemical engineering, chemistry, materials science, mathematics, nuclear engineering, nutrition and food science, and physics.

The collection consists of approximately 297,599 volumes of which about 51,574 are catalogued by the Library of Congress system. Materials in the life sciences number about 8,424 volumes. For the purpose of this study, we have defined life sciences materials to be monographs and serials with Library of Congress call numbers from QH-RS; we define "medical books" as monographs and serials with call numbers from R-RS, and those with call numbers from QH-QR we designate as "other life sciences books."

The total circulation of all materials in the Science Library for the year 1976-1977 was 61,117. Since the statistics for this total were not broken down by call number, we have no figures for the total circulation of Library of Congress-classed life sciences books for the year 1976-1977.

Materials charged out of the Science Library circulate for four weeks, and may be renewed once. Materials which do not circulate and were not included in this study are books in the Reference and Core Reference collections, items which are on course reserve, and periodicals.

MODELS AND METHODOLOGY

Our basic assumption in approaching this study was that a useful question to ask in order to help make accurate budget allocation decisions for books in the life sciences is "which books are used the most?" Or, more specifically, "are medical books needed more, less, and in what proportion compared to other books in the life sciences?" One way to answer this question is to measure the present use of medical books compared to other life sciences books, and to use a model which will allow us to predict the future use of each category of books.

The most direct way to measure the past use of books is to record their circulation histories. The usefulness of such a study is enhanced when a statistical analysis is made of the data thus obtained. Studies using circulation statistics have been reported by a number of investigators. Many of these studies are summarized and reviewed in a recent book by Lancaster (1977).

Of the methods described by these authors, we decided to use the operations research model of book use which was developed by Morse (1968), tested by Chen in the Countway Library (The M.I.T. Press, 1976) and simplified by Morse and Chen (1975).

The basic operations research model developed by Morse (1968) is based on three assumptions:

1) The process of book circulation is a random one;
2) On the average, book circulation drops off exponentially with time;
3) There is a time correlation from one time period to the next concerning the behavior of book use. So, a book may become popular after having been little used for several years; once such a book becomes popular, the circulation history from then on is as though it had been popular all along.

From data gathered at the M.I.T. Science Library, Morse found that the average behavior of a *class* of books $N(m)$ during its t+1 year depends on its previous year's circulation (year t). From this observation, he developed a linear model which uses probability theory to predict the probable future circulation of a class of books based on the present circulation:

$$N(m) = \alpha + \beta \, m$$

This model says that the average behavior of a class of books $N(m)$ in its $t + 1$ year depends on the previous circulation in year t. α and β are parameters which are measured for each class of books studied. Parameter β measures the rate at which the "popularity" of a book of the class diminishes from year to year. The parameter α is a measure of the mean circulation which a book of the class will eventually reach with time.

Morse's study used statistics which had been gathered from a random sample of books on the shelf. This "collection sample" method, while quite accurate, is tedious and time-consuming to use (Chen, The M.I.T. Press, 1976). An easier way to obtain circulation data is to use a "checkout sample" method, taking statistics from the cards of books in circulation. However, statistics collected in this way are biased toward the active books in the collection, and exclude the books which have not circulated during the sampling time period (Chen, The M.I.T. Press, 1976). The modified Morse-Chen model of book use removes this bias, allowing one to apply the probabilistic model when data are collected from the active books in circulation. The values thus obtained are less accurate than if the circulation histories of a random sample of books on the shelf were recorded, but the information resulting from such a study is said to be accurate enough to be useful in making budgeting decisions (Morse, 1968). This corrected model is expressed as:

$$N(j) = \frac{M(j)}{[1-(1-\rho)^j]} \quad \text{where } j = 1,2,3. \ . \ .$$

$N(j)$ = The expected value of all books which circulated j times this year.

$M(j)$ = The number of books which circulated j times during the sample period (last year).

$[1-(1-\rho)j]$ = The correction factor which corrects the bias.

According to Morse and Chen (1975), the advantages to using the checkout sample method with the Morse-Chen modified model are the following:

1) Data collection is relatively easy, and very quick.
2) Problems of missing data and differing circulation policies in the past are avoided.
3) By collecting a relatively small amount of data, reasonably accurate (within 25 percent) conclusions can be made about the ways in which classes of books are used in the library.
4) Several useful variables of books can be measured.
5) The model allows one to predict the probable future use of classes of books.

In order to charge out materials in the Science Library, borrowers present their embossed plastic M.I.T. identification cards to a member of the circulation staff. Each book has a blue charge card (with author, title, and call number at the top), and a charge slip in the back cover of the book with spaces for date due stamps. When a book is charged out, a member of the circulation staff runs the blue charge card and ID card through an addressograph machine, and the date due is stamped on the book's white charge slip. The blue card is filed in that day's circulation file, and then filed with the previous day's circulation the next morning.

For purposes of this study, we asked the circulation staff not to file the charge cards for books with call numbers QH to QR and all the R's each morning until we could collect the circulation data from the charge cards. Since data collection each morning took less than half an hour in most cases, it scarcely interrupted the daily filing routine of the circulation staff.

By examining the due dates on the charge cards, we were able to record on forms, as shown in Figure 1, the number of times the book circulated.

Call No.		
	1976-1977	5
	1975-1976	6
	1974-1975	5
	1973-1974	4
	1972-1973	4
	1971-1972	6
	1970-1971	__
	1969-1970	__
	1968-1969	__
	1967-1968	__

A sample form for collecting circulation history of a book. Year-pairs indicated by brackets.

FIGURE 1

Each due date represented one circulation; renewals were not counted as separate circulations unless a renewal fell in a different year, as defined below. If a card showed circulation only for the current year (1976-1977), we could use data on that card to describe current circulation behavior, but we could not include it in the year-pair data we used to determine α and β. Because this study was conducted primarily during the month of September, the due dates of most items borrowed during our sampling period fell in October. So, for purposes of this study, a year ran from October to October (Morse, 1975, p. 180).

Circulation history data from the data collection forms (Figure 1) was transferred to two year-pair entry forms—one form for QH-QR data, and one form for R data:

m	n
0	1, 0, 0, 0, 0, 2, 0, 2, 2, 0, 1, 0, 1, 1, 0, 4, 1, 0, 1, 0, 1, 0, 0, 0, 0, 0, 1, 0, 2, 1, 0, 0, 3, 1, 0, 2, 3, 1, 2, 0, 0, 2, 0
1	2, 2, 0, 6, 1, 1, 0, 3, 1, 3, 0, 2, 0, 0, 0, 0, 1, 1, 1, 0, 0, 2, 1, 0, 1, 1, 0, 0, 0, 5, 0
2	4, 0, 0, 1, 2, 0, 1, 7, 0, 0, 0, 1, 1, 3, 0, 4, 2, 2, 0, 0, 2, 3
3	0, 0, 0, 1, 3, 4, 3, 3, 2, 2, 0, 7, 2
4	2, 5, 1
5	1, 0
6	2, 3

Part of the year-pair entry form for R circulation history data, where m = number of circulations in year t, and n = number of circulations in year t +1

FIGURE 2

The data from the year-pair entry forms for QH-QR and R (Figure 2) books were summarized in a final table (Chen, The M.I.T. Press, 1976, p. 44) as shown in Tables I and II where:

M = Total number of examples in the sample

m = Number of circulations in year t

M(m) = Number of examples with m circulations in year t

n = Number of circulations in year t + 1

Nmn = Number of examples which had m circulation in year t and n circulation in year t + 1

N(m) = Average circulation during year t + 1, given that the sample had m circulation in year t. This is computed by dividing the number of books which circulated n times (M(m)) into the total circulations accounted for by those books.

TABLE I

Values of M(m), Nmn and N(m) for different values of m and n for QH-QR books checked out of the Science Library during the sampling period, September 1977.

m	M(m)	Nmn									N(m)
		n=0	1	2	3	4	5	6	7	8	
0	122	39	43	19	15	5	0	1	0	0	1.25
1	138	38	51	27	13	5	2	0	1	1	1.37
2	102	25	37	27	7	3	3	0	0	0	1.36
3	60	11	14	21	9	5	0	0	0	0	1.72
4	24	5	8	3	3	2	1	1	1	0	2.04
5	21	3	7	4	3	2	2	0	0	0	2.0
6	8	0	4	2	0	2	0	0	0	0	2.0
7	3	0	2	0	0	0	0	1	0	0	2.67
8	1	0	0	0	1	0	0	0	0	0	3.0

Total M=479

TABLE II

Values of M(m), Nmn and N(m) for different values of m and n for R books checked out of the Science Library during the sampling period.

m	M(m)	Nmn									N(m)
		n=0	1	2	3	4	5	6	7	8	
0	86	39	22	21	3	1	0	0	0	0	.893
1	60	28	17	9	4	0	1	1	0	0	.966
2	32	11	7	8	2	2	1	0	1	0	1.53
3	13	4	1	3	3	1	0	0	1	0	2.07
4	3	0	1	1	0	0	1	0	0	0	2.66
5	2	1	1	1	1	0	0	0	0	0	3.0
6	2	0	0	1	1	0	0	0	0	0	2.5

Total M=261

The different values of N(m) and m were plotted for QH-QR and R books (Figures 3 and 4). The values of parameters α and β were determined by visual observation. Parameter β is the slope of the line, and parameter α_a is the point on the y axis where m = 0. This value of α_a, must be corrected to account for books that did not circulate at all during the sample period (Chen, 1976, p. 34); this was done by using the equation:

$$^a\!l = C \times \alpha_a$$

C is the fraction of active to live books and is derived in the following way.

First, we used the Morse-Chen extended model (which corrects for the bias caused by having only active books in our sample) to obtain

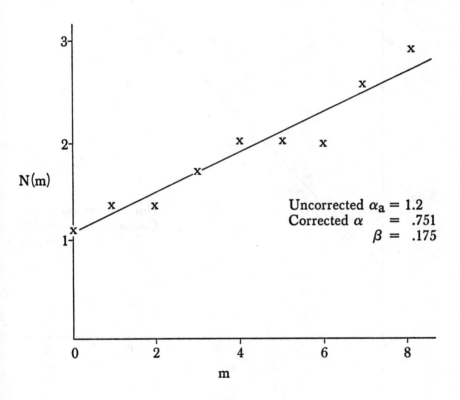

Plot of m vs. N(m) for classes QH-QR. Mean circulation N(m) for year t+1 as a function of year t for QH-QR books.

FIGURE 3

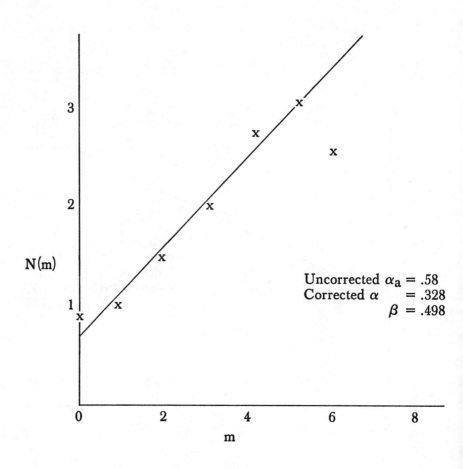

Plot of m vs. N(m) for class R. Mean circulation N(m) for year t+1 as a function of year t for R books.

FIGURE 4

the current circulation distribution. This model is expressed as (10, p. 182):

$$N(j) = M(j)/[1 - (1-\rho)^j]$$
where $j = 1,2,3. . .$

    $N(j)$ = the total corrected number of books of the class that circulated j times.

Since $M(j)$ is the number of books which circulated j times during the year preceding the end of the sample period (1976-1977), a count was made from the circulation data collection forms (Figure 1) of the number of circulations during 1976-1977 for $j = 1,2,3. . .$. The value of p in the correction factor $1/[1-(1-\rho)^j]$ was 1/11 in this study (see Figure 7 and Morse, 1975). The value of the correction factor $\rho = 1/11$ was obtained from a table (Chen, The M.I.T. Press, 1976, p. 29). Thus, for the QH-QR books, where seventy-nine books in the sample circulated one time (j=1) during 1976-1977, and the value of $1/1 - [1-(1-\rho)^j]$ provided by the table is 11:

$$N(j) = M(j)/[1-(1-\rho)^j]$$
$$N(1) = 79/[1-(1-\rho)^1]$$
$$= 79 \times 11$$
$$= 869$$

A final table of the various j, $M(j)$, and $N(j)$ values is shown in Table III:

TABLE III

Corrected circulation distribution for classes QH-QR.

j	1	2	3	4	5	6	7	8	9	10	Total
M(j)	79	55	57	20	19	8	1	1	1	1	247
N(j)	868	316	228	63	50	18	1	1	1	1	$1558 = N_a$

Corrected circulation distribution for class R.

j	1	2	3	4	5	6	7	Total
M(j)	19	22	15	4	3	1	2	66
N(j)	209	126	60	13	8	2	4	$422 = N_a$

    As expected, when the values of j were plotted versus the values of $N(j)$ (see Figure 6, Appendix), the circulation distributions for QH-QR and R books fit into a geometric distribution (Morse, 1975, p. 183).

    We were then able to proceed with the following calculations.

    The sum of the $N(j)$ values is N_a, the number of active books in the class (Morse, 1975, p. 183). The percentage of the collection which is active is expressed by the fraction N_a/N, where N is the size of the total collection of the class of books. For this study, the value of N for each sampled class was calculated by counting the number of volumes listed in the shelf list for the sampled class. Excluded from the shelf list count were missing books and books in non-circulating reference collections.

Since N_a, the total number of books that circulated at least once during the year, does not represent the total number of potentially used books, we calculated N_ρ, the number of books that potentially circulate j times but did not happen to circulate during the year 1976-77 (Morse, 1975, p. 188):

$$N_\rho{}^{(i)} = N(j)/(1-e^{-j})$$

The values for the factor $(1-e^{-j})$ for j = 1,2,3. . . were given in a table (Chen, The M.I.T. Press, 1976, p. 29). The values of N_j had been previously calculated (see Table III). The sum of the individual values of $N(j)/(1-e^{-j})$ for j = 1,2,3 . . . is N_ρ. N_l is the fraction of "live" books, and is the sum of N_a, the active books, and N_ρ, the potentially active books. The fraction of "dead" books, N_d is simply total N_l less N_l. N_l, the sum of N_a and N_ρ, is used in the equation to compute the value of C, the fraction of active to live books (Chen, The M.I.T. Press, 1976, p. 33):

$$C = \frac{N_a}{N_l}$$

C is used to correct the estimated value of α_a, as mentioned above. It is also used to calculate the mean circulation of the live books, $\overline{R}_l$ (Chen, The M.I.T. Press, 1976, p.33):

$$\overline{R}_l = C \times \overline{R}_a$$

The mean circulation of the active books, $\overline{R}_a$, is simply the sum of the circulations of active books in the class, divided by the number of active books.

The total annual circulation of the QH-QR and R classes of books was estimated using the equation (Chen, The M.I.T. Press, 1976, p. 33):

$$\overline{R}_l N_l = \overline{R}_a N_a$$

Once the values for the corrected α, β and $\overline{R}_l(t)$ were determined, the mean circulation of the class of books next year, $\overline{R}_l(t+1)$ was calculated by using the equation:

$$\overline{R}_l(t+1) = \alpha + \beta \overline{R}_l(t)$$

Finally, the value of γ for each class was calculated (Morse, 1975, p. 186):

$$\gamma(t) = 1-N(1)/N_a(t)$$

Having determined the value of γ, we could then calculate the number of books in each of the sampled categories which circulated two or more times (Morse, 1975, p. 186) and Table V:

$$N(> m,t) = N_a(t) \, [\gamma \, (t)]^m$$
$$N(> 2,t) = N_a(t) \, [\gamma \, (t)]^2$$

We chose m to be two or more circulations per year because this would represent "high circulation" books, since the mean circulation of live books $\overline{R}_a$ was approximately two for both of the sampled groups of books. We calculated the percentage of the active collection that these books accounted for:

$$\% = N(> 2,t)/N_a(t)$$

We also calculated the fraction of the total circulation that the books which circulated two or more times accounted for (Table V):

$$N(> m,t) = [m(1-\gamma) +1] \, [\gamma \, (t)]^m$$
$$N(> 2,t) = [2(1-\gamma) +1] \, [\gamma \, (t)]^2$$

LIMITATIONS OF THE STUDY

We have been able to describe the circulation behavior of categories of books in the Science Library. The usefulness of the results in evaluating how well these groups of books have met the needs of users, and in making budget allocation decisions, are limited in several ways.

First, the information we have obtained does not give a complete picture of the use of medical materials compared with the use of other life sciences materials. In order to fully evaluate the use of materials in the library, one needs to measure in-house use of books, the use of journals, and the use of Dewey-classed material. Journals do not circulate, so their use could not be included in this study. We also have not included in-house use of non-circulating book collections. Also, the data we have obtained is quantitative data only, and does not take into account other variables which affect the "value" of a book: user frustration, quality of book selection, ease of access, etc. As Chen states, (The M.I.T. Press, 1976, p. 66), "since other factors are difficult to measure in a quantitative way, this study and all other use studies take 'frequency of use' as an index of the 'value,' 'worth,' or 'usefulness' of a book," and "the recorded use of a book is considered a measure for determining whether the book has met a need."

A second limitation results from the fact that the data were collected during one month only, from circulating books only. This will affect the accuracy of our results, although not to an unacceptable degree. Morse and Chen state that the model for removing bias from the circulation desk data will give results sufficiently accurate to compare total circulation rates, and to assist in determining the need for changes in policies (Morse, 1975, p. 193).

A more serious limitation to the accuracy of our results is that we determined α and β graphically, although we corrected the α_a value with a correction factor. The fact is that we ended up with *estimated* values for the circulation of books, and *estimated* α and β values, all of which limit the absolute accuracy of the results. Nevertheless, for the purpose of comparing the same values of categories of books, the information obtained is useful.

While we were able to predict the mean circulation for the "live" and "active" books in each class for next year based on data from active books, we were not able to predict the values for active and inactive fractions of each class for future years. Thus, we were not able to separate the "zero-use" books from the live books for use in the predictive model. These values are easier to determine from unbiased data taken from shelf samples, since that sampling methodology requires the use of fewer correction factors (Chen, MLA, 1976). We simply found that we were unable to handle the greater number of correction factors which needed to be computed.

Another limitation is that our sample included both monograph and serial titles. Monographs and serials are used differently, and the circulation policy in the Science Library is different for these two types of books; serials may be borrowed for one week only, and the most recent volumes of popular review serials are placed in the non-circulating Core Reference collection. In retrospect, we realize that we should have separated the serial volumes from the monograph titles, using data from the monographs only for our study.

In addition, this study has given us no information on who uses the life sciences collections. While obtaining user information was not one of the objectives of this study, we realize that such information is essential to a thorough evaluation of the use of a collection, and it is information which is quantifiable. In an earlier study of life sciences book use in the Science Library, we tried to identify the users of a larger sample of books. Unfortunately, because users' names were often illegible on the charge cards, we were unable to identify more than half of the users who charged out the books we sampled. Because of this problem, we did not attempt to identify users in this study.

This suggests that a study of this type, while it gives one useful information, leaves questions unanswered as well. The variables which we have measured tell us something about the circulation behavior of the books we studied; it does not tell us *why* users use the books they do. For example, in order to determine how the new programs in the medical sciences at M.I.T. are affecting book use, one needs to consider results of quantitative studies such as this, as well as other information, such as ILL requests, information gleaned from applications to use Countway Library of the Harvard Medical School, and identification of specific high-use titles. In addition, this study does not evaluate the literature needs of persons who never use the library and who fill their information needs in other ways.

RESULTS

The results of this study are shown in Tables IV & V.

TABLE IV
CIRCULATION CHARACTERISTICS OF CLASSES QH-QR AND CLASS R.

	Na	Np	N_l	$\bar{R}_a$	$\bar{R}_\alpha$	$\bar{R}$ (t+1)	γ	C
QH-QR	1558	929	2487	1.79	1.12	2788	.443	.626
R	422	325	747	2.02	1.14	852	.896	.565

	Nd	N(Total)	active %	live%	α	β
QH-QR	5937	8424	18	30	.751	.175
R	1774	2521	17	30	.328	.498

TABLE V
RELATIVE NUMBERS OF HIGH CIRCULATION BOOKS FOR CLASSES QH-QR AND R.

No. books circulating 2 times or more account for *% of total circulation*

QH-QR	305 (19%)	41%
R	108 (25%)	51%

The total number of QH-QR books which were active in 1976-77 is estimated to be 1,558. This active fraction represents 18 percent of the QH-QR collection. When potentially active QH-QR books are added to the active books, one finds a total of 2,487 live books, which represents 30 percent of the QH-QR collection. The total circulation of QH-QR books in 1976-77 is estimated to be 2,788 (mean circulation of live books multiplied by the number of live books).

For the R books, the active fraction is estimated to be 422 books, which represents 17 percent of the R collection. The live R books consist of 747 books, representing 30 percent of the R collection. The total circulation of R books in 1976-77 is estimated to be 852 (the number of live books multiplied by the mean circulation of live books).

The mean circulation of active books in 1976-77 was 2.02 for medical books, and 1.79 for other life sciences books. The mean circulation for live medical books is 1.14 and 1.12 for other life sciences books.

The model predicts that the mean circulation for live medical books in 1977-78 will be .896, while this value for other life sciences books will be .947.

Table V shows that 25 percent of the medical books circulated two or more times in 1976-77, and accounted for 51 percent of the total circulation of R books. Of the other life sciences books, 19 percent of these circulated two or more times, accounting for 41 percent of their circulation.

The values for γ for each group of books studied is .443 for QH-QR books, and .505 for R books.

The estimated values for α are .751 for QH-QR books, and .328 for R books. The values of β are estimated to be .175 for QH-QR books, and .498 for R books.

CONCLUSIONS AND IMPLICATIONS

We found that we were able to quantify a number of useful circulation variables with this study. Since we assume that the circulation behavior of a group of books represents one aspect of user demand, we now have some measure of the effectiveness of the life sciences collection. In addition, we are able to compare the use of medical books in the collection to other life sciences books, and to relate this comparative use to the money budgeted for each category of books.

The central question which we wished to answer with this study was: are medical books used differently from other life sciences books? We expected to find that medical books are used more, both in proportion to the rest of the collection and in intensity. We also expected to see clear evidence that more of the life sciences book budget needed to be allocated to purchase medical books.

The information derived from this study gives a partial answer to the question asked above. While this information is useful, it raises more specific questions for which further studies are required in order to provide a more complete answer to our central question concerning the need for, and use of, medical books. Indeed, we consider the additional questions which are raised by this study to be the most valuable benefit of this project because those new questions provide specific clues to the real nature of life sciences book use in the Science Library. Thus, the information gained from this study has directed us to the additional questions which we need to ask in order to fully understand the specific use of life sciences books in our particular library. A discussion of the results, and their usefulness, as well as implications for further investigations, follows.

A category of information derived from this study which is directly useful is shown in Table IV. This shows that the mean circulation of live medical books in 1976-77 was 1.14, while that of other life sciences books was 1.12. In addition, 17 percent of the medical books were active, and 30 percent of those books were live. For other life sciences books, 18 percent were active in 1976-77, and 30 percent were live. As an indicator of book use, this means that about the same proportion of medical books and other life sciences books are active or potentially active. While a 30 percent live portion is respectable, it leads to some concern about the 70 percent of the collection which consists of "dead" books.

We had hypothesized that medical books would be seen to show more use, both in proportion and in intensity of use. It is valuable information, in terms of planning for future use, to find that this hypothesis is not borne out by this study. It is a warning to carefully consider this information in order to discover why, when we know there is a growing need for medical books at M.I.T., the medical collection here does not reflect this need.

It would seem from this discussion of the proportion of live books in the collection, and the mean circulation in 1976-77 of QH-QR and R books, that all life sciences books are needed and used in the same way, and that indeed the QH-QR and R books (based on their circulation behavior) form a homogeneous group or class.

However, if one examines Figures 1 and 2 and looks at the values of α and β for each category of book, a difference emerges in the behavior of the books. According to Chen (The M.I.T. Press, 1976, p. 67), a large α indicates that many books in that class don't go out of date quickly, and that they continue to be useful for a long time. While the α's measured for both medical and other life sciences books are in the range usually found by Morse for classes of books (1968), the α of QH-QR books is twice as high as that for R books. At first glance, this might suggest that money would be better spent on QH-QR books, since they will be used longer.

On the other hand, the measured values for β show another interesting characteristic. β measures how rapidly the popularity of a book of the class diminishes from year to year; the smaller β is, the faster the mean circulation of the books of a class will approach the final mean circulation (Chen, The M.I.T. Press, 1976, p. 67). The β for R books is much higher than that for the QH-QR books, which seems to indicate that these books lose their popularity more slowly over time, even though eventually they are less used. If one plots the predicted mean circulation of both categories of books for the past ten years (Figure 9), this pattern of decrease in popularity may be seen.

Consideration of the values of α and β for medical books compared to other life sciences books shows us that the need for these two groups of books is different. R books are initially more popular, and lose their popularity less rapidly, but when their use levels out to a steady-state circulation, that circulation is lower than that for QH-QR books. Thus, in the long run, older live QH-QR books are more heavily used than older R books. The initial popularity of R books is probably due to a number of causes: new interest in medical research with correlating new programs at M.I.T.; the possibility there are fewer medical titles which have been well chosen; and the fact that as an applied science, medicine changes more rapidly than a pure science.

Whatever the causes, it seems clear that we should look closely at the specific titles which have circulated, and carefully examine the R collection to find out why the "dead" titles are no longer used. We are also warned to use great care in book selection.

One practical application of the results of this study is its implications for weeding the library collection. In weeding books in the life sciences, it is clear that older books with R call numbers are less active than older books with QH-QR call numbers. Thus, if we looked again at the books in our sample and determined the publication date for

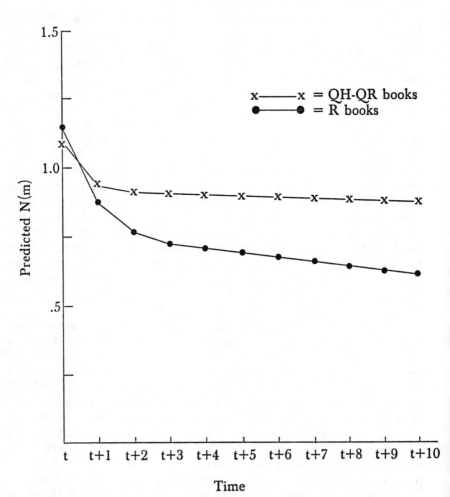

Predicted mean circulation, year t through t+10, for QH-QR and R books

FIGURE 5

each, we should get information which would be useful if a decision is made to weed on the basis of publication date for each type of life sciences book.

One of the objectives of this study was to determine whether more money needs to be allocated for buying medical books. The annual budget for books and serials in the life sciences for 1976-77 was split among four accounts, as follows:

	% of Life Sciences Budget	
Biology	54%	
		72%
Nutrition	18%	
Experimental Medicine	22%	
		28%
Physiological Psychology	6%	

Money spent from the "Experimental Medicine" and "Physiological Psychology" accounts is considered to be the medical book budget, while money from the "Biology" and "Nutrition" accounts purchases other life sciences books. Thus, 28 percent of the total life sciences book budget is set aside for medical books, with 72 percent of the budget allocated for other life sciences books. Our study has shown that 77 percent of the total circulation of life sciences books in 1976-77 was accounted for by QH-QR books, and 23 percent accounted for by R books. Also, 78 percent of the live life sciences books were QH-QR books, with 23 percent of the live books being R books. We therefore conclude that, of the funds currently budgeted for life sciences books, the proportion allocated for medical books is appropriate, based on the use of these books. We are alerted by the measured α and β values, however, to the fact that it is necessary to exercise more care in the selection of R books, choosing titles which will be used over a longer period of time in order to ensure the most efficient use of budgeted money.

In addition, we are reminded that this study, and our consideration of the allocation of budgeted funds, tells us nothing about the adequacy of the total life sciences budget allocation in the context of the total money available for books in the Science Library. The *proportion* of money set aside for medical books out of life sciences funds may be appropriate, but this does not mean that the needs of users for life sciences materials are being met, nor that we do not need more money for life sciences books. In order to more completely answer this question, we need to study the use of all books in the Science Library, and compare this use to budget allocations. The information thus obtained, plus information gleaned from a careful examination of the books which circulate, should give us the basis for a plan of book buying which is based on current need as measured by book use.

A way in which we could try to identify patterns of use of life sciences books would be to group the books in our sample differently. That is, instead of looking at books in the Library of Congress classes (i.e., QH-QR, R) only, which do not correspond to specific subject areas, we might better see patterns of use by grouping the books in our sample in a different way. We tested this idea by taking the data sheets for the sampled books and rearranging them according to the following randomly chosen topics: cancer, immunology, neurology, and biochemistry (books for each topic were identified by consulting the *Classified Library of Congress Subject Headings* and noting the call numbers assigned to each topic) (Williams, 1972). We then recorded the number of active books which circulated in each topic. As it turned out, there were not enough books in each category for us to see patterns of use. One thing we can do is to track down the books which circulated, and from them, identify specific titles to tell us which ones are used the most.

It would be extremely useful to compare such information with the limited information which we have on user requests. We keep records of interlibrary loan requests for medical and other life sciences materials and also record the titles which are requested for purchase by the Science Library. Our records of the requests of users to recall books for personal reserves and to locate books which they seek in the library but do not find are another source of information. In recent years we have also begun to tabulate the research interests and literature needs which are listed on the application forms of M.I.T. users who apply for Countway Medical Library courtesy cards. When all of these types of information are combined, we should be able to discern categories of books which are most often sought by users in the Science Library.

Further studies which are suggested to us in order to determine categories of materials which are needed by users include studies of the in-house use of Core, Reference, and Reserve books, as well as the use of journals. Such studies require more staff time and effort to conduct. Until the time when it is possible for us to study the in-house use of life sciences materials, we can rely on circulation desk data to serve as indicators of the use of books in this area.

The procedures we used in collecting and recording the data for this study are easy to implement, and we did not need to modify them to suit our library system. The collection of circulation data each day took less than half an hour, depending on the volume of circulation the previous day. When we used the method suggested by Chen (The M.I.T. Press, 1976) for the recording of data, we found that transferring circulation histories from charge cards to the form was straightforward and easy to do. This is a task we feel support staff could be trained to do with no problem.

Once the data was collected, it was a simple matter to use it in the appropriate equations after we had determined the proper sequence in which to use the equations of the models. For the benefit of those who may be interested in conducting a similar study in their own libraries, we have included at each step in our methodology, the reasons for each measurement, and an indication of the sequence in which the equations were used. The calculations are not difficult, requiring only a hand calculator to perform.

We were struck by the variety of types of information which it is possible to obtain from this simple procedure, using this one model of book use. We recommend the model and methodologies reported here as a useful technique for evaluating a collection, especially in light of the minimal staff time and effort which are required.

The technique and model which we have used in this study are only one example of a variety of quantitative techniques which have been described in the literature for use by library managers. We chose these particular types because of the ease in implementing them in our particular library situation. Our recommendation does not exclude other quantitative methods, but rather is meant to show our satisfaction with the types of useful information which a quantitative study can provide. We believe such studies can be used to find out about general behavior characteristics of classes of books. In addition, the information which is gained from such studies point out what else should be looked at in order to obtain more complete information about the need for, and use of books. This is especially useful when one uses a model which can predict the future behavior of books, because this allows one to evaluate how successful one is in making changes in policy which will affect such behavior. For example, if we want the β value for medical books to drop, i.e., choose medical books which lose their popularity less rapidly, we can make an effort to do a better job of book selection, or to find out what other conditions are responsible for this phenomenon. If we then repeat the study at a later time, we will be able, by again measuring β, to tell if our changes in policy have been successful. It is valuable to be able, with a minimum amount of time spent in the collection of a relatively small number of quantitative data, to obtain this type of information about our book collections and their use.

The usefulness of the information gained from this particular model has been further illustrated in the M.I.T. library system. As part of a Collection Analysis Project conducted within the Libraries between November 1977 and January 1978, a Task Force on Collection Effectiveness applied the Chen model in the five divisional libraries at M.I.T. After considering the available utilization methodologies that have been reported in the literature, task force members chose to use this model as one component of an overall evaluation of techniques used to measure collection effectiveness. The purposes of this study were to provide an overall behavior norm for books in the library system as a whole, and for books in each divisional library (including the Science, Engineering, Humanities, Social

Science and Management, and Architecture and Urban Studies Libraries).

The variables which were measured by the task force included active and live fractions; the mean circulation of active and live fractions; and the parameters α and β. Data collected from books in the humanities and social sciences disciplines fit the requirements of the model in terms of statistical validity as well as did data from books in the sciences. This finding implies that the three basic assumptions upon which the Morse model is based seem to hold true for non-science books as well as for those in the scientific and technical disciplines. We anticipate that this will be verified in other non-science collections, extending the usefulness and applicability of the Morse-Chen model. The task force's experience with applying this model was that, on a sampling basis, the technique is quick, easy to implement, and feasible for use as part of an on-going evaluation of collection effectiveness.

Had it been designed differently, other types of information could be obtained from this type of study including the effects which a duplicate copy of a book of a certain class would have for an estimation of additional circulations (Chen, 1976, p. 110); and the effect which a change in loan or renewal policy would have on the use of a collection (Chen, The M.I.T. Press, p. 127). Finally, new questions which are raised by such studies serve to focus our attention on policies and on qualitative aspects of book use which need our attention.

BIBLIOGRAPHY

Chen, Ching-chih. *Applications of Operations Research Models to Libraries.* Cambridge, MA: The M.I.T. Press, 1976.

_____. *Applications of Operations Research to Library Decision Making* (Medical Library Association Courses for Continuing Education, CE19). Chicago, IL: Medical Library Association, 1976.

Fussler, H. H., and Simon, J. L. *Patterns in the Use of Books in Large Research Libraries.* Chicago, IL: University of Chicago Press, 1969.

Jain, A. K. *A Sampled Data Study of Book Usage in the Purdue University Libraries.* Lafayette, IN: Purdue University, 1965.

_____. *Report on a Statistical Study of Book Use.* Lafayette, IN: School of Industrial Engineering, Purdue University, 1965.

_____. "Sampling and Short-Period Usage in the Purdue Library." *College and Research Libraries* 27 (1966):211-218.

_____. "Sampling and Data Collection Methods for a Book-Use Study." *Library Quarterly* 39 (1969):245-252.

Lancaster, F. W. *The Measurement and Evaluation of Library Services.* Washington, DC: Information Resources Press, 1977.

Morse, Philip M. *Library Effectiveness: A Systems Approach.* Cambridge, MA: The M.I.T. Press, 1968.

Morse, Philip M., and Chen, Ching-chih. "Using Circulation Desk Data to Obtain Unbiased Estimates of Book Use." *Library Quarterly* 45 (April 1975):179-194.

Raffel, J. A., and Shishko, R. *Systematic Analysis of University Libraries.* Cambridge, MA: The M.I.T. Press, 1969.

Raisig, L. M., et al. "How Biomedical Investigators Use Library Books." *Bulletin of the Medical Library Association* 54 (1966):104-107.

Trueswell, R. W. "A Quantitative Measure of User Circulation Requirements and Its Possible Effect on Stack Thinning and Multiple Copy Determination." *American Documentation* 16 (1965):20-25.

Williams, James G.; Manheimer, Martha L.; and Daily, Jay E., eds. *Classified Library of Congress Subject Headings,* Vols. 1 and 2. New York: Marcel Dekker, Inc., 1972.

APPENDIX

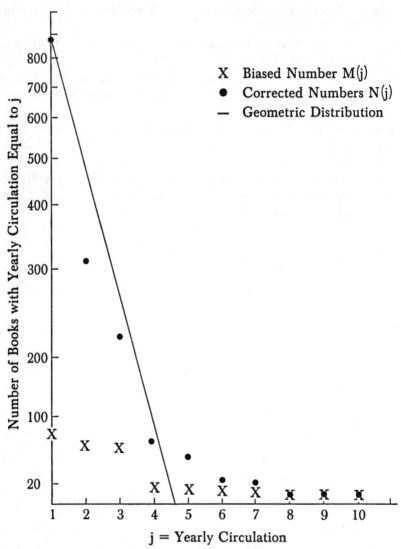

X   Biased Number M(j)
•   Corrected Numbers N(j)
—   Geometric Distribution

Corrected and uncorrected circulation distribution for
QH-QR books

FIGURE 6A

APPENDIX

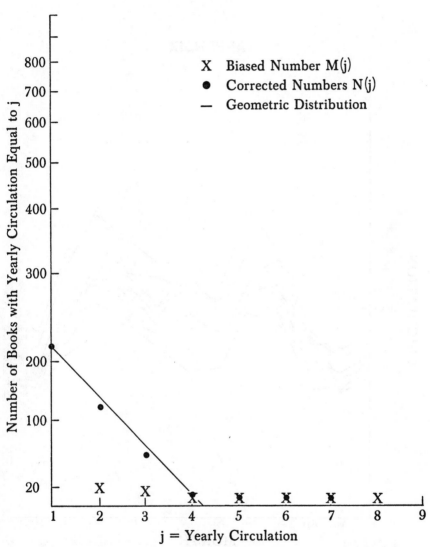

Corrected and uncorrected circulation distribution for R books

FIGURE 6B

APPENDIX

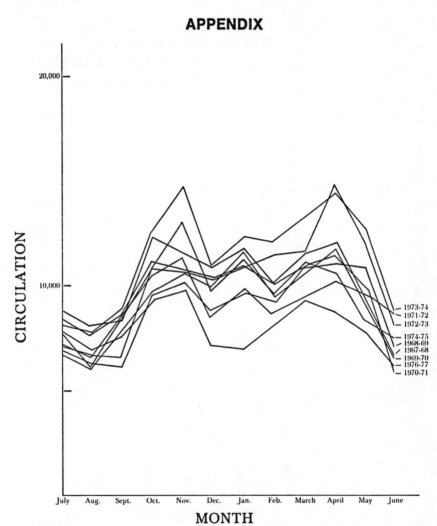

MONTH

Circulation distribution for books in the Science Library, 1970-1975

FIGURE 7

Monograph Duplication in the Kresge Center for Teaching Resources at Lesley College

by Andrea C. Hoffman

THE PROBLEM

With the continuing pressures of rising book prices and the increasing number of materials published each year, the service-oriented librarian must consider the thoughtful formulation of a book duplication policy. All too often librarians succumb to unsystematic and intuitive duplication, short-lived trends and, in the academic library, pressures from friendly faculty members. It is difficult to overcome these obstacles without a reasonable policy, and equally difficult to formulate such a policy without some quantitative assistance. One must be able to balance present and future user needs as well as to measure the benefit of adding a new title to a collection as compared to spending that same money on a duplicate title. Intuition and foresight may work in certain limited situations but it is impossible to make such decisions systematically for the entire collection. Therefore, the problem of monograph duplication would appear to be a fertile area for the application of operations research models. This is not to suggest that decisions should be made purely on quantitative information. Rather, quantitative information should be used to help make better decisions and provide better service to library users.

RELEVANT FACTORS

In approaching a book duplication problem, one must first ask the question: "What factors should be considered in the formulation of a book duplication policy?" Those factors which appear most important to consider are:

1) *High circulation*
   Purchase of duplicate copies for those titles which experience a

relatively high circulation should be considered. Obviously, if a book circulates only once or twice per year, it would probably not warrant duplication;

2) *The future circulation of a book*
   In order to spend money most effectively, one would want to purchase duplicates for those books which would enjoy a higher than average circulation not only during the present year, but in subsequent years as well;

3) *The length of time which a book is off the shelf during one circulation*
   Some books, due to their nature or content, are likely to experience longer periods of circulation than others. Therefore, the time which one group of books is off the shelf during one circulation could equal the amount of time which another group of books is off the shelf during two or three circulations.

Ideally, a methodology for book duplication would consist of a combination of all three of the above factors.

PREVIOUS RESEARCH EFFORTS—A SURVEY OF THE LITERATURE

A number of different approaches to book duplication have been reported in the literature. Some, such as Franklin (1966), suggest an intuitive approach to duplication. He feels that the number of copies of a title should be determined by such factors as the size of the library, the size and nature of the community and available book funds. Moreland (1968) suggests mass purchase of paperbacks for selected popular titles.

Others have applied more systematic and quantitative techniques to the duplication problem. Goyal (1972) presents a procedure for dealing with the problem of over-ordering copies of titles. Grant (1971), Trueswell (1965) and Buckland (1975) suggest the identification of a "core" of heavily used books for multiple-copy purchase.

Probably the most comprehensive and authoritative book duplication technique was proposed by Philip Morse (1968). The theoretical basis of his approach lies in the basic assumptions of his own Markov models for book use. These assumptions are:

1. Book circulation is random, and it is impossible to predict the circulation of an *individual* book during a future year, but it is possible to predict the average use of a *class* of books;

2. Book circulation, on the average, drops off exponentially with time;

3. There is, on average, a "memory" involved in book circulation.

From data gathered at the M.I.T. Science Library, Morse found that the average circulation N(m) of a class of books during its t + 1 year depends on its previous circulation (year t). He then developed a simple linear model, based on probability theory, to predict the average future circulation of a class of books from past circulation history of that class as a whole. His assumptions and observations are translated into the equation (see page 232 for notation equivalents)

$$N(m) = \alpha + \beta m$$

where α and β are parameters measured for each class of books studied. β measures the rate at which the "popularity" of a book diminishes, and α is a measure of the mean circulation which a class of books will eventually reach with time. The variable m is the number of circulations in the tth year.

In addition to predicting the future circulation for a particular class of books, it is also necessary, in considering book duplication, to determine the mean fraction of a year that a given class of books is off the shelf. Morse suggests that $^{52}/w$ is the mean number of weeks that a book is off the shelf during the year and that

$$w = \frac{RN}{J}$$

where w is the mean return rate for all books in a class, R is the mean yearly circulation per book in a class, N is the total number of circulating books in a class and J is the mean number of books out on loan at any time (Morse, 1968). The circulation "interference," or the mean amount of time that a class of books is off the shelf is measured by $R\mu$ (Chen, 1976). One may decide if a particular book is worth duplication by determining the increase in circulation, in addition to the first copy, produced by having a second copy in the collection from year t + 2 through t + 5. That increase is computed by (Chen, 1976):

$$Ri = \mu \left\{ \left(\frac{\alpha}{1-\beta}\right)^2 \left(5 + \frac{1+\beta}{1-\beta}\right) + \left[\frac{\alpha}{1-\beta} + \beta R(1)\right]^2 \left(\frac{1}{1-\beta^2}\right) \right\}$$

Where α and β are parameters for a class of books and μ is the mean loan period for that class of books.

Finally, Chen (1976) applied Morse's book use models in the Countway Library at Harvard University. Her purpose was to test, broaden and modify the models and to demonstrate the usefulness and implications of operations research techniques in various library decision-making processes. Among the latter was the formulation of a book duplication policy.

Morse's approach to the book duplication problem has been selected as the theoretical basis for this study for the following reasons:

1) The approach comprehensively addresses all of the relevant factors detailed in Section II.
2) The Markov model has been correctly tested and verified (Chen, 1976) in an academic library.

OBJECTIVES AND PROPOSED HYPOTHESES

Objectives

The objectives of this study are as follows:

1) To test the applicability of Philip Morse's Markov model already tested in science collections, to a broader collection including the humanities, social and pure sciences. Specifically, it will be tested in an academic collection of children's literature in the Kresge Center for Teaching Resources at Lesley College;

2) To apply, if valid, the Markov model, illustrated in Ching-chih Chen's study of monograph use in the Countway Library (Chen, 1976), together with a queueing model in order to establish some guidelines for book duplication.

Hypothesis

This study has attempted to accomplish these objectives through the test of the following hypothesis:

—The Morse model for book use can be applied in the children's literature collection at Lesley College to predict average circulation behavior for a class of books. The model can predict the average number of circulations for the average book in a particular class during n number of years.

It was reasoned that if the above hypothesis is valid, Morse's equations for determining the fraction of the year that a book is off the shelf and for book duplication could be used by this researcher. The required test of these formulas against empirical evidence is not within the time frame of this study.

METHODOLOGY

Deduction from Hypothesis

If the previously stated hypothesis were valid, then the gathered experimental and theoretical data would correspond. In other words the theoretical and experimental mean number of circulations $N(m)$ for books circulating m number of times during the year $t + 1$ would be approximately the same.

Kresge Center for Teaching Resources

To better understand the environment in which this study was conducted and the specific collection in which the models were applied, a brief description of the Kresge Center for Teaching Resources is here detailed. The Kresge Center is a curriculum resource center located in the Lesley College Library. Though it is administered by the Library, the Center has its own public services staff and circulation desk. Its raison d'être is to serve the curriculum materials and audio-visual needs of the students and faculty at Lesley College, a teacher-training institution. The Center is located on the second floor of the Library and consists of one large room for the curriculum materials, an audio-visual production room and a classroom for viewing films.

The Collection. The Center has one of the most comprehensive elementary curriculum materials collections in New England. The collection numbers approximately 12,000 items, and consists of 5,000 volumes of children's literature and 7,000 volumes of textbooks, games, kits, realia and audiovisuals (records, study prints, filmstrips, films, etc.). Each year nearly 1,500 volumes are added to the collection, of which approximately 400 are children's books. With the exception of a few reference materials, the entire collection circulates. During 1975-76, the Kresge Center circulated approximately 35,000 volumes, of which 16,000 were children's literature.

Arrangement. Different types of materials in the collection are cataloged with different classification systems: children's literature is cataloged in the Library of Congress system, teaching materials (texts, games, kits) in the HEW textbook system, records in the ANSCR system and the audiovisuals in Dewey Decimal.

Borrowing Policies. The charge-out time for each circulating item is two weeks. Materials may be renewed twice if they are not on hold for another user. There is a fine of five cents per day charged on each item that is overdue.

Procedures for Charging and Discharging Materials. To charge out materials, the borrowers must present their embossed library card to the assistant at the Kresge circulation desk. Each item is equipped with a blue charge-out card which has identifying data typed on the top, and a book pocket with spaces for due date stamps. When charging out a book, the circulation assistant runs the blue book card and library card through an addressograph machine and stamps the due date on the charged-out item's book pocket. The blue card is then filed in the present day's circulation file, which is interfiled with the past days' circulation the following morning. When an item is returned, the appropriate blue card is pulled from the circulation file, the last user's name is crossed off the blue card and the last due date is crossed off the book pocket. When a blue book card is fully used it is discarded, and a duplicate is made.

Users of Kresge. The users of the Kresge Center consist of approximately 750 full-time undergraduate students, 800 full-time equivalent graduate students, various faculty members and 100 paying alumni. These people generally use the Kresge materials when involved in education materials and methods courses, children's literature courses and student teaching experiences.

Acquisitions Budget. Annual budgets for print and non-print materials in the Kresge Center have continued to rise in recent years. The Library has not been afflicted with the severe fiscal problems experienced by other private colleges. During 1975-76, the print budget was $3,600 and the non-print $6,500. The print budget is to accommodate all children's books and text books and the non-print budget all other materials. While budgets increased, so did prices. Hence, the 1975-76 budget had the same purchasing power as it did several years ago. A problem faced by the Center which is more pressing than money is space. Though the Library and Kresge Center moved to a new building in April, 1973, the Kresge Center outgrew its under-programmed quarters within two years. In August 1976, it was relocated to a larger floor of the Library, but has far from unlimited space for growth. Therefore, it is important to make judicious selections for Kresge not only due to money but due to space. Both this and the high circulation rate (approximately 2.5 circulations per item in 1975-76) causes one to question whether the Kresge money and space are best utilized by purchasing new materials or duplicating presently owned titles.

Methodology

In order to apply Morse's Markov model, certain book use data must be gathered. This study will deal only with recorded book use, and will not consider in-house use of materials. Book-use data was gathered by the "collection method" of sampling. This appeared to be a more feasible method than the "check-out sample" due to the nature of the library's circulation system and the time limit in which this study was to be completed. Also, this method could give a reasonably unbiased and accurate circulation account for a whole year. The collection studied lent itself well to sampling, as all due dates were consistently recorded on book pockets. Circulation histories were gathered only between the dates of July 1, 1973 and June 30, 1976. Before July 1973, materials were charged out under a different circulation system which did not record due dates on the present book pockets. Since the size of the collection studied was small, the time involved in sampling was not immense. However, this method could become burdensome with a larger collection.

The Sample Scope. The materials examined in this study were limited to the 5,000 volumes of children's literature housed in the Kresge Center. All books examined for circulation histories were in the collection since July 1, 1973, were single copies, had never needed replacement and had never been on reserve. Verification of these constraints was easily retrieved from the shelf list. The shelf list was used as a master file for selection of samples, as it contained all necessary information and provided an accurate representation of what was on the shelf. The "misplaced" rate in the juvenile literature collection is quite small (less than 1 percent a year), so that almost all sampled books could be located.

Since the study was to run between November and March, it seemed logical to do the sampling when most of the books were on the shelves. From the graph of the circulation histories of the children's literature, the low January circulations marked that month as ideal for sampling. See Table I.

The next step was to select the classes to be sampled. Since the children's literature collection is classified in the Library of Congress System, it seemed reasonable to define the classes by main class letter. Some classes were grouped together or divided more specifically depending on the number of books in each class. The defined classes are as follows:

L. C. Class	# in Class	Approximate % of Total Collection
PZ1-7	1,610	32.5%
PZ8	720	14.5
PZ10	720	14.5
Q	420	8.5
E	210	4.2
F	110	2.2
T-Z	220	4.4
PL-PX	180	3.6
D	160	3.2
G	140	2.8
H	85	1.7
S	66	1.3
B	57	1.1
N	55	1.1
M	46	.9
PZ9	45	.9
P-PJ	40	.8
R	33	.6
J	13	.2
C	8	.1
K	7	.1
L	7	.1

TABLE I

To test Morse's models on a general collection, at least one class from the sciences, humanities and social sciences was selected for study: H class (social sciences); PZ1-7 (children's fiction) and Q (science). Others chosen for additional comparison included: PZ8 (fairy tales) D (history) and E (American history). Approximately 65 percent of the entire collection was sampled.

Determining the size of the sample was a more difficult problem. As there had been no past history of sampling size for this particular collection, there were no guidelines to consider. The largest class (PZ1-7) was sampled first, and data continued to be gathered until the calculations for the mean number of circulations for year t + 1 stabilized. It then followed that the sample number of books, and hence, year-pairs of circulation history, had to be no larger for the other classes. In all cases, samples continued to be taken until numerical results stabilized.

The data collection itself was fairly simple and straightforward. Appropriate shelf list cards (i.e., those of single copy books which had been in the collection since July 1, 1973) were randomly tagged, and the class number and the fiscal year dates 1973-74, 1974-75, 1975-76 were written on a blank card. The book was then retrieved, and the appropriate circulation history recorded from the due dates stamped on the book pocket.

Problems involved in data collection were minimal. Illegible due date stamps accounted for the greatest number of difficulties in recording the histories. Replaced book pockets or due date slips did occur two or three times. If an accurate history could not be recorded, that particular book was not included in the sample.

Analysis and Interpretation of Data

Throughout this study the author shall adopt approximately the same notation as used in the Chen study (1976), i.e.:

M = total number of examples (year-pair) in the sample

m = number of circulations in the tth year

$M(m)$ = number of examples with m circulations in the tth year

n = number of circulations in the $(t + 1)$ th year

Nmn = number of examples that have m circulations in year t and n circulations in year t + 1

$N(m)$ = mean number of circulations during year t + 1 given that the sample has m circulations in year t

α and β = Markov circulation parameters which must be determined for each class of books studied

R = mean circulation rate

μ = mean fraction of a year that a book is off the shelf during one circulation

Returning to Morse's basic assumptions, we are reminded that the future average circulation of a given class of books is dependent on its past circulation. Basically this is summarized by:

$$N(m) = \alpha + \beta m$$

So, if a class of books circulates m times in year t, it will circulate $N(m)$ times in year t + 1, all being dependent on the values of m and the parameters α and β. To determine these values and to illustrate the relationships of the circulations from one year to the next, the circulations for Q class have been charted and are shown in Exhibit II. It may be concluded from the chart that on average a Q class book which circulates twice in year t will circulate 1.81 times in year t + 1. The mean number of circulations in year t + 1 was derived by:

$$N(m) = \frac{1}{M(m)} \sum_{n=o}^{\infty} nN_{mn}$$

The calculations for $N(m)$ may be plotted on a graph, as the equation
$$N(m) = \alpha + \beta m$$
signifies a linear relationship. This is also shown in Exhibit II.

Note that theoretical quantities of $N(m)$ have also been calculated, and correspond fairly well with experimental results. This appears to confirm the validity of Morse's Markov model for the Q class. Identical procedures were followed for the remainder of the classes sampled. Again, experimental and theoretical results corresponded well. Some classes studied, particularly the H class, were not large enough to produce an ideal number of circulations for comparison. However, enough data was obtained for books with lower circulations to produce a clear pattern. The data shown in Exhibits III-VII for classes PZ, H, D, Q and E appear to support the applicability of Morse's Markov model to a general book collection.

It should be noted that for an accurate test of the Markov model a linear regression analysis should be performed to determine α (Y axis intercept) and β (slope). There should be a reasonable relationship between the experimental and theoretical values, indicated by acceptable correlation coefficients. Such an analysis was not done in this study. Instead, a less formal visual graphic comparison was made.

PROCEDURE BASED ON THE VERIFIED HYPOTHESIS

Since the Markov model was successfully tested in the children's literature collection, it is possible to proceed with use of the book duplication models.

Book Duplication Models

According to Chen's study, the most effective approach to book duplication is the combination of Morse's Markov model with a queueing model for circulation interference (Chen, 1976). To determine circulation interference, or the fraction of a year that a given class of books is off the shelf, it is necessary to calculate the mean circulation rate for that class. Morse suggests that the mean number of weeks that a book is off the shelf may be derived by:

$$w = \frac{RN}{J}$$

Where w is the mean return rate, R is the mean yearly circulation per book in a class, N is the total number of circulatable books and J is the mean number of books out on loan at any time. Therefore, 52/w is the mean number of weeks a book is away from the library during one circulation. An alternative model to Morse's is:

$$\frac{RN}{D} = C \text{ and } \frac{J}{C} = \text{Average loan period (in days)}$$

Where D = the number of days in a year of library circulation and C = average daily circulation for a class of books. Either model generates the same answer, with Morse's being in terms of weeks and the alternative being in days. For the purposes of this study a year has been defined as 36 weeks as opposed to 52, even though the Library is open year round. The year has been defined as such due to the fact that the vast majority of circulation behavior takes place during only 36 weeks of the year. The graph of circulation indicates that circulation is extremely low during the months of June, July and August. In 1975-76 the circulation for those three months accounted for only 7.4 percent of the entire circulation. Therefore, since these months would have biased the calculations, they were excluded.

It should also be noted that w must be calculated numerous times during the year as the number of books out on loan will vary from one time period to another. For the sake of this report, calculations were completed on the basis of a single time sampling. The true mean number of books out on loan will continue to be calculated and will undoubtedly differ from the single time results. The "temporary" mean loan periods calculated are:

Class	Mean Loan Period (w) In Weeks
D	1.93
E	3.45
H	5.54
PZ7	1.20
PZ8	1.46
Q	2.40

According to Chen's report, Morse's claim is that circulation interference $(R\mu)$ becomes serious at approximately one-half. At this point, one may determine whether or not a duplicate copy is "worth" purchasing (Chen, 1976). The key figure is the increase in circulation over the next five years, in addition to that generated by the first copy, produced by having a duplicate present. This is calculated by:

$$R_i = \mu \left\{ \left(\frac{\alpha}{1-\beta} \right)^2 \left(5 - \frac{1+\beta}{1-\beta} \right) + \left[\frac{\alpha}{1-\beta} + \beta R(1) \right]^2 \left(\frac{1}{1-\beta^2} \right) \right\}$$

If the results of this calculation, divided by five to give the average yearly circulation, is equal to or greater than the predicted mean circulation of that class of books for the next year, it would be worthwhile to consider purchase of a duplicate copy.

Advance calculations offer assistance in forming guidelines for duplication. In other words, a book must circulate at least X times before it is worth considering a second copy. X has been calculated for each class.

Class	# of Circulations of 1st Copy Before Worth Duplicating
D	13
E	7
H	6
PZ7	25
PZ8	39
Q	25

Recommendations and Policy Changes

If the above calculations are assumed to be correct (and they are probably not, due to the deficient sample for the mean loan period), one may conclude that little or no duplication is warranted in classes PZ, Q and D. After a book in the E or H class circulates six or seven times in one year duplication should be considered. As a simple working rule of thumb, staff at the circulation desk may be asked to pass all E and H books to the librarian after a blue charge-out card has been filled. A filled blue card holds approximately seven names. If after examining the card the librarian sees that the book has circulated six or seven times during the *past year*, a duplicate purchase of the book will be considered.

An alternative to duplicate purchasing may be variable loan periods, as suggested by Buckland (1975). However, the number of books with which we are dealing here is so small that duplicate purchasing is the most feasible course of action.

It should also be noted that a wealth of information was collected in the process of this study. Such data can and will be used to aid in the formulation and change of policies other than those concerned with book duplication.

Limitations of the Study

Like Chen's study, this project does admit to some inherent limitations. First, the value of duplicating a book is considered only in a quantitative way. The study does not take any qualitative judgments or unusual situations into consideration. Second, the accuracy of the sampling could not be perfect, and some classes were too sparsely populated for fully adequate data. Third, the calculations for α and β were probably not as accurate as possible as no computer was available to assist with this study. Finally, some of the calculations of R_i are undoubtedly inaccurate, as they were computed on the basis of a single loan period taken from a single sample in time.

Conclusions

It may be concluded that the objectives of this study were fulfilled as follows:

1) Morse's Markov model was tested (and verified) in the children's literature collection in the Kresge Center for Teaching Resources;
2) A book duplication policy, based on the Markov model together with a queueing model, was developed for application in the Kresge Collection of children's literature.

GENERALIZATIONS

One may conclude that the implications of this study, and the techniques employed, are more far-reaching than a single study of book duplication in a particular library. It is believed that the following generalizations may be drawn:

1) Libraries should *not* duplicate books simply on the basis of high circulation. Projected future demand and the length of a single circulation must also be considered;
2) The statistical information gained from a study of this nature may be helpful to the functions of collection development and resource allocation. It would seem that a larger portion of book budgets should be assigned to those subject classes which are *expected* to receive a higher than average circulation. The utilization of past use-records may also effectively assist the process of "weeding" or thinning a collection.
3) Morse's predictive models offer librarians an invaluable tool to aid in the increase of book availability. If the reports that show a 40-50 percent failure rate in finding a book in the card catalog on the shelf (Gore, 1972; Trueswell, 1965) are accurate, the book availability problem should be aggressively attacked. As it is believed that a very small percentage of a collection accounts for most user requests, librarians should welcome this systematic procedure to assist in objectively making book purchase decisions.

EXHIBIT I

JUVENILE LITERATURE CIRCULATION

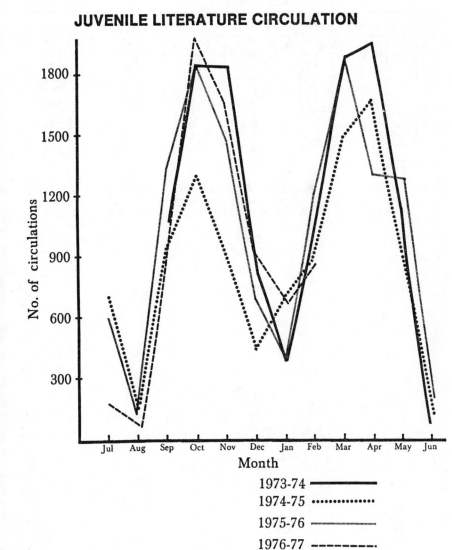

EXHIBIT II

Q Class - Values for M(m), N_{mn}, and N(m)
for different values of m and n

		N_{mn}														N(m)	
		n=															
m	M(m)	0	1	2	3	4	5	6	7	8	9	10	11	12	13	Experimental	Theoretical
0	36	18	11	3	2	2	0	0	0	0	0	0	0	0	0	.86	.95
1	43	10	16	10	2	3	1	1	0	0	0	0	0	0	0	1.50	1.37
2	32	5	8	10	6	3	0	0	0	0	0	0	0	0	0	1.81	1.79
3	16	1	4	4	2	3	0	1	0	0	1	0	0	0	0	2.80	2.21
4	17	1	6	2	3	2	1	2	0	0	0	0	0	0	0	2.60	2.63
5	8	2	1	0	1	3	1	0	0	0	0	0	0	0	0	2.60	3.05
6	12	0	2	3	2	2	0	0	1	1	1	0	0	0	0	3.80	3.47
7	3	0	0	1	0	0	0	1	0	0	0	0	0	0	1	7.00	3.89
8	1	0	0	0	0	0	0	0	1	0	0	0	0	0	0	7.00	4.31
9	2	0	0	0	0	0	0	1	1	0	0	0	0	0	0	6.50	4.73

$\overline{M}=170$

Plots of N(m) for m year-pairs 1973-76—
Mean circulation N(m) for year t+1
as function of circulation m for year t

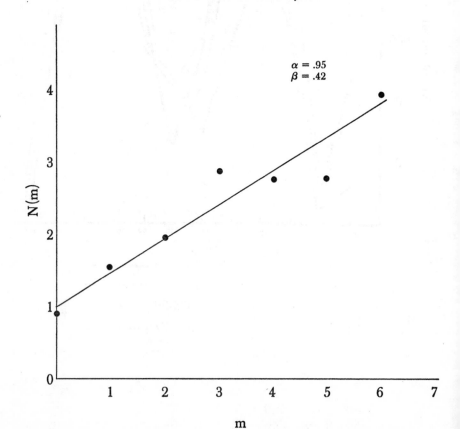

$\alpha = .95$
$\beta = .42$

N(m)

m

EXHIBIT III

PZ1-7 Class - Values for $M(m)$, N_{nm}, and $N(m)$
for different values of m and n

		N_{mn}													$N(m)$	
m	M(m)	n=0	1	2	3	4	5	6	7	8	9	10	11	12	Experimental	Theoretical
0	88	44	28	6	7	2	0	0	0	0	0	0	0	1	.92	.88
1	51	22	9	8	7	2	1	2	0	0	0	0	0	0	1.39	1.46
2	37	11	12	5	3	4	2	0	0	0	0	0	0	0	1.54	2.04
3	40	9	8	7	6	5	2	1	1	1	0	0	0	0	2.27	2.62
4	22	3	5	3	2	2	3	1	1	0	0	0	1	1	3.30	3.20
5	22	2	3	2	3	2	5	3	0	0	0	0	2	0	3.86	3.78
6	14	1	1	0	1	3	3	3	1	0	0	0	1	1	5.42	4.36
7	13	2	0	0	1	5	3	1	1	0	0	0	0	0	3.90	4.94
8	9	0	0	1	0	0	2	3	0	1	0	0	1	1	6.40	5.92
9	7	0	0	0	3	0	1	1	2	0	0	0	0	0	4.80	6.50
10	3	0	1	0	0	0	1	0	1	0	0	0	0	0	4.30	7.08

$\overline{M=306}$

Plots of $N(m)$ for m year-pairs 1973-76
Mean circulation $N(m)$ for year t+1
as function of circulation m for year t

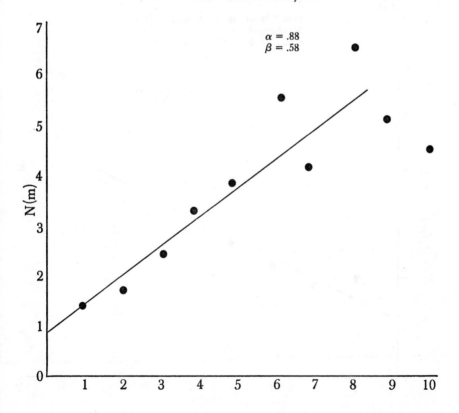

$\alpha = .88$
$\beta = .58$

EXHIBIT IV

PZ 8 Class — Values for M(m), N$_{mn}$, and N(m) for different values of m and n

| | | N_{mn} | | | | | | | | | | | | | N(m) | |
m	M(m)	n= 0	1	2	3	4	5	6	7	8	9	10	11	12	Experimental	Theoretical
0	29	11	12	1	4	0	0	1	0	0	0	0	0	0	1.10	1.20
1	23	5	6	6	2	2	1	0	1	0	0	0	0	0	1.90	1.60
2	20	5	4	4	5	1	0	1	0	0	0	0	0	0	1.85	2.00
3	16	3	6	2	1	1	1	2	0	0	0	0	0	0	2.12	2.40
4	12	2	4	2	0	0	2	0	2	0	0	0	0	0	2.66	2.80
5	11	3	1	3	0	0	0	3	1	0	0	0	0	0	2.90	3.20
6	7	0	1	2	1	1	2	0	0	0	0	0	0	0	3.14	3.60
7	5	0	1	0	2	1	0	0	0	1	0	0	0	0	3.80	4.00
8	4	0	0	0	0	1	2	0	0	0	1	0	0	0	5.75	4.40
9	2	0	0	0	0	2	0	0	0	0	0	0	0	0	4.00	4.80
10	2	0	0	0	1	0	0	1	0	0	0	0	0	0	4.50	5.20
11	3	0	0	0	0	0	0	0	1	1	0	0	0	1	9.60	5.60
12	1	0	0	0	0	0	0	0	0	0	0	0	1	0	11.00	6.00
13	1	0	0	0	0	0	0	0	0	0	0	0	1	0	11.00	6.40

M=136

Plots of N(m) for m year-pairs 1973-76 —
Mean circulation N(m) for year t+1
as function of circulation m for year t

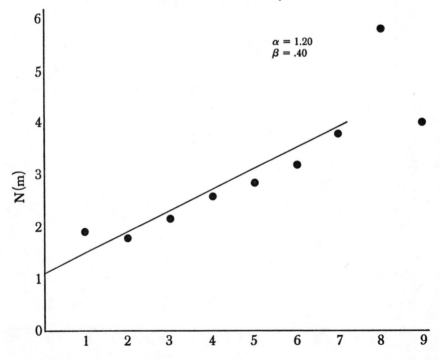

$\alpha = 1.20$
$\beta = .40$

EXHIBIT V

H Class — Values of M(m), N_{mn}, and N(m) for different values of m and n

| | | N_{mn} | | | | | | | | | | N(m) | |
| | | n= | | | | | | | | | | | |
m	M(m)	0	1	2	3	4	5	6	7	8	9	Experimental	Theoretical
0	14	9	2	0	2	1	0	0	0	0	0	.86	.86
1	16	5	4	4	2	1	0	0	0	0	0	1.37	1.46
2	8	1	2	2	1	2	0	0	0	0	0	2.12	2.06
3	9	1	2	4	2	0	0	0	0	0	0	1.77	2.66
4	7	1	0	1	1	0	2	0	2	0	0	4.10	3.26
5	2	0	0	0	0	1	0	0	0	0	1	6.50	3.86
6	1	0	1	0	0	0	0	0	0	0	0	1.00	4.46
7	2	0	0	1	0	1	0	0	0	0	0	3.00	5.06
8	1	1	0	0	0	0	0	0	0	0	0	1.00	5.66
9	1	0	0	0	0	0	0	0	1	0	0	7.00	6.26

$\overline{M=61}$

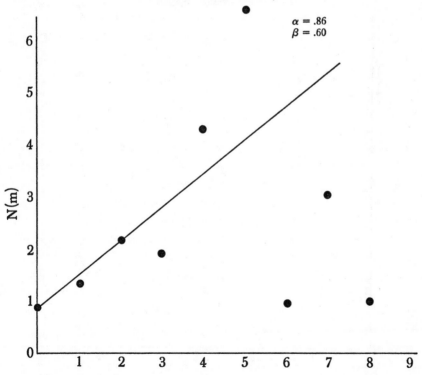

Plots of N(m) for m year-pairs 1973-76
Mean circulation N(m) for year t+1
as function of circulation m for year t

$\alpha = .86$
$\beta = .60$

N(m)

m

EXHIBIT VI

D Class — Values for M(m), N_{mn}, and N(m) for different values of m and n

		N_{mn}										N(m)	
m	M(m)	n= 0	1	2	3	4	5	6	7	8	Experimental		Theoretical
0	42	26	13	1	2	0	0	0	0	0	.50		.50
1	26	11	8	4	2	1	0	0	0	0	1.00		1.10
2	24	5	5	7	5	0	2	0	0	0	1.83		1.70
3	16	3	6	4	2	0	1	0	0	0	1.56		2.30
4	11	0	1	2	4	2	2	0	0	0	3.18		2.90
5	5	1	0	0	1	0	2	0	0	1	4.20		3.50

$\overline{M=124}$

Plots of N(m) for m year-pairs 1973-76 —
Mean circulation N(m) for year t+1
as function of circulation m for year t

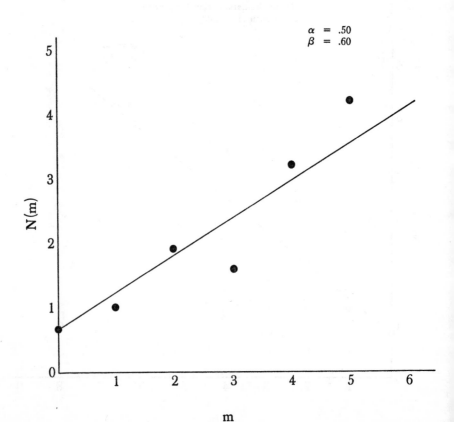

$\alpha = .50$
$\beta = .60$

EXHIBIT VII

E Class — Values of M(m), N$_{mn}$, and N(m)
for different values of m and n

		N_{mn}												N(m)	
m	M(m)	n=0	1	2	3	4	5	6	7	8	9	10	11	Experimental	Theoretical
0	32	18	7	5	2	0	0	0	0	0	0	0	0	.71	.35
1	21	10	9	1	1	0	0	0	0	0	0	0	0	.66	1.07
2	9	3	3	1	1	0	1	0	0	0	0	0	0	1.44	1.79
3	10	0	1	2	3	2	0	2	0	0	0	0	0	3.40	2.51
4	5	0	1	0	1	2	0	0	1	0	0	0	0	3.80	3.23
5	3	0	2	0	1	0	0	0	0	0	0	0	0	1.66	3.95
6	2	1	0	0	1	0	0	0	0	0	0	0	0	1.50	4.67
7	2	0	0	0	1	0	0	1	0	0	0	0	0	4.50	5.39
8	1	0	0	0	1	0	0	0	0	0	0	0	0	3.00	6.11
9	1	0	0	0	0	0	0	0	0	0	0	0	1	11.00	6.83
10	1	0	0	0	0	0	0	0	1	0	0	0	0	7.00	7.55
11	1	0	0	0	0	0	0	0	0	0	0	0	0	8.00	8.27

M=88

Plots of N(m) for m year-pairs 1973-76 —
Mean circulation N(m) for year t+1
as function of circulation m for year t

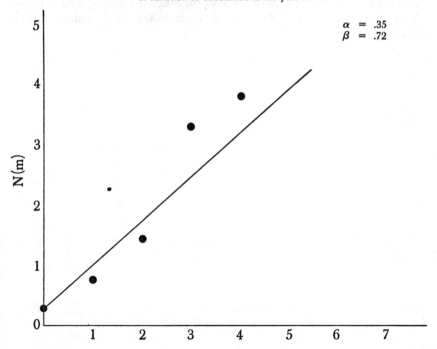

α = .35
β = .72

REFERENCES

Buckland, Michael K. *Book Availability and the Library User.* New York: Pergamon Press, 1975.

Chen, Ching-chih. *Applications of Operations Research Models to Libraries.* Cambridge, MA: The M.I.T. Press, 1976.

Franklin, R.D. "How Many Copies are Enough?" *Library Journal* 91 (October 1, 1966):4573-78.

Gore, Daniel. "Let Them Eat Cake While Reading Catalog." *Library Journal* 100 (January 15, 1975):93-8.

Goyal, S. K. "A Systematic Method for Reducing Over Ordering Copies of Books." *Library Resources and Technical Services* 16 (Winter, 1972):26-32.

Grant, Robert S. "Predicting the Need for Multiple Copies of Books." *Journal of Library Automation* 4 (June, 1971):64-71.

Moreland, George B. "Operation Saturation." *Library Journal* 93 (May 15, 1968):1975-79.

Morse, Philip M. *Library Effectiveness: A Systems Approach.* Cambridge, MA: The M.I.T. Press, 1968.

Trueswell, Richard W. "A Quantitative Measure of User Circulation Requirements and Its Possible Effect on Stack Thinning and Multiple Copy Determination." *American Documentation* 16 (January, 1965): 20-25.

A Conceptual Framework for the Performance Measurement of a Canadian Federal Government Health Sciences Library Network

by Sandra Parker

INTRODUCTION

Service-oriented institutions throughout society are currently experiencing budgetary difficulties. These financial constraints appear to be the trend for the future, and have prompted such organizations to seek techniques by which to support their funding requirements, particularly where public funds are involved. This concern is reflected in the recent interest in performance measurement and evaluation as evidenced by the attention given it in the social sciences literature. Specifically, this trend is evident in the library and information science field. Here the question of library performance measurement and evaluation has been demonstrated by an increased research emphasis since the late 1960s.

In keeping with this trend, the Health Protection Branch Library of Health and Welfare Canada took part in a performance measurement experiment on a pilot project basis from April 1973 to March 1975. The pilot project employed the Operational Performance Measurement System (OPMS) as defined and developed by Treasury Board's Planning Branch (*Organization of.* . . 1976). As a generalized technique, OPMS (or Performance Measurement, to cite the current term) is designed to be sufficiently flexible to meet the particular requirements of any organizational unit regardless of its level within the bureaucratic hierarchy. The performance indicator selection, interpretation and measurement are the responsibility of the organizational unit utilizing this management tool.

The Health Protection Branch Library's involvement in the OPMS pilot project lapsed with a turnover in Branch personnel. How-

ever, the imperative need for a performance measurement and evaluation technique is still recognized by the Branch's Chief of Library Services and the financial administrators to whom she is responsible. This
need is felt both internally, in terms of the effective allocation and
management of resources within the library services' unit, and exter-
nally, in terms of fiscal accountability to the financial administrators.

In keeping with this continued concern in the Branch, the long-
range planning of the Health Protection Branch Library is to rein-
troduce performance measurement. However, the specific concepts of
the 1973-1975 pilot project reflect a library organization and structure
which is no longer valid. This is due to the centralization within the
Health and Welfare Departmental Library of several activities for-
merly associated with the Branch Library. The future implementation
of the performance measurement technique thus demands a redefini-
tion of the conceptual base of the 1973-1975 OPMS project in order
that it may reflect the present Branch Library organization and
activity structure.

PERFORMANCE MEASUREMENT: DEFINITION OF THE PROBLEM

Performance measurement is an analytical tool which provides a
manager with the means to evaluate the activities of his/her organization as to the results produced and the extent to which these results
fulfill predesignated objectives. This evaluative aid supports the management processes of resource planning, control and reporting. The
development and implementation of any such technique demands the
establishment of clearly defined and agreed upon objectives as well as
reliable indicators, measures and standards of performance. The objec-
tives-setting process is, in fact, a contractual agreement between the
manager and his/her superiors as to the performance expectations of
the particular organizational unit in return for needed resources. In
this way, the manager is accountable to his/her superiors for the organization's performance, or the results achieved based on predetermined goals.

However, performance measurement is not a technique which can
supplant the judgmental process of a manager. Its role is solely sup-
portive in its provision of "hard" data derived from the organization's
output as related to the input associated with their production. In
addition, the evaluative process cannot determine whether the organization's objectives as set out are appropriate or realistic, nor can it
determine if alternate means are available to better achieve these
objectives. Finally, as a technique which focuses on the performance
measurement of organizations, it is not designed to measure the performance of individuals within that organization.

Indicators of "performance expectations or preferences in terms of which value judgements can be made" (Swanson, 1975) exist in the library and information science literature, but lack a "total system performance" approach to measurement and evaluation. In addition, they exist primarily as the result of an academic research effort rather than a practical endeavor by a practicing library manager.

Measures of these performance yardsticks also exist in the literature. However, the conventional library approach to quantitative measurement, apart from the results of specific research projects, reveals a tendency to measure that activity or aspect of an activity which is easiest to quantify (e.g., number of books catalogued, number of items circulated). This counting syndrome makes little attempt to interpret the meaningfulness of the data gathered or any measurement interrelationships. Problems in this quantitative area have been succinctly summarized in a 1967 study submitted to the United States National Advisory Commission on Libraries (*Mathematics*, Aug. 1967) in which it was concluded that "available statistical data might be described with little exaggeration as a collection of gaps interspersed by an occasional bit of reliable information." The critique considered library statistical data systems at the local, state, and national levels. Similar surveys reveal a continuing statistical deficiency despite recent major attempts to quantify, measure and evaluate library performance.

Library performance standards, those units of measurement which provide "a norm or base of reference" (Terry, 1967) or the evaluative guidelines, do not presently exist. Those library standards which are available are at best descriptive. They are often based on value judgements as opposed to absolute or relative values derived from the actual work situation, and are directed in emphasis toward the measurement of input alone rather than the relationship of output to input.

ENVIRONMENT: HEALTH PROTECTION BRANCH LIBRARY

The Branch

The Health Protection Branch consists of some 2,000 field inspectors, applied research scientists, technical support, administrative and management staff. The Branch is composed of six major Directorates—Food, Drugs, Environmental Health, Laboratory Centre for Disease Control, Nonmedical Use of Drugs, and Field Operations. Functioning primarily as a regulatory body, the Branch is responsible for the enforcement, in full or in part, of many acts, among them the "Food and Drug Act, the Narcotic Control Act, the Hazardous Products Act, the Atomic Energy Control Act, the Canada Labour Code, the Radiation Emitting Devices Act, and the Department of National Health and Welfare Act." (*Organization of . . .* 1976).

The Library Network

The HPB Library is composed of a multi-site network of Reading Centres. Four staffed Ottawa Reading Centres serve the research, administrative and management clientele of the Food, Drugs, Environmental Health, Laboratory Centre for Disease Control, and Nonmedical Use of Drugs Directorates. Three Regional Reading Centres, one each in Toronto, Montreal and Vancouver, serve the inspectors and allied personnel of the Field Operations Directorate. In addition, there are unmanned collections in Halifax, Winnipeg and at least four separate sites in Ottawa, all of which have the potential to be organized as reference collections as demand and Branch staff resources dictate. At the present time, the library network's organizational responsibilities do not extend to these unmanned collections.

The Library Staff

The Chief of Library Services for the network reports to the Branch Director of Finance and Administration. She has line responsibility for thirteen professional/clerical staff (in a ratio of 6:7) in the three Ottawa Reading Centres which serve the Food, Drugs, Environmental Health and Laboratory Centre for Disease Control Directorates. In addition, she has functional responsibility for the Nonmedical Use of Drugs Reading Centre in Ottawa, and the three manned Regional Reading Centres Serving the Field Operations Directorate. The organization of the library network staff in terms of their levels, distribution, and the responsibility relationship of the Chief to them is depicted in Figure 1. The largest staff complement of the network is attached to the Reading Centre serving the Food and Drugs Directorates (from here on known as the Main Reading Centre).

The Library Collection

Organized and maintained as a working current awareness collection geared to meet the immediate information needs of Branch users, the library collection presently contains some 900 serial titles, and approximately 15,000 monographic volumes. Well over half of the serial subscriptions and the monographic collection are housed in the Main Reading Centre. This Reading Centre also contains the major reference indexes and abstracts for the network, as well as serial and monographic works of an interdisciplinary nature. The other Reading Centres have collections specific to the subject needs of the Directorate they serve. The Departmental Library of Health and Welfare Canada serves as the archive for older (i.e., six years or more in most cases) materials. The subject orientation of this collection covers such major areas as Pharmacology, Food Science, Food and Drug Technology, Nutrition, Toxicology, Virology, Drug Abuse, Food and Drug legislation, and Biomedicine. Primarily due to its relative currency, the serial collection is the major information resource for the Branch users and the library staff as they respond to the users' expressed information needs.

HEALTH PROTECTION BRANCH
LIBRARY ORGANIZATION CHART

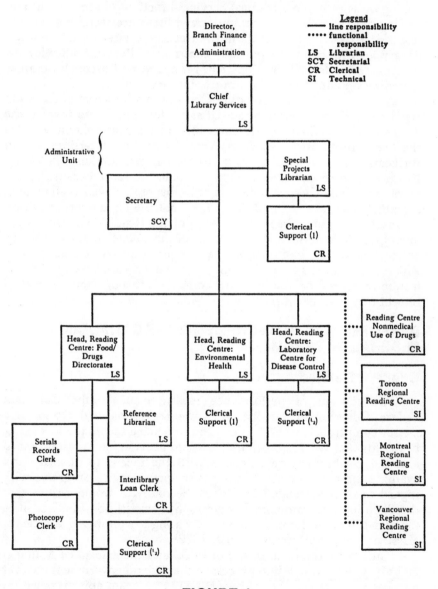

FIGURE 1

The Library's Activities

Following the 1973 restructuring of the Health Protection Branch Library, several activities were completely or partially centralized with those of the Health and Welfare Departmental Library. Primary among these were the Technical Services functions of acquisitions and cataloguing, as well as the computerized literature searching services (e.g., MEDLINE, TOXLINE) in the Reader Services area. The interlibrary loan function was partially centralized. Responsibility for the functions of collection development, reference, and manual literature searching remained with the Branch Library system.

Each Branch Library Reading Centre is a microcosm of the Main Reading Centre in terms of activities performed. These involve the professional functions of reference and collection development, plus the clerical activities associated with kardexing, interlibrary loan verification and processing, and circulation of materials. The Main Reading Centre provides backup reference support because of the more extensive reference collection at its disposal, as well as all manual literature searches. It should be noted that the circulation of library materials is a minimal activity in each of the Reading Centres as the monographic material is the only part of the collection allowed to circulate. The majority of the document requests are for journal articles which are fulfilled by a photocopy from the network's own serial collection resources, or from external collections through the established interlibrary loan network.

PERFORMANCE MEASUREMENT: THE CANADIAN FEDERAL GOVERNMENT

Concept Defined

The concept of performance measurement in the Canadian Federal Government was defined by the Treasury Board, the government's comptroller, in 1970. The need for such a technique was felt to be essential for two reasons. First, it would provide the Treasury Board and the government departments with the means to quantify and evaluate the performance of the government's many programs with regard to their associated objectives. Secondly, it would ensure that the Planning Programming Budgeting System (PPBS), in effect since the mid-1960s, "did not become merely a slightly improved vehicle for classifying expenditures." (Hartle, 1972)

Until 1970, the main thrust of PPBS and the associated Management by Objectives (MBO) process in the Federal government context had been the clarification of departmental program objectives within their related activity structure with little attention paid as to how well these objectives were being met. Performance Measurement, like PPBS and MBO, is an objectives-oriented technique; however, the rationale for each approach complements that of the others. To paraphrase Frederiksen (1975), PPBS addresses itself to the cost-benefit analysis of alternative courses of action at the program level of departmental operations. MBO, on the other hand, seeks to establish clearly defined and mutually appropriate organizational goals and to develop and implement the plans necessary to achieve these goals. Performance measurement, the latest technique, was implemented to make up for the lack of a process to quantify and qualitatively rank the program output and organizational performance vis á vis their objectives.

Concept Implemented

This analytical tool developed and implemented in an experimental testing mode from 1971-1973, and introduced as of April 1973, had two basic functions:

1) to "relate output to input" (Treasury Board, 1974) in order to determine organizational efficiency, where input are the resources (e.g. manpower or dollars) utilized in the production of that output;

2) to focus on the results achieved in order to determine organizational effectiveness, where effectiveness is defined as "the extent to which an objective or goal is achieved." (Treasury Board, 1974)

The basic performance measurement concepts of the Treasury Board are thus *efficiency* and *effectiveness*.

Current Status

From the beginning of the 1973/74 fiscal year to the end of the 1975/76 fiscal year, performance data were utilized by many departmental managers to support their Program Forecasts, or the long-term budgetary plan of resources required to carry out future programs. The emphasis on the performance indicators up until that time was on the efficiency aspects of departmental programs. The technique was viewed primarily as a mechanism for budgetary support of increased resource allocations. Gordon Osbaldeston (1976), Secretary of the Treasury Board, reviewed the implementation progress of performance measurement in the Canadian Federal Government in 1976, and concluded that although efficiency indicators and measures were fairly widespread in their implementation, the definition and measurement of effectiveness indicators of performance were still inadequate.

Robert Andras (1976), President of the Treasury Board, reaffirmed the government's commitment to improve the efficiency and effectiveness of its programs in his November 1976 report to the Canadian House of Commons. In it, he outlined the Treasury Board's Policy Statement (1976) which requires that all Departments and Agencies whose programs are subject to the Treasury Board funding review will support their program forecasts with efficiency and effectiveness performance data by 1980.

The 1976 Policy Statement and the two progress reports cited above mark the second phase of Performance Measurement implementation by the Treasury Board. This phase will focus on the effectiveness indicators and measures of performance. In doing so, it will allow the Treasury Board Ministers to make more rational decisions with regard to departmental resource allocation. The emphasis on effectiveness performance factors also underscores the government's concern with the provision of a mechanism to reveal the accountability of its managers.

Concept Problems/Limitations

The performance measurement concept as initially developed and applied has posed certain difficulties, particularly in the experimental stages. Treasury Board staff have worked closely with the departmental staff involved, and many of the problems and/or limitations have been resolved. To provide an historical perspective, some of these earlier difficulties are highlighted below:

1) The technique, as first implemented by some departments, was designed and developed in a manner far too detailed to administer. Analysts are now warned of the complexity pitfalls;

2) The technique was originally viewed as having optimum advantage in the efficiency measurement of repetitive, labour-intensive activities yielding uniform outputs. In practice, although such activities are the easiest to define, quantify and measure, the qualitative aspects of the technique as it pertains to effectiveness are now being successfully investigated and implemented;

3) The technique had failed in instances where those responsible for its implementation and monitoring had not taken into account organizational change, the resultant change in output, and adjusted the technique's performance indicators and measures accordingly. Again, analysts are cautioned about this problem area;

4) The technique had not initially been considered amenable to measure such administrative overheads as personnel, as well as project-oriented work as research or consulting. However, several recent attempts to develop indicators and measures in these two areas have been successful.

Despite these and other initial difficulties, the Treasury Board has taken steps in close cooperation with the government departments involved to improve the application of the technique. To date, the results indicate that the performance measurement concept as developed and used in the Canadian Federal Government has and will continue to provide an effective tool for management planning, control and accountability and the Treasury Board's resource allocation decisions.

PERFORMANCE MEASUREMENT: THE LIBRARY AND INFORMATION SCIENCE LITERATURE

Library performance measurement and evaluation can best be described as embryonic in terms of the concepts developed and the measurement methodology employed. The pre-1964 published literature indicates a concern with the need for performance evaluation but lacks specification of the concepts and measurement methodology. Most of the substantive research has been conducted and the results reported in the literature since 1968.

A 1972 study by Evans et al. (1972) isolated and identified six performance indicators and associated measures employed in the evaluative research up until 1969, and grouped them according to the aspect of the library system appraised. Implicit in this grouping is the lack of research consideration to develop indicators and measures of total library performance. The Evans survey also pinpointed a second weakness in the pre-1970 literature—that is, much of the reported research failed to address the basic concept of performance evaluation rationale and methodology.

Figure 2 highlights some of the major research efforts reported in the literature since 1968. Specifically, the matrix attempts to relate their reported performance indicators and associated measures with the efficiency/effectiveness criteria of the Treasury Board Performance Measurement technique. The research matrix and a critical review of the pre-1969 literature covered by Evans prompt the following general statements about the state-of-the-art in library performance measurement and evaluation research:

1) The research studies have not been cumulative. For the most part they are project-oriented (involving one-time support by a funding agency), and follow-up is not provided by the funding agency and/or the original research objectives. The one outstanding exception is the Orr and Schless (1972) report of the employment of Orr's standardized Document Delivery Test (DDT) to assess the capability of ninety-two medical school libraries to meet the document needs of their bio-medical researchers and the capability of fifteen major resource libraries to fill the interlibrary loan requests from biomedical libraries. Independently, two researchers have utilized Orr's DDT with considerable success. Penner (1972) reports his efforts with the technique to measure the document delivery capability of a library and information science collection. Piternick (1972) used the DDT to measure the journal capability of a Canadian academic biomedical library.

2) The research results (performance indicators selected, data gathering and analysis methodology) have not been consistently tested as to their practicality in actual library situations. The project conducted by Wessel et al. (1967, 1968, 1969) is a prime

PERFORMANCE EVALUATION RESEARCH MATRIX

Researcher	Categorization		Type of Library			No. of Libraries Considered		Performance Indicators
	Libr	Non Libr	Acad	Pub	Spec	Mult	Sing	
Chen	X		X				X	Collection use
DeProspo et al.	X			X		X		Collection, Staff and Facilities use
Durham University Study		X	X			X		Cost and benefit of library services.
Fussler and Simon		X	X			X		Collection use
Hamburg et al.		X	X	X		X		Collection use
Morse		X	X				X	Collection use
Orr et al.	X	X	X			X		Document and/or information delivery response time
Wessel et al.		X			X	X		Library use

FIGURE 2

example. Although the models developed have been described as theoretically sound, they have yet to be implemented in the actual measurement of total library efficiency and effectiveness of the United States Army Technical Libraries for which they were designed.

3) The studies reported reveal an orientation to one type of library (notably large academic research libraries), or to one library in particular. The narrowness of the research scope limits the generalization of the research results. Researchers as Chen (1976) and DeProspo et al. (1973) indicate in the discussion of their research results that their concepts and measurement methodologies are applicable with or without modification to other types of libraries. They do not support these statements; however, this applicability aspect was not part of their original research concern.

4) The research reported indicates a tendency to treat the library as an isolated entity, and to ignore its relationship to the larger

figure 2, continued

Performance Measures	Classification of Indicators and Measures		Remarks
	Efficiency	Effectiveness	
Book use/manipulation of recorded data	N/A	N/A	Quantitative presentation of present book use to predict future use with no relationship to total resources available.
Gross use to services available	N/A	X	Research objective to define and develop effectiveness ratios only.
Interrelationship of services provided to costs incurred	X	N/A	Importance and value weighting of services provided judged only by library administrator. No definitive benefit measures developed.
See Chen above	N/A	N/A	See Chen above
Document exposure hours related to dollar costs	X	N/A	Assumes benefit of material used is equated with amount of contact time, but indicator and measure essentially concern efficiency.
See Chen above	N/A	N/A	See Chen above
Ratio of library capability to delivery	N/A	X	Research objective to define and develop effectiveness ratio only.
Cost and value of library operations and services	X	X	Theoretical discussion only. Complex efficiency and effectiveness models never implemented to measure the actual capability of libraries for which they tested.

FIGURE 2

information complex in terms of its ability to provide information and/or documents. Again, the research of Orr et al. (1968) is the notable exception. Their DDT was designed to determine user satisfaction in terms of the library's capability and turnaround time to deliver materials likely to be required by its users. The measuring procedure equates the library's capability on the basis of its actual holdings and the effectiveness of its interlibrary loan activities.

5) The studies reveal a lack of consideration for total library performance in that most concentrate on one or two evaluative concepts and their measures relating to one or two service functions performed by the library or type of library in question. Only Wessel et al. (1969) attempt to depart from such partial measures of effectiveness to consider the efficiency and effectiveness of the library system as a whole.

6) The majority of the innovative research projects have been carried out by non-librarians with little experience in or

knowledge of libraries and their activities. The frequent result has been the utilization of management science techniques as in Wessel et al. (1969) and the development of sophisticated mathematical models such as those reported by Morse (1968) which are virtually incomprehensible to the average practicing librarian. In addition, the associated data collection is often too time-consuming and expensive for practical implementation.

7) Many of the studies, particularly those involving large academic libraries, display a tendency to overconcentrate on the use and manipulation of circulation data. Such researchers as Morse (1968), Chen (1976), and Fussler and Simon (1969) focus on recorded circulation usage, information which is not only readily available in most libraries, but is easy to quantify and amenable to model construction. However, such data are biased to recorded use only, thus ignoring the in-house use made of library materials. In addition, their research perspective disregards those library activities which provide information and/or documents from external sources, and the all-important variable of response time regardless of source fulfillment.

8) Most of the reported research projects concentrate on output indicators of performance. That is, they do not attempt to establish a relationship between the output and the input (i.e. manpower resources or costs) associated with their production, nor the extent to which the output achieve their objectives. There are two noteworthy exceptions. Hamburg et al. (1972, 1974) developed the concept of Document Exposure Time and related the costs incurred to output measured in terms of exposure hours—that is, actual time spent by readers in consulting library materials. This research represents a similar but more refined approach based on Meier (1961). The Durham study (1974) attempted to define the worth of a university library to its parent institution. Benefits were derived from models which measured the unit costs and the relationship of the cost of one library service to another. The importance of the various library services was weighted in accordance with a scheme determined by the value judgements of the library administrator. This lack of involvement of user expectations underlines the inherent weakness of the research project. It also failed to achieve its objective to develop definitive benefit measures.

It is evident that this survey review of the recent evaluative research does not provide a suitable framework for the HPB special library network in terms of its approach to the efficiency and effectiveness of the total library system. This is due in part to the narrowness of the research objectives and thus the evaluative concepts and measures of existing studies. It is also due in part to the complexity of many of the measurement and analysis techniques utilized. On the other hand, the Treasury Board's Performance Measurement technique previously outlined, geared as it is toward the evaluation of the efficiency and effectiveness of non-profit institutions, appears to be a viable alternative. The conceptual framework for the development of the technique for the HPB Library network will be detailed in the next chapter.

PERFORMANCE MEASUREMENT: THE HEALTH PROTECTION BRANCH LIBRARY

The evaluative model depicted in Figure 3 represents the interrelationships between the performance evaluation components and their associated performance indicators within the Treasury Board technique. The efficiency-effectiveness interrelationship illustrated in Figure 3 identifies the five specific performance indicators to be measured and upon which the evaluative judgements as to the library's performance will be made. The five indicators are defined as follows:

Operational Efficiency (b/a) : the quantitative ratio of operational output units (b) to the operational input (a) expressed as units of output per man-year or dollar costs associated with the output production. In this context, the operational output are the goods and services provided by the individual work processes of the library. An illustration of this ratio could be the number of interlibrary loan requests handled per year to the number of man-years associated with their handling, e.g.,

$$\frac{2,500 \text{ requests}}{2 \text{ man-years}} = 1,250 \text{ requests handled per man-year}$$

The figure 1,250 represents an efficiency indicator for that annual period in relation to relative performance standards previously established.

EFFICIENCY-EFFECTIVENESS MODEL (TREASURY BOARD, 1974) FOR THE EVALUATION OF THE HEALTH PROTECTION BRANCH LIBRARY

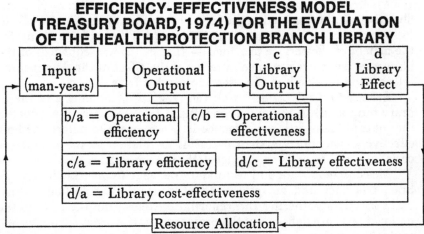

FIGURE 3

Operational Effectiveness (c/b): the quantitative ratio of library output units (c) to operational output units (b), or the extent to which the operations meet their objectives. In this context, library output are those which have been successfully provided by the operational work processes and which have an impact external to its operations. In terms of an example, this ratio could be illustrated as the number of interlibrary loan requests satisfactorily fulfilled annually (by the internal collection resources or the back-up resources of the larger information community) in an average of *n* man days in relation to the total number of interlibrary loan requests handled per man year, e.g.,

$$\frac{2{,}025 \text{ successful requests}}{2{,}250 \text{ requests handled}} = 90\% \text{ operational effectiveness in an average } n \text{ man-day turnaround}$$

The 90% average *n* man-day turnaround operational effectiveness indicator for the annual period in question is then evaluated relative to past performance standards.

Library Efficiency (c/a): the quantitative ratio of library output units (c) to operational input units (man-years or dollars). For example, this ratio could be expressed as the number of interlibrary loan requests successfully processed per year in an average of *n* man-days in relation to the number of man-years associated with their successful handling, e.g.,

$$\frac{2{,}250 \text{ successful requests}}{2 \text{ man-years}} = 1{,}125 \text{ requests successfully handled per man year in an average } n \text{ man-day turnaround}$$

Again, this efficiency indicator can be related to pre-established library efficiency performance standards expressed in relative terms.

Library Effectiveness (d/c): the extent to which the library meets its objectives. It is expressed as the ratio of the effect of the library output (d) per unit of such output (c). This indicator attempts to account for the benefit of the service provided — that is, the consequences of the library system's performance in terms of the effect of the documented information received on the user's research efforts.

Library Cost-effectiveness (d/c): the relation of the effects of the library output (d) to the operational input (a) expended in producing that output. This fifth performance indicator seeks to determine how effectively the library system performs in relation to the manpower costs incurred to achieve that level of performance.

Measurement data and techniques relevant to operational and library efficiency and operational effectiveness do not presently exist. Statistical data gathering and reporting systems from the local to the national level are deficient at the present time. However, such a system could be developed within a reasonable time frame for the library system concerned. Inherent in its development is a requirement to identify and to define for the library system the resource input, the major operational and library output, and to relate the quantitative input so defined to its appropriate output activities.

The concepts of library effectiveness and library cost-effectiveness do not appear to be so readily amenable to direct quantification. The value of a library at present defies definition and thus measurement as indicated in the review of the literature. Some of the definitions approach serendipity — e.g., stimulation of research or invention. Until the effect of the library can be approached more definitively, instruments to directly or indirectly measure the library effectiveness and cost-effectiveness concepts will remain elusive.

SUMMARIZATION

The flexible framework of the Treasury Board's Performance Measurement technique is recommended as the viable resource planning, control, and evaluative tool for the Health Protection Branch Library network. With a commitment by management to the concept of performance measurement and to its potential role in the manager's decision-making processes, certain operational and user information will be required in order to successfully develop and implement the technique. In particular this includes:

1) determination of the user population's needs, and their use of the current library service unit in terms of type of use, usage patterns and user groups;
2) determination of the extent of user satisfaction with the library output now offered in terms of volume and turnaround time required to meet their needs;
3) identification and definition of the major activities and associated operational and library output, weighted according to their importance to the users;
4) determination of the measurable aspects of the operational and library output, and their associated input resources;
5) determination of the unmeasurable activities of the library organization;
6) development of quantifiable measurable goals and objectives in keeping with the library's scope, authority and users' needs.

The implementation of the management tool requires the concomitant design and development of a statistical input and output data gathering system to "feed" the performance measurement indicators defined in the preceding chapter. The final requirement is a two-level reporting format. The first-level report aimed at library management must be sufficient in detail to aid in the evaluative and resource allocation process. The second-level report, to senior management, should reflect the librarian's accountability for the performance of his/her organization—that is, the extent to which the mutually agreed upon objectives have been met by the organization's performance.

CONCLUSION

Three Canadian Federal Government libraries are in various stages of implementation with this performance measurement technique. Several other libraries are in the initial planning stages—the Health Protection Branch Library network included. The emphasis to date, in those libraries where implementation has begun, is on the efficiency indicators and measures—in other words, those aspects of the technique which are most amenable to identification and quantitative manipulation. As this relatively new approach becomes more familiar to those responsible for its design and implementation, and the value of its results realized by library managers, an emphasis shift will no doubt take place to incorporate the technique's effectiveness indicators and measures.

Currently, those key library resource people involved in the planning and/or development of the Treasury Board's Performance Measurement have established an informal working group for the exchange of ideas and practical implementation problems. It is planned that this arrangement will provide a continuing information forum to encourage the progressive implementation of the technique within those libraries presently involved and its spread to those libraries not yet actively committed and participating.

REFERENCES

Andras, Robert. "Progress Report on the Measurement of Performance in the Public Service of Canada." Document tabled in the House of Commons, November 17, 1976. (Typewritten.)

Canada. Treasury Board. "Measurement of the Performance of Government Operations." Policy and guidelines. Ottawa, July 22, 1976. Circular Letter No. 1976-25.

Canada. Treasury Board. *Operational Measurement, Vol. 1: A Managerial Overview*. Ottawa, 1974.

Chen, Ching-chih. *Applications of Operations Research Models to Libraries: A Case Study of the Use of Monographs in the Francis A. Countway Library of Medicine, Harvard University*. Cambridge, MA: The M.I.T. Press, 1976.

DeProspo, E. R. et al. *Performance Measures for Public Libraries*. Chicago, IL: Public Library Association of ALA, 1973.

Durham University. "Project for Evaluting the Benefits from University Libraries. Final Report, 1969." In *Measuring the Quality of Library Service: A Handbook*. Metuchen, NJ: Scarecrow Press, 1974.

Evans, Edward et al. "Review of Criteria Used to Measure Library Effectiveness." *Bulletin of the Medical Library Association* 60 (January, 1972):102-110.

Frederiksen, Henning. "Is Operational Performance in Government Measurable?" *Optimum* 6 (1975):24.

Fussler, H. H. and Simon, J. L. *Patterns in the Use of Books in Large Research Libraries.* Chicago, IL: University of Chicago Press, 1969.

Hamburg, Morris. *Library Planning and Decision-Making Systems.* Cambridge, MA: The M.I.T. Press, 1974.

Hamburg, Morris et al. "Library Objectives and Performance Measures and Their Use in Decision-Making." *Library Quarterly* 42 (January, 1972):107-127.

Hartle, D. G. "Operational Performance Measurement in the Federal Government." *Optimum* 3 (1972):5.

Meier, Richard L. "Efficiency Criteria for the Operation of Large Libraries." *Library Quarterly* 31 (July, 1961):215-234.

Morse, Philip M. *Library Effectiveness: A Systems Approach.* Cambridge, MA: The M.I.T. Press, 1968.

"On Library Statistics." *Mathematics* (August, 1967):1.

Organization of the Government of Canada, Sect. 9005, Sect. 9050. Ottawa, 1976.

Orr, R. H. et al. "Development of Methodological Tools for Planning and Managing Library Services: I. Project Goals and Approach." *Bulletin of the Medical Library Association* 56 (July, 1968):235-240.

_____. "Development of Methodological Tools for Planning and Managing Library Services: II. Measuring a Library's Capability for Providing Documents." *Bulletin of the Medical Library Association* 56 (July, 1968):241-267.

_____. "Development of Methodological Tools for Planning and Managing Library Services: III. Standardized Inventories of Library Services." *Bulletin of the Medical Library Association* 56 (October, 1968):380-403.

Orr, R. H., and Schless, A. P. "Document Delivery Capabilities of Major Biomedical Libraries in 1968: Results of a National Survey Employing Standardized Tests." *Bulletin of the Medical Library Association* 60 (1972):382-422.

Osbaldeston, Gordon. "Implementation of Performance Measurement in the Federal Public Service: A Progress Report." *Optimum* 7 (1976):5-11.

Penner, R. J. "Measuring a Library's Capability." *Journal of Education for Librarianship* 13 (1972):17-30.

Piternick, Anne Brearley. "Measurement of Journal Availability in a Biomedical Library." *Bulletin of the Medical Library Association* 60 (October, 1972):534-542.

Swanson, Rowena Weiss. "Performing Evaluation Studies in Information Science." *Journal of the American Association for Information Science* 26 (May-June, 1975):142.

Terry, George R. *Principles of Management*, 6th ed. Homewood, IL: Irwin, 1972.

Wessel, C. J. et al. *Criteria for Evaluating the Effectiveness of Library Operations and Services; Phase I: Literature Search and State of the Art.* Washington, DC: John I. Thompson and Co., 1967.

_____. *Criteria for Evaluating the Effectiveness of Library Operations and Services; Phase II: Data Gathering and Evaluation.* Washington, DC: John I. Thompson and Co., 1968.

_____. *Criteria for Evaluating the Effectiveness of Library Operations and Services; Phase III: Recommended Criteria and Methods for Their Utilization.* Washington, DC: John I. Thompson, 1969.

Appendix I

Report on Capitol Region Library Council
Study to develop management system for use
in measurement of library services—February
22, 1978.

A committee from the Capitol Region Library Council, Hartford, Connecticut were participants in the Institute on Quantitative Measurement and Dynamic Library Service, Simmons College. Their study involved the development of a data management system for use in measurement of library service. During Unit II of the Institute in March, 1977, the Capitol Region Library Council group presented the goals and purposes of their study and their progress to date towards obtaining a grant to fund Phase I of their proposed project. The participants were Mr. Richard Akeroyd, then Director, Department of Planning and Research, Connecticut State Library, Hartford, Connecticut (currently, Consultant, White House Conference on Libraries and Information Services, National Commission on Libraries and Information Science, Washington, D.C.); Ms. Barbara H. Gibson, Director, Village Library, Farmington, Connecticut; and Ms. Dency Sargent, Executive Director, Capitol Region Library Council, Hartford, Connecticut.

The following is a current report on the study by Ms. Dency Sargent.

BACKGROUND

The Capitol Region Library Council is a private voluntary association of public, school, academic, and special libraries in the Hartford, Connecticut area formed in 1969 to further library service through cooperative projects and programs. It has a history of active programs to improve access to existing resources, to acquire new skills, to cooperatively offer programs and services to the public, and to encourage better communications between member libraries and with the public.

In the fall of 1976 the Board of Directors of the Capitol Region Library Council discussed the development of a performance measurement system for use by libraries. The interest was generated by the publication of *A Data Gathering and Instructional Manual for Performance Measures in Public Libraries* by Ellen Altman, Ernest R. DeProspo et al. (Chicago: Celadon Press, 1976) and an ALA conference program by DeProspo on the extended study which produced the *Manual.* The decision by the Board of Directors to explore the development of a system of data management to measure library service arose from direct interest by the member libraries.

The members of the study committee formed by the Council were Mr. Richard Akeroyd, and Ms. Barbara Gibson. In the fall of 1977, Ms. Leslie Berman replaced Mr. Akeroyd at the State Library and became a member of this CRLC project committee.

THE STUDY

The primary need identified by the committee was for affordable techniques to acquire meaningful data for planning and evaluation of library services. Thus the goal of the study became the development of an efficient, cost-effective data management system to measure library services. It was decided to use *A Data Gathering and Instructional Manual for Performance Measures in Public Libraries* as a guide in the development of the proposed data management system.

The collection of data concerning the delivery of library service presents certain problems; however, the most difficult step in acquiring meaningful information on library services is the manipulation of the data once collected. To meet the goal of efficiency, it was an initial decision that the data would be processed by computer. Then the question became one of access and cost. Could a data management system be developed that uses a computer to manipulate the data, produces a report useful to a library, and is within a price range that the library can afford? Thus Phase I of the Project became a feasibility study to determine the time and cost coefficients for data collection, inputting, sorting, and reporting. It calls for a sample of field collected data.

Phase I of the proposed project was funded by a Library Services and Construction Grant awarded to the Capitol Region Library Council in June, 1977. A user study was selected for the feasibility phase because this study has the highest number of individual items of data and the highest number of possible correlations between the items of data. A "Library User Ticket" was developed to determine user characteristics including town of residence, occupational or student status, use of staff assistance, time and length of stay, and satisfaction with service. Library user data was collected from four varying sized public libraries within the Capitol Region Library Council. A sample of the user data collected was used to test the data management system and determine the time and cost coefficients.

As of February, 1978, sample reports for all four libraries were nearly ready. The quantitative information provided by the reports are of definite value to the libraries in identifying the characteristics of their users. The information does meet the goal of acquiring meaningful data for planning and evaluation of library services. The system also appears to meet the goal of cost-effectiveness.

The Capitol Region Library Council is awaiting the final report of the feasibility study. If Phase I shows the system is viable, two directions are likely to result. The first is for the Council to move to Phase II of the proposed project. Phase II calls for the development of a computer software package capable of processing additional library performance data. Phase III is a pilot study of the resulting data management system in libraries of the Capitol Region Library Council. Further development also projects application of the system to nonpublic libraries. Since the results appear to support moving to Phase II of the study, a search for sources of funding and preparation of a written grant request has begun.

Given the probable positive report on the Phase I feasibility study, the second direction which is likely is that the user study developed for Phase I of the project will be made available to libraries within and outside of the region through the Capitol Region Library Council.

Glossary

by Ching-chih Chen

Average: a value which is typical or representative of a set of data. Averages are also called measures of central tendency. There are three kinds of averages:

1. **Mean:** the total of the values of a set of observations divided by their number.

2. **Median:** the value of the central item when data are arranged by size.

3. **Mode:** the observation that occurs with the greatest frequency.

Biased Sample: a biased sample is not random, i.e., it is a sample drawn in such a way that it is not representative of the population as a whole.

CHI Square Method: a statistical method used to determine whether a statistically significant difference between the two sets (observed and expected) of data exists.

Computability: a measure of the extent to which something can be described mathematically, especially with regard to being handled by machine, such as a computer.

Confidence Interval: range of precision.

Confidence Level: level of risk involved.

Correlation: indicates how two variables are related.

Correlation Coefficient: a measure of the degree of association between two variables.

Cost-Benefit Analysis: the attempt to relate the worth or benefit of a service to the cost of providing it. Ideally benefits exceed costs.

Cost-Effectiveness: a measure of how efficiently in terms of cost a system is meeting its goals. A means of relating the cost of a project to effective performance or goal attainment.

Cumulative Frequency Distribution: the total frequency of all values less than the upper class boundary of a given class interval.

Decision Theory: a more recent name for the theory of statistical inference. Methods by which one makes inferences or generalizations about a population based on information obtained from a sample group of the population.

Descriptive Statistics: one of the most widely known statistical methods that summarize numerical data in terms of average and other kinds of measures for descriptive purpose.

Effectiveness: a measure of how well a service satisfies the demands made on it by its users.

Exponential: involving numbers raised to powers.

Figure: usually a chart, illustration, or graph which is used to present statistical data.

Flow Chart: utilizes a very limited number of symbolic conventions to describe the flow of forms or data and the sequence of operations on them.

Forecasting: making predictions.

Frequency Distribution: the pattern of data grouped into classes and the number, i.e., the frequency, of cases that fall in each class.

Function: an association between a pair of variables so that for every possible value of the first, the independent variable, there corresponds a unique value of the second, the dependent variable.

Game Theory: a mathematical theory that deals with the problem of decision-making under uncertainty in situations where some or all of the uncertainty is due to the as-yet-unknown actions of one or more other decision-makers.

Inferential Statistics: a kind of statistical method which draws inferences from a particular set or sets of data collected by using modern analytical techniques.

Input: the information or data supplied to a device or system.

Interface: a shared boundary; a storage area that can be accessed in two or more ways.

Interval Estimate: the probability that the mean will occur in a given range.

Linear Programming: problems involving allocating scarce resources among activities that vary in profitability and in the amounts of each resource needed.

Logarithm: of a positive number, the exponent indicating the power to which a positive number (the base) must be raised in order to produce the given number.

Macroevaluation: a study of how well a system operates.

Management Data System: a system that provides data to assist management in the decision-making process.

Markovian Book-Use Model: a probabilistic model of book use developed by Philip Morse. It shows that there is a time correlation, or "memory," from one time period to the next in book use.

Mathematical Model: a model which describes as accurately as possible a real physical system or process by using mathematical languages.

Matrix Operations: a matrix is a tabular array of data, organized in a standard form, which may be handled as a package in mathematical calculation. A matrix's size is called its **order,** and is denoted by its rows m and its columns n. The size of a matrix is m x n.

Median: see **Average.**

Mean: see **Average.**

Methodology: the processes, techniques, or approaches employed in the solution of a problem or in doing something.

Microevaluation: a study of how and why a system functions.

Mode: see **Average.**

Model: a model is a conceptual idealization and representation, in abstract form, of a complicated actual physical system or process. It helps to visualize in a simplified way something that cannot be directly observed.

Morse-Chen Model: a probabilistic model on book use modified by Philip Morse and Ching-chih Chen to enable the use of biased circulation data to predict book use.

Mutually Exclusive: the occurrence of one event excludes the occurrence of the other.

Normal Distribution: a symmetrical curve, bell-shaped, and asymptotic to the horizontal axis. It is used to explain a great number of phenomena in the world.

On-Line: of or indicating peripheral hardware that is under direct control of a central processing unit.

Operation Research: the quantitative study of how an organization functions for the purpose of improving the operations. It usually applies mathematical modelling techniques by using statistics and probability theory.

Optimization: the process of finding the optimal solution (most profitable, least costly, most efficient) to a problem that has been formulated and represented by a mathematical model.

Output: that which is produced as a result of some process or operation.

Parameter: a quantitative characteristic.

Performance: the level of effectiveness.

Population: the entire group or collection of things or people being examined (see universe).

Predictive Model: a mathematical model to which analytical and probabilistic techniques are used for predictive purposes.

Probabilistic Model: see **Predictive Model.**

Probability: the relative frequency of the occurrence of an event (which can be defined mathematically). It is the study of purely chance phenomena (the chance that a certain event or outcome will occur.)

Quantitative Methods: generally these involve the use of statistics to attempt to quantify a process of activity.

Random Sample: a sample drawn in such a way that every combination of the possible sample elements of the population has an equal chance of being selected.

Random Variable: a variable outside the scope of the variables under study that by chance interferes with the study.

Range: the difference between the largest and smallest numbers of the data.

Raw Data: recorded information in its original collected form.

Regression Analysis: methods by which estimates are made of the values of a variable from the knowledge of the value of one or more other variables.

Sample: a small part of the population or universe.

Sampling Theory: an inferential statistical method which is based on the fact that the arithmetic means of all possible samples of a population follow a normal distribution, and the mean of all possible sample means equals the mean of the population.

Scientific Management: scientific approach to managerial problems. It generally involves problem solving and reflective inquiry.

SDI: an acronym for selective dissemination of information, a method of making people aware of information of potential interest to them.

Standard Deviation: the square root of the variance. Generally it is used to measure the dispersion in the units of the original data.

Statistical Estimation: an estimation of a population parameter on the basis of a sample.

Statistics: scientific methods for collecting, organizing, summarizing, presenting, and analyzing data, as well as drawing valid conclusions and making reasonable inferences on the basis of such analysis. In a narrower sense, the term is also used to denote the data themselves or numbers derived from the data. See also **Descriptive Statistics and Inferential Statistics.**

Stochastic: random.

System Analysis: the organized, step-by-step study and analysis of the detailed procedure for collection, manipulation, and evaluation of information about an organization with the goal of improving control over its total operation or segments of it.

Systems Theory: a theory concerned with developing a systematic, theoretical framework for describing general relationships of the empirical world.

Table, Statistical: a presentation of numbers in a logical arrangement (tabular format).

Universe: the population.

Variable: a symbol that can represent any one of a given set of numbers or quantities. A quantity that may assume any of a specified set of values.

Variance: the arithmetic mean of the squared deviation from the population mean.

Bibliography

Compiled by Joy McPherson

BIBLIOGRAPHIES

A selection of bibliographies or lists of readings on statistical approaches to librarianship was consulted in construction of the present work. The aim of the present work is to update bibliographies presented below, therefore duplication of citations have been kept to a minimum.

Chen, Ching-chih. "Applied Statistics Methods in Library Management." (Course objectives and reading list for L.S. 642.) Boston: Simmons College School of Library Science, Winter 1978. And "Further Readings." (Internal document.)

Lists twelve core readings in the field written between 1961 and 1977. Sixteen supplementary references are found in "Further Readings."

Chen, Ching-chih. *Applications of Operations Research Models to Libraries: A Case Study of the Use of Monographs in the Francis A. Countway Library of Medicine, Harvard University.* Cambridge, MA: The M.I.T. Press, 1976.

Bibliography (pages 199-207) contains over 150 references spanning 1961-1975.

Chen, Ching-chih. "Selected Reference List: Institute on Quantitative Measurement and Dynamic Library Service." Boston: Simmons College School of Library Science, Spring 1976. (Internal document.)

Contains 17 basic references including several bibliographies spanning period 1965-1976.

Hamburg, M.; Clelland, R. C.; Bommer, M. R. V.; Ramist, L. E.; and Whitfield, R. M. *Library Planning and Decision-Making Systems.* Cambridge, MA: The M.I.T. Press, 1974.

Bibliography on pages 243-268 contains over 300 monograph and journal articles from 1934 to January 1972. Literature covers statistical applications to over 30 library operations.

Kraft, Donald H. and McDonald, Dennis. "Library Operations Research: A Bibliography and Commentary on the Literature." *Information Reports and Bibliographies* 6 (March-April, 1977):2-10.

Bibliography of library operations research. Contains descriptions of the field, commentary on the state of the literature and a selected bibliography of over 200 items covering full range of material from theoretical models to applied analysis. Bibliographies span 1964-1976.

Lancaster, F. W. *The Measurement and Evaluation of Library Services.* Washington, DC: Information Resources Press, 1977.

Lancaster concludes each of his thirteen major chapters of the book with a reading list containing classic and contemporary readings for each aspect of library service. Number of references vary from 40 to 300 per chapter, most written between 1960 and 1975.

Leimkuhler, F. F. "Operations Research," In *Encyclopedia of Library and Information Science*, Vol. 20, edited by Allen Kent, Harold Lancour and Jay E. Dailey. New York: Marcel Dekker, 1977.

Bibliography on pages 434-439 contains over 100 references to operations research in libraries covering the period 1968 to 1976.

INTRODUCTORY TEXTS IN STATISTICS

A sampling of text books in basic statistical methods published since 1970.

Auslander, Louis, et. al. *Mathematics through Statistics.* Baltimore, MD: Williams and Wilkins, 1973.

Blalock, Hubert M. *Social Statistics.* 2nd ed. New York: McGraw-Hill, 1972.

Campbell, Stephen K. *Flaws and Fallacies in Statistical Thinking.* Englewood Cliffs, NJ: Prentice-Hall, 1974.

Derman, Cyrus et al. *A Guide To Probability and Application.* New York: Holt, Rinehart and Winston, 1973.

Guilford, Joy Paul. *Fundamental Statistics in Psychology and Education.* 5th ed. New York: McGraw-Hill, 1973.

Hamburg, Morris. *Basic Statistics: A Modern Approach.* New York: Harcourt, Brace, Jovanovich, 1974.

Hoel, Paul G. *Elementary Statistics.* 4th ed. New York: Wiley, 1976.

Hollander, Myles and Wolfe, Douglas A. *Nonparametric Statistical Methods.* New York: Wiley, 1973.

Loether, Herman J. and McTavish, Donald G. *Inferential Statistics for Sociologists: An Introduction.* Rockleigh, NJ: Allyn and Bacon, 1974.

Lovejoy, Elijah P. *Statistics for Math Haters.* New York: Harper and Row, 1975.

Marascuilo, Leonard A. *Statistical Methods for Behavioral Science Research.* New York: McGraw-Hill, 1971.

Phillips, John L. *Statistical Thinking: A Structural Approach.* San Francisco: W. H. Freeman, 1973.

Welkowitz, Joan. *Introductory Statistics for the Behavioral Sciences.* New York: Academic Press, 1976.

Wetherill, G. B. *Elementary Statistical Methods.* New York: Halsted Press, 1972.

Willemsen, Eleanor W. *Understanding Statistical Reasoning: How to Evaluate Research Literature in the Behavioral Sciences.* San Francisco: W. H. Freeman, 1974.

STATISTICAL REPORTING IN LIBRARIES— GENERAL SOURCES AND CONSIDERATIONS

Flowers, H. "New Perspective on School Library Media Center Statistics." *Unabashed Librarian* 18 (Winter, 1976):25-26.

Gilford, D. M. and Schick, F. L. "LIBGIS and Other U.S. Library Statistics Programs," *Bowker Annual of Library and Book Trade Information.* 20th ed. New York: R. R. Bowker, 1975, pp. 195-198.

Ladd, B. "Statistics for Planning National Information Services." *Bowker Annual of Library and Book Trade Information.* 20th ed. New York: R. R. Bowker, 1975, pp. 198-201.

Leach, Steven. "The Growth Rates of Major Academic Libraries." *College and Research Libraries* 37 (November, 1976):531-542.

Mathematica. "On Library Statistics." Unpublished report. Princeton, NJ: Mathematica, 1967.

Moore, Nick. "The Need for Library Statistics." *Liber Bulletin* 7 (May, 1977):24-29.

_____. "Quantitative Information in Library Management: National and International Needs." *Liber Bulletin* 7 (May, 1977):124-127.

Packer, K. H. "Collecting Canadian Library Statistics." Bibliography. *Canadian Library Journal* 34 (June, 1977):203-207.

Piternick, George. "ARL Statistics—Handle with Care." *College and Research Libraries* 38 (September, 1977):419-423.

Pratt, A. D. "Analysis of Library Statistics." *Library Quarterly* 45 (July, 1975):275-286.

Salverson, Carol A. "The Relevance of Statistics to Library Evaluation." *College and Research Libraries* 30 (July, 1969):352-361.

Schick, F. L. "Statistical Reporting of Library Developments by the Federal Government." *Library Trends* 25 (July, 1976):81-88.

United States. National Center for Educational Statistics. "Library Statistics Publication, 1962-1975." *Bowker Annual of Library and Book Trade Information.* 20th ed. New York: R. R. Bowker, 1975.

"STATE-OF-THE-PRACTICE"

General concepts, methods, and techniques in library statistical analysis, with emphasis on practical applications.

American Library Association. *Library Statistics: A Handbook of Concepts, Definitions and Terminology.* Edited by Joel Williams. Chicago: ALA, 1966.

American Library Association. LAD LOMS Statistics Coordinating Committee. "Using Statistics as an Internal Management Tool." ALA Conference Cassette 77/24. Chicago: ALA, 1977.

Bookstein, A. "How to Sample Badly." *Library Quarterly* 44 (1974): 124-33.

Burns, R. W., Jr. "A Generalization Methodology for Library Systems Analysis." *College and Research Libraries* 32 (July, 1971):295-303.

Chapman, E. A.; St. Pierre, P. L.; and Lubans, J., Jr. *Library Systems Analysis Guidelines.* New York: Wiley, 1970.

Chester, Leonard, and Magoss, George. "Evaluating Library Services by Sampling Methods: a Project at the North York Public Library." *Canadian Library Journal* 34 (December, 1977):439-443.

Fischer, T. B. ("Methods for Carrying Out Tests in Libraries") "Metodik zur Durehfuhrung Reprasentativer Stichproben im Bibliothekswesen." *Zentr Bibl.* 88 (April, 1974):193-204.

Fitzner, Dieter. *(Random Sample Methods in Library Statistics.) Stichprobenverfahren in der Bibliotheksstatistik.* Berlin and Leipzig: Zentralinstitut fur Bibliothekswesen and Fachschule fur Bibliothekare 'Erich Weinert', Abt. Fernstudium, 1975.

Frana, Anton and Reinhard Krieg. "Some Principles Underlying the Application of Statistical Methods in Librarianship." *Bibliothekar* 30 (December, 1976):806-812.

Glazer, N. "Linear Programming for Libraries." *Chemical and Engineering News.* 35 (1957):142-3.

Goldberg, R. L. *Systems Approach to Library Program Development.* Metuchen, NJ: Scarecrow, 1976.

Hayes, R. M. and Becker, J. *Handbook of Data Processing for Libraries: Sponsored by the Council on Library Resources.* 2nd ed. Los Angeles, CA: Melville Publishing Co., 1974.

Hoadley, I. B., and Clark, A. S., eds. *Quantitative Methods in Librarianship: Standards, Research, Measurement.* Westport, CT: Greenwood Press, 1972.

(Investigative Methods in Library Statistics: An Introduction to Statistical Methods and Their Possibilities for Application in Library Practice.) Untersuchungsmethoden der Bibliotheksstatistik: eine Einfuhrung in Bibliothekspraxis. Berlin and Leipzig: Zentralinstitut fur Bibliothekswesen and Fachschule fur Bibliothekare 'Erich Weinert', Abt. Fernstudium, 1975.

Krejci, Frantisek. ("The Use of Statistical Methods in Information Centers.") "Vyuziti Statistickych Metod v Informacnich Strediscich," *Kniznice a Vedecke Informacie* 8 (1976):74-82.

Line, Maurice B. *Library Surveys: An Introduction to Their Use, Planning, Procedure and Presentation.* Hampden, CT: Archon, 1967.

Machlup, F. "Our Libraries: Can We Measure Their Holdings and Acquisitions." *AAUP Bulletin* 62 (October, 1976):303-7.

Morrison, Elizabeth. "Library System Measurement." *LASIE* 7 (Nov.-Dec., 1976):3-20.

Nwoye, S. C. "Essence of Library Statistics." *Nigerbiblios* 1 (April, 1976):17-18.

Olson, Edwin E. "Quantitative Approaches to Assessment of Library Science Functions." Unpublished paper. Philadelphia, Pa: Institute for the Advancement of Medical Communication, 1968.

Rader, Vasil. "Assessment of Public Libraries by Means of a Mathematical Formula." *Bibliothekar* (Sofia) 23 (1976):34-39.

Raffel, L. J., and Shisko, R. *Systematic Analysis of University Libraries: An Application of Cost-Benefit Analysis to the MIT Libraries.* Cambridge, MA: The M.I.T. Press, 1969.

Rorvig, Mark Evan. *The Effect of State and Federal Grants on Local Library Funding Support: A Statistical Analysis of Six Rural Arizona Counties.* Phoenix, AZ: Arizona State Dept. of Library and Archives, 1977. ED 135 398.

Rouse, William B., ed. *Applications of Operations Research Techniques in Tufts University Libraries.* Medford, MA: Tufts University College of Engineering, 1973. ED 087 480.

Simpson, I. S. *Basic Statistics for Librarians.* CT: Linnet, 1975.

Srikantaiah, T., and Hoffman, H. H. *Introduction to Quantitative Research Methods for Librarians.* 2nd ed. CA: Headway Publications, 1977.

Stock, K. F., ed. *(Principles and Practice of Library Statistics.) Grundlagen und Praxis der Bibliotheksstatistik.* Verlag Dok: 1974.

Taylor, Robert S. and Hieber, C. E. *Library Systems Analysis: Manual for the Analysis of Library Systems.* Report No. 3. Bethlehem, PA: Lehigh University Center for the Information Services, 1965.

Voigt, Melvin J. *Advances in Librarianship: Vol. 5.* New York: Academic Press, 1975. ED 119 708.

"STATE-OF-THE-ART"

Theoretical developments in library systems analysis and operations research.

Adeyemi, N. M. "Library Operations Research—Purpose, Tools, Utility, and Implications for Developing Libraries." *Libri* 27 (March, 1977):22-30.

Brookes, B. C. "Theory of the Bradford Law." *Journal of Documentation* 33 (September, 1977):180-209.

Chen, Ching-chih. *Applications of Operations Research Models to Libraries: A Case Study of the Use of Monographs in the Francis A. Countway Library of Medicine, Harvard University.* Cambridge, MA: The M.I.T. Press, 1976.

Daiute, Robert Kenneth. *On the Relationship Between the Epidemic Theory and the Bradford Law of Dispersion.* Ph.D. Thesis. Case Western Reserve University, 1974.

Drake, Miriam A. *Academic Research Libraries: A Study of Growth.* West Lafayette, IN: Libraries and Audio-Visual Center, Purdue University, 1977.

———. "Forecasting Academic Library Growth College and Research Libraries 37 (January, 1976):53-59.

Goldberg, R. L. *PIES (Planning, Implementation, and Eon, and Evaluation System) Model: A Systems Approach to Library Program Development.* Ph.D. Thesis. Rutgers University, 1975.

Gore, Daniel, ed. *Farewell to Alexandria: Solutions to Space, Growth, and Performance Problems of Libraries.* Westport, CT: Greenwood Press, 1976. ED 119 742.

Hamburg, M.; Clelland, R. C.; Bommer, M. R. V.; Ramist, L. E.; and Whitfield, R. M. *Library Planning and Decision Making Systems.* Cambridge, MA: The M.I.T. Press, 1974.

King, D. W., and Bryant, E. C. *Evaluation of Information Services and Products.* Washington, D.C.: Information Resources Press, 1971.

Korzon, Krystyna. "The Application of the Delphi Method to the Forecasting of Information Activity Development." *Akt. Probl. Inf. Dokum.* 21 (1976):16-21.

Leimkuhler, F. F. "Operational Analysis of Library Systems." *Information Processing and Management* 13 (1977):79-93.

Lied, Terry R., and Tolliver, Don L. "A General Statistical Model for Increasing Efficiency and Confidence in Manual Data Collection Systems Through Sampling." *Journal of the American Society for Information Science* 25 (Sept.-Oct., 1974):327-331. EJ 104 617.

Liesener, J. W. *Systematic Process for Planning Media Programs.* Chicago: ALA, 1976.

Listowski, David. *Work Estimate at an Information Center.* Syracuse, NY: State University of New York, 1976. ED 135 363.

Mason, D. "Management Techniques Applied to the Operation of Information Services (with discussion)." *Aslib Proc* 25 (November, 1973):445-458.

Mayerhofer, Josef. "The Scientific Library—A Cybernetic System." *Liber* 7 (1977):156-179.

Mohamed, Oli. *Development of a Behavioristic Model for the Quantitative Measurement of Academic Library Effectiveness.* Ph.D. Thesis. University of Pittsburgh, 1976.

Morse, P. M. *Library Effectiveness. A Systems Approach.* Cambridge, MA: The M.I.T. Press, 1969.

Nozik, Barbara Sayles. *A Stochastic Model to Predict Demand for Library Services.* Berkeley, CA: University of California, 1974.

Robertson, S. E. "Progress in Documentation: Theories and Models in Information Retrieval." *Journal of Documentation* 33 (June, 1977): 126-148.

Shields, Dorothy McDonald. *A Fault Tree Approach to Analyzing School Library Media Services.* Ph.D. Thesis, Brigham Young University, 1977.

Surace, Cecily J. et al. *Rand Library Evaluation Survey.* Santa Monica, CA: Rand Corp., 1976. ED 135 375.

Ward, Patricia Layzell. *Exploratory Modeling of Library and Information Systems in the UK: Report Of the Feasibility Study, January 13-July 13, 1975; report to the British Library R & D Department on project no. SI/G/118.* London: University College, School of Library, Archive and Information Studies, (BLRDR 5280), December, 1975.

White, G. Travis, "Quantitative Measures of Library Effectiveness." *Journal of Academic Librarianship* 3 (July, 1977):128-136.

STATISTICAL APPROACHES BY SPECIFIC AREA OF OPERATION

Bibliometrics

Bookstein, Abraham. "Patterns of Scientific Productivity and Social Change: A Discussion of Lotka's Law and Bibliometric Symmetry." *Journal of the American Society for Information Science.* 28 (July, 1977):206-210.

Brennen, Patrick W. "Citation Analysis in the Literature of Tropical Medicine." *Bulletin of the Medical Library Association* 66 (January, 1978):24-30.

Clark, C. V. "Obsolescence of the Patent Literature." *Journal of Documentation* 32 (March, 1976):32-52.

Corth, Annette. "Coverage of Marinebiology Citations." *Special Libraries* 68 (December, 1977):439-446.

Dikeman, Robert K. "A Use of Bibliometric Techniques in Serials Management for Libraries." *Information Revolution: Proceedings of the 38th ASIS Annual Meeting,* Vol. 12, Boston, MA, October 26-30, 1975; edited by Charles W. Husbands and Ruth L. Tighe. Washington, DC: American Society for Information Science, 1975, pp. 55-56.

Doi, Makiko. "Pattern of Current Periodical Usage: Yule Curve." *PNLA Quarterly* 41 (Fall, 1976):14-17.

Donohue, J. C. *Understanding Scientific Literatures: a Bibliometric Approach.* Cambridge, MA: The M.I.T. Press, 1973.

Elmore, C. H. "Application of Bradford's Law to the Journal Literature of the Annual Review of Information Science and Technology." Research Paper. Columbia, MO: University of Missouri, 1975.

Funk, M. E. "Correlation of Quality and Quantity in a Bradford Distribution." Research Paper. Columbia, MO: University of Missouri, 1976.

Halperin, Michael. "Waiting Lines." *RQ* 16 (Summer, 1977):297-299.

Halsey, Richard Sweeney. "A Bibliometric Analysis of the Serious Music Literature on Long Playing Records." Ph.D. Thesis, Case Western Reserve University, 1972.

Hawkins, D. T. "Unconventional Uses of On-line Information Retrieval Systems: On-line Bibliometric Studies." *American Society for Information Science Journal* 28 (January, 1977):13-18.

Kashafutdinova, E. S. et al. ("Analysis of the Call Frequency of Periodicals on Electrical and Power Engineering from VINITI's Information Centre Stock.") "Analiz Zaprasivaemosti Zhurnalov po Elektrorekhnike i Energetike iz Fonda Informatsionno-Spravochnogo tsentra VINITI," *Nauch.-Tekh. Inf.*, Series 2:8-11, 1975.

Maursted, Betty Louise. *Concerning Structural Properties in the Literature of the Art Historian-A Bibliometric Study.* Cleveland, OH: Case Western Reserve University, 1972.

Nicholas, David and Ritchie, Margaret. *Literature and Bibliometrics.* Hamden, CT: Shoe String Press, 1978.

Singleton, Alan. "Journal Ranking and Selection: a Review in Physics." *Journal of Documentation* 32 (December, 1976):258-289.

Small, Henry G., and Koenig, Michael E. D. "Journal Clustering Using a Bibliographic Coupling Method." *Information Processing and Management* 13 (1977):277-288.

Subramanyam, Krishnappa. *A Bibliometric Investigation of Computer Science Journal Literature.* Pittsburgh, PA: University of Pittsburgh, 1975.

Tobias, Audrey Sylvia. "The Yule Curve Describing Periodical Citations by Freshmen: Essential Tool or Abstract Frill?" *Journal of Academic Librarianship* 1 (March, 1975):14-16.

Vervliet, Hendrik D. L. *(Bibliometrics and Library Allocation.) Bibliometric en Bibliotheekbudgetten.* Brussels; Koninklijke Academie voor Wetenschappen Letteren en Schone Kunsten var Belgie, 1976.

Vlachy, Jan. "Time Factor in Lotka's Law." *Probleme de Informare si Documentare.* 10 (March-April 1976):44-87.

Worthen, Dennis Brent. *Clinical Drug Literature: A Bibliometric Analysis.* Ph.D. Thesis, Case Western Reserve University, 1976.

Wyllys, Ronald E. "Measuring Scientific Prose with Rank-Frequency ("Zipf") Curves: a New Use for an Old Phenomenon." In: *Information Revolution: Proceedings of the 38th ASIS Annual Meeting,* Vol. 12, Boston, MA, October 26-30, 1975; edited by Charles W. Husbands and Ruth L. Tighe. Washington, DC: American Society for Information Science, 1975, pp. 30-31.

Collection Development—Selection and De-acquisition

Aiyepeku, Wilson O. "The Bradford Distribution Theory: The Compounding of Bradford Periodical Literatures in Geography." *Journal of Documentation* 33 (September, 1977):201-219.

Ashworth, Wilfred. "Self Renewing Libraries." *New Library World* 78 (March, 1977):47-48.

Broadus, Robert N. "The Applications of Citation Analysis to Library Collection Building." *Advances in Librarianship.* Vol. 7, edited by M. J. Voigt and M. A. Harris. New York: Academic Press, 1977.

Brooks, B. C. "Obsolescence of Special Library Periodicals: Sampling Errors and Utility Contours." *Journal of the American Society for Information Science* 21 (September-October, 1970):320-329. EJ 025 993.

Cooper, William S. et al. "The Duplication of Monograph Holdings in the University of California Library System." *Library Quarterly* 45 (July, 1975):253-274. EJ 122 926.

Greenberg, Harvey J., and Kraft, Donald H. "On Computing a Buy/Copy Policy Using the Pitt-Kraft Model." *Information Processing and Management* 13 (1977):125-134.

Holland, Maurita Peterson. "Serial Cuts vs. Public Service: a Formula." *College and Research Libraries* 37 (November, 1976):543-548.

Lewkowicz, Linda B. et al. "Acquisitions Analysis Employing a Statistical Package for the Social Sciences." In *Information Revolution: Proceedings of the 38th ASIS Annual Meeting,* Vol. 12, Boston, MA, October 26-30, 1975, edited by Charles W. Husbands and Ruth L. Tighe. Washington, DC: American Society for Information Science, 1975, pp. 53-54.

Maxin, Jacqueline A. "Weeding Journals with Informal Use Statistics." *De-acquisitions Librarian* 1 (Summer, 1976):9-11.

Raghavan, K. S. and Shalini, R. "Economics of Periodicals in Special Libraries: an Application of Bradford's Distribution to CFTRI Library Periodicals Holding." *Annuals of Library Science and Documentation.* 24 (March, 1977):34-41.

Windsor, Donald A. "De-acquisitioning Journals Using Productivity/ Cost Rankings." *De-acquisitions Librarian* 1 (Spring, 1976):8-10.

Collection Evaluation

Baughman, James C. "Toward a Structural Approach to Collection Development." *College and Research Libraries* 38 (May, 1977):241-248.

Goldstein, Marianne and Sedransk, Joseph. "Using a Sample Technique to Describe Characteristics of a Collection." *College and Research Libraries* 38 (May, 1977):195-202.

Ifidon, Sam E. "Qualitative/Quantitative Evaluation of Academic Library Collections: A Literature Survey." *International Library Review* 8 (June, 1976):299-308. EJ 141 567.

McInnis, R. Marvin. "The Formula Approach to Library Size: an Empirical Study of Its Efficacy in Evaluating Research Libraries." *College and Research Libraries* 33 (May, 1972):190-198. EJ 059 364.

Shabowich, Stanley A. *An Approach to Assessment of Duality of a University Library Collection.* Hammond, IN: Purdue University Calumet Campus Library, 1975. ED 107 308.

Virgo, Julie A. "A Statistical Procedure for Evaluating the Importance of Scientific Papers." *Library Quarterly* 47 (October, 1977):415-430.

Collection Use

Bookstein, Abraham. "Comments on the Morse-Chen Discussion of Non-Circulating Books." *Library Quarterly* 45 (April, 1975):195-198.

Bruce, Daniel R. "A Markov Model to Study the Loan Dynamics at a Reserve-Loan Desk in a Lending Library." *Library Quarterly* 45 (April, 1975):161-178.

Harris, C. "A Comparison of Issues and In-Library Use of Books." *Aslib Proceedings* 29 (March, 1977):118-126.

Jain, A. K. "Sampling In-Library Book Use." *Journal of the American Society for Information Science* 2 (May-June, 1972):150-155. EJ 060 824.

Jenks, George M. "Circulation and Its Relationship to the Book Collection and Academic Departments." *College and Research Libraries* 37 (March, 1976):145-152.

Jones, William G. "A Time-Series Sample Approach for Measuring Use in a Small Library." *Special Libraries* 64 (July, 1973):280-284. EJ 084 906.

Morse, Philip M. and Chen, Ching-chih. "Using Circulation Desk Data to Obtain Unbiased Estimates of Book-Use." *Library Quarterly* 45 (April, 1975):179-194.

Pan, Elizabeth Lim. *Citation and Use Patterns of Scientific Journals in Biomedical Libraries.* Ph.D. Thesis, Rutgers University, 1976.

Turner, Stephen J. "The Identifier Method of Measuring Use as Applied to Modeling the Circulation Use of Books From a University Library." *Journal of the American Society for Information Science* 28 (March, 1977):96-100.

Literature Searching and Information Retrieval

Barrette, Pierre P. *An Exploratory Study of the Contents of Non-Fiction Young Adult Book Reviews.* Harrisonburg, VA: Madison College, 1973. ED 094 799.

Bichteler, Julie, and Eaton, Edward A., III. "Comparing Two Algorithms for Documentation Retrieval Using Citation Links." *Journal of the American Society for Information Science* 28 (July, 1977):192-195.

Bookstein, Abraham. "When the Most "Pertinent" Document Should Not Be Retrieved—An Analysis of the Swets Model." *Information Processing and Management* 13 (1977):377-383.

Brookes, B. C. "A Measure of Categorical Dispersion." *The Information Scientist* 11 (March, 1977):11-17.

Cooper, Michael D. "Input—Output Relationships in On-Line Bibliographic Searching." *Journal of the American Society for Information Science* 28 (May, 1977):153-160.

Doszkocs, Tamas E. et al. "Analysis of Term Distribution in the TOXLINE Inverted File." *Journal of Chemical Information and Computer Science* 16 (August, 1976):131-135.

Gor'kova, V. I., and Khodzha-Bagirova, A. E. "Corrections of Search Specifications as a Problem of the Theory of Statistical Decisions." *Nauch. - Tekh. Information* Series 2 (1975):18-21.

Griffiths, Jose-Marie. "Index Term Input to IR Systems." *Journal of Documentation* 31 (September, 1975):185-190.

Guazzo, Mauro. "Retrieval Performance and Information Theory." *Information Processing and Management* 13 (1977):155-165.

Guy, Louis-Gavet. "A Mathematical Formulation of Keyword Compression for Thesaurus." *Information Processing and Management* 13 (1977):189-200.

Hickey, Thomas Butler. *Superimposed Coding Versus Sequential and Inverted Files.* Ph.D. Thesis, University of Illinois of Urbana-Champaign, 1977.

Lancaster, F. W. *Vocabulary Control for Information Retrieval.* Washington, DC: Information Resources Press, 1972.

Lancaster, F. W. "The Cost-Effectiveness of Information Retrieval and Dissemination Systems." *Journal of the American Society of Information Science* 22 (1971):12-27.

Radecki, Tadenz. "Mathematical Model of Time-Effective Information Retrieval System Used on the Theory of Fuzzy Sets." *Information Processing and Management* 13 (1977):109-116.

Travis, I. L. "Design Equations for Citation Retrieval Systems: Their Role in Research Analysis." *Information Processing and Management* 13 (1977):49-56.

Wilys, Ronald Eugene. *The Measurement of Jargon Standardization in Scientific Writing Using Rank-Frequency ("ZIPF") Curves.* Ph.D. Thesis, The University of Wisconsin-Madison, 1974.

Management and Budget Applications

Bates, Marcia J. "Factors Affecting Subject Catalog Search Success." *Journal of the American Society for Information Science* 28 (May, 1977):161-169.

Brazell, Troy V., Jr. "Comparative Analysis: A Minimum Music Materials Budget for the University Library." *College and Research Libraries* 32 (March, 1971):110-120. EJ 034 963.

Cohen, Jackson B. "Science Acquisitions and Book Output Statistics." *Library Resources and Technical Services* 19 (Fall, 1975):370-379.

Cole, Diane Davis. *Mathematical Models in Library Management: Planning, Analysis and Cost Assessment.* Ph.D. Thesis, The University of Texas at Austin, 1976.

Cotton, Ira W. "Cost-Benefit Analysis of Interactive Systems." *Computer Networks* 1 (November, 1977):311-324.

Genova, B. K. L. et al. *A Study of Salary Determinants within the SUNY Librarians Association between 1973 and 1977.* 1977. ED 134 189.

Haslam, Dan. "Books in a Seige Economy, II: Library Statistics." *The Bookseller* 3650 (December 6, 1975):2586-2589.

Hewitt, Joe A. "Sample Audit of Cards from a University Library Catalog." *College and Research Libraries* 33 (January, 1972):24-27. EJ 050 863.

Moore, Nick. "Too Many Books? An Economic View of Library Operations." In *Survival 76:* papers read at the one-day conference of the London and Home Counties Branch of the Library Association held at the Library Association May 12th, 1976. Edited by V. Whibley. London: The Library Association, 1976. pp. 30-42.

Singleton, Allen. "Scientific Journal Budgeting: Where Does the Money Go?" *Aslib Proceedings* 29 (March, 1977):127-132.

Spencer, Carol C. "Random Time Sampling with Self-Observation for Library Cost Studies: Unit Costs of Interlibrary Loans and Photocopies at a Regional Medical Library." *Journal of the American Society for Information Science* 22 (May-June, 1971):153-160. EJ 039 711.

Welwood, R. J. "Book Budget Allocations: An Objective Formula for the Small Academic Library." *Canadian Library Journal* 34 (June, 1977):213-219.

Physical Access and Ease of Use

Carroll, Hardy. *Metric Spaces Applied to Locating Library Collections.* Ph.D. Thesis, Case Western Reserve University, 1974.

Cooper, Michael D. and Wolthauser, John. "Misplacement of Books on Library Shelves: a Mathematical Model." *Library Quarterly* 47 (January, 1977):43-57.

Hindle, A. et al. *The Effects of Satisfaction Time for Inter-Library Loans in a Research Laboratory: A Pilot Study.* Lancaster: University of Lancaster, Department of Operational Research (BLRD Report 5315), 1976.

Huttner, Marian A. "Measuring and Reducing Book Losses." *Library Journal* 98 (February, 15, 1973):512-513. EJ 070 894.

McClure, Charles R. "Linear Programming and Library Delivery Systems." *Library Resources and Technical Services* 21 (Fall, 1977):333-344.

Niland, Powell and Kurth, William H. "Estimating Lost Volumes in a University Library Collection." *College and Research Libraries* 37 (March, 1976):128-136.

Piternick, Anne B. "Derivation of a Sample of Journal Issues for Tests of Availability and Use." *Journal of the American Society for Information Science* 26 (September-October, 1975):269-270. EJ 126 249.

Saracevic, W. M. et al. "Causes and Dynamics of User Frustration in an Academic Library." *College and Research Libraries* 38 (January, 1977):7-18.

Stout, Chester Bernard. "Measurement of Document Exposure Time Distributions at a Small Public Library." Ph.D. Thesis, Case Western Reserve University, 1976.

Stuart, M. "Some Effects on Library Users of the Delays in Supplying Publications." *Aslib Proceedings* 29 (January, 1977):35-45.

Reference Services

American Library Association. Library Administration Division, Library Organization and Management Section. *Statistics for Reference Services Committee. Preconference Institute on Statistical Methods for Reference Services.* Chicago: ALA, 1977.

Caldwell, G. H. "Preconference Statistics for Reference Services Committee." *Library of Congress Information Bulletin* 36 (August 12, 1977):551.

Howell, Benita J. et al. "Fleeting Encounters - A Role Analysis of Reference Librarian-Patron Interaction." *RQ* 16 (Winter, 1976):124-129.

Morgenshtern, I. G. "Visual Presentation of Statistics of Reference Work." *Nauchnye i Teckhnicheskie Biblioteki SSSR* 7 (1976):3-7.

Pings, Vern M. "Reference Services Accountability and Measurement." *RQ* 16 (Winter, 1976):120-123.

Regazzi, John J. and Hersberger, Rodney M. *Library Use and Reference Service: A Regression Analysis.* 1976, ED 129 219.

Technical Services

Atwood, Virginia Woll. "Relationship of College and University Size to Library Adaption of the 1967 Anglo-American Cataloging Rules." *Library Resources and Technical Services* 14 (Winter, 1970):68-83. EJ 020 572.

Ayers, F. H. "The Universal Standard Book Number (USBN): Why, How, and a Progress Report." *Program* 10 (April, 1976):75-80.

Bevan, Allen. *Report of a Pilot Bibliometric Analysis of Extra-MARC Material Using the Statistical Package for the Social Sciences: a British Library Research and Development Department Funded Project-January to April 1976.* London: London and South Eastern Library Region (BLRDR. 5281) 1976.

Black, George W. "Selected Annual Bound Volume Production." *Special Libraries* 67 (November, 1976):534-536.

Bookstein, Abraham and Fouty, Gary. "A Mathematical Model for Estimating the Effectiveness of Bigram Coding." *Information Processing Management* 12 (1976):111-116.

Miller, Bruce and Sorum, Marilyn. "A Two Stage Sampling Procedure for Estimating the Proportion of Lost Books in a Library." *Journal of Academic Librarianship* 3 (May, 1977):74-80.

Miller, G. and Coleridge, F. "A Conceptual Model for Circulation Control Systems." *Journal of the American Society for Information Science* 28 (July, 1977):196-205.

Planton, Stanley. *A Methodology for Decision-Making in Serials.* South Dakota: Dakota Wesleyan University, 1976. ED 135 399.

Reid, Bruce J. and Green, Betty. "An Analysis of LC Retrospective Cataloguing Data to Determine Its Relevance for the British." *Journal of Librarianship* 6 (January, 1974):28-45. EJ 101 148.

Reid, Marion T. "Effectiveness of the OCLC Data Base for Acquisitions Verification." *Journal of Academic Librarianship* 2 (January, 1977):303-326.

Rocke, Hans Joachim. "Analysis of the Data From a Technical Processing Cost Study." Master's Thesis in Librarianship, California State University. 1974. ED 140 795.

Index